# The Bully at Work

Second Edition

## What You Can Do to Stop the Hurt and Reclaim Your Dignity on the Job

Gary Namie, PhD
and Ruth Namie, PhD

SOURCEBOOKS, INC.
NAPERVILLE, ILLINOIS

Copyright © 2000, 2003, 2009 by Gary Namie and Ruth Namie
Cover and internal design copyright © 2009 by Sourcebooks, Inc.
Cover design © Noelle Stransky © Workplace Bullying Institute
Internal images © Workplace Bullying Institute
Sourcebooks and the colophon are registered trademarks of Sourcebooks, Inc.

This publication is designed to provide accurate and authoritative information in regard to the subject matter covered. It is sold with the understanding that the publisher is not engaged in rendering legal, accounting, or other professional service. If legal advice or other expert assistance is required, the services of a competent professional person should be sought. —*From a Declaration of Principles Jointly Adopted by a Committee of the American Bar Association and a Committee of Publishers and Associations*

All brand names and product names used in this book are trademarks, registered trademarks, or trade names of their respective holders. Sourcebooks, Inc., is not associated with any product or vendor in this book.

Published by Sourcebooks, Inc.
P.O. Box 4410, Naperville, IL 60567-4410
(630) 961-3900
Fax: (630) 961-2168

Library of Congress Cataloging-in-Publication Data for the first edition:
Namie, Gary
    The bully at work: what you can do to stop the hurt and reclaim your dignity
    on the job / Gary Namie, Ruth Namie.
        p. cm.
    Includes bibliographical references and index.
    1. Bullying in the workplace. I. Namie, Ruth. II. Title.

HF5549.5.E43 N348 2000
650.1'3—dc21
                            00-024737

Printed and bound in the United States of America
VP 10 9 8 7 6 5 4 3 2 1

In memory of Lillian and Florence and to Pat,
the three women who always gave unconditional love and support.

In memory of Heinz Leymann and Andrea Adams, pioneers.

*Each time a man stands up for an ideal, or acts to improve the lot
of others, or strikes out against injustice, he sends forth a tiny ripple of
hope, and crossing each other from a million different centers of energy
and daring, those ripples build a current which can sweep down the
mightiest walls of oppression and injustice.*
—Robert F. Kennedy

# Disclaimer

·············································································

Dear Reader:

This book contains information, suggestions, and opinions about improving the quality of people's lives from the authors. The use, misuse, understanding, or misunderstanding of the material, in whole or part, is the sole responsibility of the reader.

Neither the publisher nor authors assume responsibility or liability, jointly or individually, to any person, group, organization, or entity regarding any emotional or material loss, damage, or injury caused or alleged to be caused directly or indirectly by the information contained in this book. The authors do not represent themselves as licensed psychologists or mental health professionals.

Readers are advised to use this material in a safe and logical manner. In some cases, this material is most effective when used in conjunction with professional legal and/or counseling services.

# Table of Contents

..................................................

# Acknowledgments

......................................................................

Some of the most beautiful things in Nature are the giant sequoia and redwood trees that grow in Ruth's native California. Nature, in her wisdom, only allows new growth of these trees to come from destruction of the seed pod by fire. It was through personal destruction and pain that our cause was born.

At the top of the list to thank are the thousands of anonymous people who visit with us virtually at the website or by telephone to share their stories, seek advice, or look for support. They, in turn, launched the Workplace Bullying Institute, the U.S. anti-bullying movement, with their sacrifices.

Friend and ally David Yamada, Suffolk University law professor, is the legal pioneer whose treatise on workplace bullying in 2000 launched the legal reform aspect of our work. He authored the language for the *Healthy Workplace Bill* introduced in state legislatures throughout America. We are also blessed by the friendship of overseas experts who encourage the introduction of bullying awareness to the United States—Andy Ellis, Susan Marais-Steinman, Michael Sheehan, Charlotte Rayner, Helge Hoel, and Ståle Einarsen—and domestic academicians Loraleigh Keashly and Joel Neuman. The growing group of citizen lobbyist volunteers who comprise the WBI-Legislative Campaign Coordinators inspire and motivate us constantly.

We especially acknowledge Cindy Waitt, director of the Waitt Institute for Violence Prevention, for support including sponsorship of the first national scientific prevalence poll—the 2007 WBI-Zogby U.S. Workplace Bullying Survey—and the national project to demonstrate that reducing adult bullying in schools creates an anti-abusive climate for everyone so learning can occur.

Thanks to the Sourcebooks team who embraced the anti-bullying movement and have published three editions of this book.

We acknowledge the support of those closest and dearest to our hearts, sons Rob, Sean, and Macario.

Finally, thanks for the steadfast love from Ike Namie. He made WBI and all the dreams possible.

# Preface

........................................................

L ife for the Namies changed in 1996 when Dr. Ruth ran into a horrific woman supervisor as an employee in a psychiatric clinic. In her life before completing a PhD in clinical psychology and specializing in chemical dependency treatment, Ruth had been a corporate training director, management consultant, and retail manager. Gary (PhD, social psychology) was a professor at several universities, the director of two corporate training departments, and a management consultant.

The couple's fight for justice began in 1998 with the founding of the Campaign Against Workplace Bullying. The nonprofit organization morphed during its first decade into the Workplace Bullying Institute, which serves Americans and Canadians. The accomplishments of which we are most proud are that we imported the British term "workplace bullying" to the United States, started the national dialogue, and sustain it in more ways than originally imagined.

Research—data from empirical surveys and over 5,000 intensive interviews—distinguishes WBI from well-intentioned newcomers to the fight against bullying. Surveys started with a modest set of questions in 1998, growing to the national scientific survey conducted with partner Zogby International, and continuing with state-of-the-art descriptive empirical studies, scientific conference presentations, and publications in peer-reviewed academic journals. Interviews began when we offered toll-free advice starting in 1998. Financial complications from the practice compelled its termination, but we learned much of what we know from those who shared their suffering.

The Namies educate the public. Their bullying-related research and work have been featured numerous times on network TV—CNBC, *The Today Show, Good Morning America, The Early Show, Nightline,* CNN—on local TV, and in the national press—*New York Times, Washington Post, Los Angeles Times, San Francisco Chronicle, Chicago Tribune, Wall Street Journal, National Post, Financial Post, Toronto Star, Maclean's*—and radio across the United States and Canada. Appearances total over 700 in all media.

Work Doctor, Inc., is the premier consulting firm that focuses on employer solutions to correct and prevent workplace bullying. The firm, established in 1985, has focused exclusively on bullying-related organizational problems since 1998.

The original website grew into the Namie network of eight websites reflecting the breadth of their services and information on the topic. The portal site is *www.workplacebullying.org.*

# Introduction

．．．．．．．．．．．．．．．．．．．．．．．．．．．．．．．．．．．．．．．．．．．．．．．．．．．．．．．．．．．．．．．

A simple truth: to stop a bully from turning you into a Target, "just" coldly and unemotionally announce that the irrational, unwanted conduct you are experiencing is unacceptable. Suggest that it will be reported to the company's legal team. Offer the bully one chance to stop at the outset, with your hand raised for effect. Hold up a mirror to the bully's childish and seemingly embarrassing behavior.

Easy to say, right? Easy to understand and dream about, too. But nearly impossible to do. If it were "just" that simple, you would have done it in the first place and skipped all the misery from being the bully's Target. Targets are targeted because they are not BullyProof, for reasons to be explained in detail in this book.

Much of the pain you now feel comes not from that single missed opportunity, but from beating yourself up over not taking sufficient action to right the wrong. The fact is that it was your employer who set the stage for the bully to operate as a loose cannon, failed to constrain him or her when told about it, and made you fend for yourself, isolated at work. The true culprit is the employer, and you never could have taken on that reform task alone.

Based on the thousands of individuals we have coached and interviewed during the first decade of the Workplace Bullying Institute, we developed an action plan for individuals. It is not the most obvious set of suggestions. The three-step plan (in chapter 17) flies in the face of conventional wisdom. Our principal purpose is to help individuals caught in the web of lies spun by a bully at work to escape to safety as quickly as possible, to minimize harmful effects from exposure to undeserved stress. Take a peek at chapter 17 to see where you should be headed.

Section One introduces the bullying phenomenon and its prevalence. Bullying is the scourge of the contemporary workplace but is too easily ignored by the people who could eradicate it if they were motivated, the residents of the C-suites—executives, administrators, and owners. The section ends with a test of your readiness to fight back. You will not be successful if you act prematurely. Readiness is determined more by how strongly bullying has affected you than your willingness to fight.

If you have a spouse or partner who also shares the experience, the journey out of Targethood should be taken by you both. Therefore, it is a good idea to have that person and other caring acquaintances become familiar with the first section of the book, to be able to share the terminology and to appreciate the seriousness of your situation.

Section Two contains exercises designed to help you understand the uninvited hurricane that overwhelmed your life. Some readers will need to visit and revisit this section before being able to move on. For others, these are chapters that will be more applicable after you've undertaken the action plan.

Section Three describes our approach to getting safe or stopping the bullying, sometimes accomplishing both goals.

Section Four squarely places the burden for stopping bullying where it belongs—on employers who design and assign tasks and positions, hire the mix of people who comprise the pool of exploitable targeted individuals and the few malicious exploiters, and who either encourage or stop the bullying when it is reported. One chapter demonstrates that the rest of the western industrialized (some say civilized) world blames the work environment for fostering and sustaining bullying. All international laws firmly fix responsibility for prevention and correction on employers. The United States is dead last. The final chapter shares the hopeful story of the WBI-Legislative Campaign and its attempt to have U.S. worker protections catch up with the rest of the world.

......................................................

# The Workplace Bullying Phenomenon: Silent Epidemic

# Chapter One:

# Bullying at Work

*All the great things are simple, and many can be expressed in a single word: freedom, justice, honor, duty, mercy, hope.*
—Sir Winston Churchill

Bullying at work is repeated, health-harming mistreatment of a person by one or more workers that takes the form of verbal abuse; conduct or behaviors that are threatening, intimidating, or humiliating; sabotage that prevents work from getting done; or some combination of the three. Perpetrators are bullies; those on the receiving end are Targets.

It is psychological violence—sublethal and nonphysical—a mix of verbal and strategic assaults to prevent the Target from performing work well. It is illegitimate conduct in that it prevents work from getting done. Thus, an employer's legitimate business interests are not met.

The bully puts her or his personal agenda of controlling another human being above the needs of the employing organization. That control is typically a combination of deliberate humiliation and the withholding of resources that the Target requires to succeed in the workplace. As a result of pressure from the bully's campaign of unremitting pressure, the Target's health—physical and psychological—social support network, family, and career are jeopardized.

If this is what is happening to you, you are not alone!

To answer how big a problem bullying is, the Workplace Bullying Institute (WBI) and Zogby International, prestigious pollsters, surveyed 7,740 adult Americans just prior to Labor Day 2007. That study became the U.S. Workplace Bullying Survey, the first national scientific poll, representing the experiences of all Americans.

The main question was whether or not the survey respondent experienced or witnessed any or all of the following types of repeated mistreatment: sabotage by others that prevented work from getting done, verbal abuse, threatening conduct, intimidation, or humiliation.

The startling result was that 37 percent of American workers have been bullied at work—13 percent said it was either happening now or had happened within a year of the polling, and 24 percent said they were not now being bullied but had been bullied in the past. Adding the 12 percent who witnessed bullying but never experienced it directly, nearly half (49 percent) of adult Americans are affected by it.

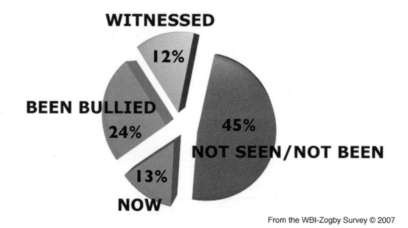

From the WBI-Zogby Survey © 2007

According to the Bureau of Labor Statistics, 146 million Americans were employed in July 2007. That means an estimated 54 million Americans have been bullied at work, using the 37 percent rate. Even the more conservative 13 percent rate (those currently experiencing it) places 19 million American workers at risk. It's an epidemic.

The epidemic is hardly discussed, though. It is shrouded in silence because the other half of Americans (45 percent) claim to neither have experienced it nor seen it. It is a silent epidemic.

Half of the bullying happens in front of witnesses; but half does not. There might be a plausible explanation for not noticing. According to the WBI-Zogby Survey, male bullies prefer public bullying more than female bullies (57.8 percent vs. 48.6 percent), while female bullies prefer to abuse behind closed doors (47.2 percent vs. 38.3 percent).

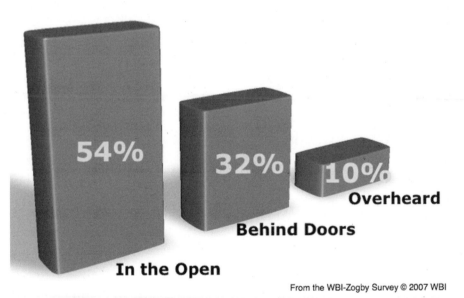

From the WBI-Zogby Survey © 2007 WBI

Perpetrators are women and men who torment women and men of all races and ages, in all workplaces, regardless of size or type of business. The majority of bullies are men (60 percent), the majority of Targets are women (57 percents). However, men and women target others differently based on gender.

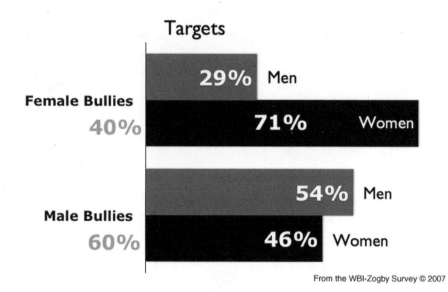

Targets

Female Bullies
40%

29% Men

71% Women

Male Bullies
60%

54% Men

46% Women

From the WBI-Zogby Survey © 2007

Women target women in 71 percent of cases, targeting other women 2.5 times as frequently as they target men, whereas male bullies are equal opportunity abusers, showing a slight preference toward bullying men.

Each inappropriate or inadequate response to the reported cruelty by employers, institutional helpers, and the legal system add to the troubles Targets face. All contribute to sustaining the cruelty. Remarkably, the organization's resources are predictably marshaled to defend the bully instead of the wronged Target. From the Target's perspective, the work world has colluded against her to do her harm.

It always begins with one-on-one aggression, but soon escalates as the bully engulfs others in the laser-focused campaign of interpersonal destruction directed against the Target.

Unchecked bullying quickly escalates into an abusive, toxic work-place where everyone suffers. If ignored long enough, the entire organization is placed at risk.

# Targets and Bullies

Out of respect to those being abused, we capitalize the word *Target*. Targets are people who merely had the bad fortune to run into a bully too lazy to acquire the insight about her own personal list of deficiencies, her lack of self-esteem. A Target drifts in, and hopefully out of, the crosshairs of the bully's scope. Target status can be temporary or it can drone on for years.

# Targets, Not Victims

Bullies select Targets to harm. Targets are recipients of unrelenting verbal and tactical assaults that cut to the core of the Target's being. Over time, the Target's personality gets trampled, bent out of recognition even to herself. When Targets see themselves as victims, two undesirable things can happen:

1. If they have a personal history of being exploited by others in their family or in other relationships, victimhood instantly re-creates a painful time. Once there, victims find it harder to act to reverse their situation. Bullying is certainly traumatizing for those with prior experience. This affects the intensity of the damages done; it does not justify the bully's actions nor relieve the employer of responsibility for putting the Target in harm's way and not protecting her once the bullying is reported.
2. Victimhood begets powerlessness, helplessness, and an inability to change matters for the better. Once out of the crosshairs, the Target can again enjoy safety and work.

# Targets Don't Deserve or Want What They Get.

# Bullies Are Liars and Cowards!

BullyProofing is about reclaiming dignity and self-respect. Unfortunately, the reclamation project seems to require that Targets make tremendous sacrifices to stop the bullying. In our WBI-Zogby Survey, we asked what stopped the bullying. Forty percent of Targets quit their jobs, which represents the preventable loss of 21.6 million workers (based on the estimated 54 million who are bullied) at a time when employers face critical shortages of skilled workers. Further, if one makes the conservative estimate that half of the bullied employees' terminations are the result of a bullying boss and not *just cause* separations, an additional 6.5 million employees lose their jobs to preventable bullying. The total turnover estimate attributable to bullying can be reasonably stated to be 28 million American workers.

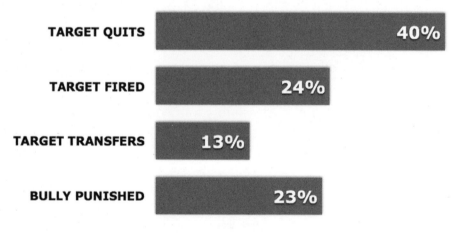

From the WBI-Zogby Survey © 2007 WBI

While attempting to escape bullying, female Targets were more likely to quit than men (45 percent vs. 32.3 percent). WBI has found that the sooner targeted individuals restore safety, by any means, the healthier they remain or the more quickly they recover from their injuries.

The British author Andrea Adams coined the phrase "workplace bullying." It is an instantly recognizable term to Americans. Every time we stand in line at a store, sit at an airport, or talk to a reporter, we get to hear someone's tale of torment at work, either theirs or a friend's. It is that common, a "silent epidemic" ready to be pushed into the light of day (or to face press and media scrutiny as defined in the modern world).

# Bullying—Familiar Yet Different

## A Different Type of Harassment

When we say "harassment," most of us automatically think of sexual harassment, which we all know is illegal by state and federal laws. In order for harassment to be illegal and actionable in court, the recipient/victim/Target's civil rights must be violated. Further, that person must be a member of a recognized "protected status" group. In the United States there are seven civil rights–protected status groups (*gender* and *race* being the most prominent) to which a person may belong in order to file a discrimination complaint or lawsuit. In addition, discrimination is prohibited if *age* or *disability* can be shown to be the reasons for the harassment. Illegal harassment is *status-based*. In Canada, it's called grounds-based harassment.

Bullying cuts across boundaries of status group membership. Bullying is *status-blind* harassment. It must be distinguished from illegal varieties of harassment. Bullying happens when harassment is same-gender or same-race or when the bully enjoys potential legal protection because he or she is a member of a status-protected group.

According to the WBI-Zogby Survey, bullying most often involves same-gender harassment, totaling 61 percent of cases—32 percent man-on-man and 29 percent woman-on-woman.

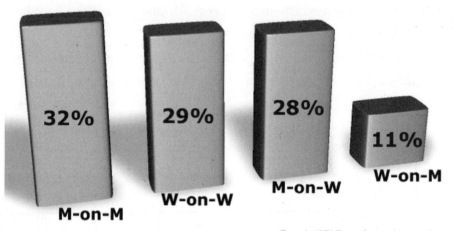

32% M-on-M
29% W-on-W
28% M-on-W
11% W-on-M

From the WBI-Zogby Survey © 2007 WBI

Bullying is four times more prevalent than illegal, discriminatory harassment. (Based on the 80:20 ratio; in only 20 percent of harassment incidents would the targeted person have been eligible for a potential discrimination complaint or lawsuit.) Bullies enjoy civil rights protection in 31 percent of all cases. And from WBI's anecdotal experience, they, the bullies, are the ones to threaten employers with lawsuits to stop investigations or attempts to curb the mistreatment.

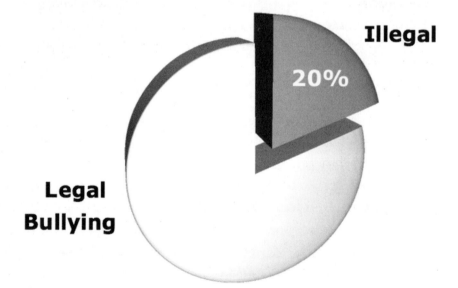

Illegal
20%
Legal Bullying

From the WBI-Zogby Survey © 2007 WBI

Bullying is rarely illegal. The attitude held by many employers seems to be "don't like it, sue me."

Employers must respond appropriately when employment laws exist. Since bullying is not currently illegal, how do employers react to bullying? In 62 percent of cases, when employers are made aware of bullying, they escalate the problem for the Target or simply do nothing. Doing nothing is not a neutral act when an individual explicitly asks for help. When nothing is done, the employer becomes the bully's accomplice, either deliberately or inadvertently, by allowing it to continue unabated. Employers rendered help in less than a third of situations.

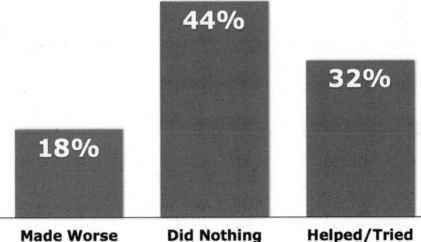

From the WBI-Zogby Survey © 2007 WBI

Please understand that the presence of a law simply gives one the "right to sue." In turn, that means placing yourself in financial jeopardy at the hands of an attorney, pro-corporate judge, or a jury whose decisions can be overruled easily over the course of several years. Even when the settlement or award is paid, the payoff hardly justifies prolonging the agony that bullying started. Legal solutions are rarely satisfying.

*Psychological violence.* Bullying operates most similarly to domestic violence (DV). In DV, the battered victim endures at least verbal abuse.

11

She is told she is undeserving of respect, is worthless, is incompetent and not lovable. The batterer, feeling more powerful, keeps his victim guessing about when the next episode will occur. Between bouts of violence, during the honeymoon phases, kindness is granted. All aspects of the victim's life are controlled by the abuser. He isolates his victim, keeping away friends who can provide social support and a reality check during stressful times. Eventually, friends tire of the victim's inability to get out by herself. They do not appreciate the imprisonment that binds the victim. They only see her futility and helplessness.

Bullying is DV in which the abuser is on the payroll. Co-workers are the do-nothing witnesses. Executives and senior managers are apologists for the bully. Soon, the Target comes to doubt her or his ability to get to safety again. The paycheck and the perception, real or imagined, that no alternatives exist form the bars that imprison the Target.

In 2005, the National Institute for Occupational Safety and Health (NIOSH) convened a special meeting on workplace aggression and workplace bullying. NIOSH recognizes bullying as a form of workplace violence. Bullying is violence whose impact is inevitably emotionally based on assaults which may or may not be psychological in nature (e.g., mind games played by the bully).

Critics say that strong words do not harm people. The notion is that Targets just need to grow a thicker skin to withstand the inevitable assaults that are a routine part of working.

Jeff Tannenbaum, a lawyer at the national employment law firm Littler Mendelson, told the *San Francisco Business Times* (7/19/99) that bullying has its benefits. "This country was built by mean, aggressive sons of bitches," said Tannenbaum. "Inappropriate bullying is in the eye of the beholder. Some people may need a little appropriate bullying in order to do a good job."

People like the educated and licensed, yet ignorant, Tannenbaum assert that those who claim to be bullied are really just wimps who can't handle "a little constructive criticism." He and others like him need to familiarize themselves with recent research that dramatizes the destructive power of verbal abuse and social exclusion.

You are probably familiar with MRI scanners, which help diagnose many physical problems. The MRI can also take pictures of the brain while it is processing information. Areas of the engaged brain light up because oxygen is rushing to those areas. In real time, we can see how the brain is functioning.

Relevant to bullying is a set of studies by Kip Williams and his colleagues at Purdue University in which people were insulted while being scanned (real-time MRI is called fMRI, or functional MRI). It turns out that insults, a form of verbal abuse, trigger neuronal pain pathways. It literally hurts to be insulted. Furthermore, when people in a social experiment are inexplicably and without warning excluded from a fun activity with others, the brain responds in ways that mirror trauma and pain. Social exclusion is painful; it's real.

Are bullied Targets weak? According to the WBI-Zogby Survey, no whiners or complainers in this group. They endure much stress in silence. Bullied individuals rarely confront or act in an adversarial

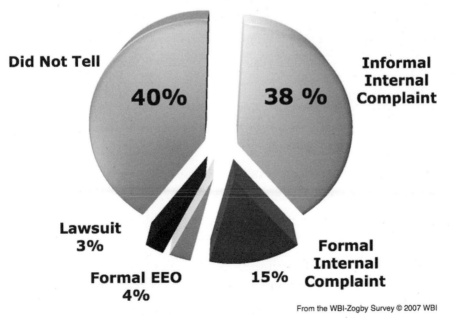

From the WBI-Zogby Survey © 2007 WBI

manner. They sued in only 3 percent of cases and filed a formal complaint in only 4 percent of cases; 38 percent *informally* notified their employers, and 40 percent did not even tell their employers.

Some gender differences surfaced. Male Targets were more likely than women to take no action (45.5 percent vs. 37 percent). Targets were more likely to informally complain to their employer when the bully was a woman than when it was a man (42.6 percent vs. 35.6 percent) and more likely to do nothing when the bully was a man than when it was a woman (43.8 percent vs. 36 percent).

Targets are not whiners. They stay "under thumb" for a long time, far too long in most cases. The survey showed that 73 percent of bullied Targets endure bullying for more than six months; 44 percent for more than one year.

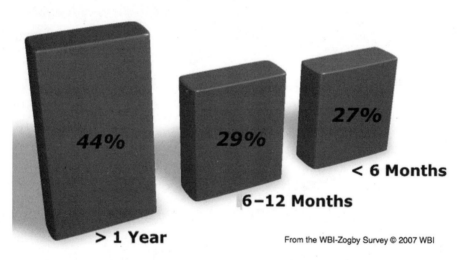

From the WBI-Zogby Survey © 2007 WBI

*Schoolyard bullying*—the torment of one child by another—is often compared to workplace bullying. Both types share common underlying principles: the desperate grab for control by an insecure, inadequate person, and the exercise of power through the humiliation of the Target. School-age bullies, if reinforced by cheering kids, fearful teachers, or ignorant administrators, grow up as dominating people. If it works for them, there is no reason to change. At work as adults, they do what they do best—bully others. An unknown percentage of workplace bullies have a lifelong record of disrespecting the needs of others. Of course, the cues given off in a super-competitive workplace will draw out the dark side of many others who were not bullies in a prior life, witnesses perhaps, but rarely Targets.

The stakes for workplace bullying are more serious than in school. Bullying threatens the economic livelihood not only of the Target but the Target's family. When a bully decides to capriciously destabilize a Target's career, years of investment in terms of time and money are at risk. Finally, the most important difference—the one that distinguishes our approach to solutions—is that the child Target must have the help and support of third-party adults to reverse the conflict. Bullied adults have the primary responsibility for righting the wrong themselves, for engineering a solution. When others intervene on their behalf—as when a more aggressive, well-intentioned spouse takes over finding the solution—the Target suffers additional consequences from giving away her independence.

Ironically, bullying among students in school happens in a location that just happens to be the workplace for adult teachers and staff. It is logical that if kids witness adults being bullied and see the impact on the Targets, the adults are modeling aggression for the kids, showing them "how to." A toxic environment for adults in schools certainly interferes with successful learning. Perhaps before launching the state law–mandated anti-bullying programs for school kids, district administrators and school boards should stop the systemic bullying that is constantly reported to them. WBI has launched the national demonstration project in a pilot school district in the Midwest to introduce our program to an entire school district and to measure its impact on a variety of indicators of school success. Progress and results can be tracked at the WBI website.

*Incivility and rudeness.* These rarely trigger stress in the people who experience them. Toe picking, knuckle cracking, belching, and nostril reaming are all offensive and undignified. However, they reflect only on the socialization of the picker, cracker, belcher, and reamer. It's not bullying until the bully does something to the Target. If the bully picks the Target's toes (against her wishes) or picks her nose (without permission) and this offensive behavior hurts her emotionally, it could be bullying. Social mistakes not expressly done to affect another person may be cute to talk about, but they do not qualify as bullying according to our criteria.

Chris Pearson, PhD, is an "incivilities" researcher. Her survey of workers who admitted they were the Targets of rudeness or disrespect revealed that 12 percent felt compelled to leave their jobs. The WBI-Zogby Survey found that 77 percent of bullied individuals lost the jobs they once loved in order to stop the bullying. Incivility pales when compared to bullying with respect to negativity, severity, and impact.

*Workplace violence.* Violence includes homicides and battery—physically striking a person. A bullying-prone workplace can be quite pathological, gripped in fear, with everyone, including management, too petrified to hold the bully accountable for unforgivable behavior. The bully routinely practices psychological violence against his Target. Yet, he rarely has to resort to physical violence or threats of it to satisfy his control needs. Some bullies do threaten violence, but nearly all bullies are content to damage people without fists or weapons.

> *Violence in the workplace begins long before lethal weapons extin-*
> *guish lives. Where resentment and aggression routinely displace*
> *cooperation and communication, violence has occurred.*
> —Bernice Fields, Arbitrator

Zero-tolerance workplace violence policy clauses enable a manager to provoke workers over the course of several years and to terminate them immediately if they dare to counter with an emotional verbal threat. The workplace has become a police state for some based on irrational fears.

*One federal worker, a mother with kids in childcare, was dragged away unceremoniously from work in handcuffs when she innocently commented that since her workplace was hell (and she had her bully to blame for that) she could sympathize with postal workers who had become violent because no one listened to them either. She not only lost her job, she was prohibited to contact her children while she wrangled with law enforcement that night.*

Are bullied Targets a violence risk? In the rarest of circumstances, a Target, after years of mistreatment at the hands of a tyrant and inaction by the employer, saw no alternative and turned to violence.

*One man killed himself and his branch manager on the day of his return from recuperation from a heart attack induced by that manager. The manager greeted him in the parking lot and provoked him before entering the office. The man, described as very gentle and caring by all who knew him, got in his car and drove away, only to return minutes later with a loaded gun. His co-workers considered the killings a tragedy only because of the suicide. It turns out that the branch manager was a favorite in the state capitol. His reputation was as a "turnaround guy" who cracked the whip in each of the several offices to which he was assigned. Staff turnover, workers' compensation, and disability claims were his legacy. He was hated by employees, though encouraged and respected by the folks in the central office who generally disrespected their workforce.*

Post-shooting analysts carefully have to dissect each episode of workplace violence. If the shooter selects certain people, then we at WBI are reasonably sure that those victims had previously frustrated the person by ignoring or denying repeated complaints about mistreatment at work. That is, when the victims are an EEO officer, a Human Resources staffer, or the boss of the bully, then we can attribute the violence to unaddressed bullying. Sadly, the knee-jerk, simplistic story told is that the shooter was a wacko. Reporters interview the bullying supervisor who defames the employee as a poor performer "with troubles" as the body is being loaded into the coroner's wagon.

It is more common for Targets to direct the violence inward and commit suicide. Given the roles shame and humiliation play in their lives, Targets have great difficulty getting out of bed and often suffer from depression. By the time they kill themselves, they have lost their marriages, their homes, their children, and all hope of surviving economically. It was bullying that probably drove them out of the job and started the decline in the quality of their lives in the first place. Unfortunately, the link between the suicide and the cruel mistreatment and subsequent loss of the job is less obvious than the trail of bodies in a public shooting rampage. A federal agency union representative knew of nine suicides in one year in her region directly attributable to bullying.

On a scale of damage one could suffer at work, incivilities would fall near the low end. Bullying would cover a wide middle range of destructive, intimidating workplace practices. Physical violence appears at the high end, score 10.

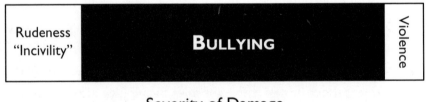

Severity of Damage

# The Workplace Bullying Institute, Catalyst for Change

Workplace bullying is a serious threat to:

- Freedom from fear and trauma
- Employee health and safety
- Civil rights in the workplace

- Dignity at work
- Personal self-respect
- Family cohesion and stability
- Work team morale and productivity
- Employment practices liability
- Retention of skilled employees
- Employer reputation

Bullying is a multi-faceted problem that requires multi-disciplinary solutions:

- Behavioral and organizational researchers
- Medicine
- Mental health practitioners
- Legal resources
- Organized labor
- Employee advocates
- Management and Human Resources
- Dispute-resolution specialists
- Education
- Government

Target silence and shame coupled with the permanence of human aggression probably ensure that bullying will never be completely stopped. Notwithstanding these realities, we must aim to create a bullying-free world of work, contenting ourselves with any accomplishments along the journey.

> *Do not wait for leaders; do it alone, person to person.*
> —Mother Teresa

*Chapter Two:*

# Understanding Bullies

*There is overwhelming evidence that the higher the level of self-esteem, the more likely one will be to treat others with respect, kindness, and generosity.*
— Nathaniel Branden

It takes two to make a relationship grow from an initial spark. This is true for love and for some exploitative relationships, too. In most couples, each person wants something, otherwise nothing develops. Ideally, in a partnership, each person needs the other in some way.

However, the Target–bully pathological "relationship" is different because:

- The Target is swept into the relationship involuntarily, simply because the employer put the Target in harm's way by work assignment and then insisted that the battered partner not be allowed to escape without significant sacrifice.
- The bully controls every aspect of the reign of terror—when to attack, when to hold back, the place, and the audience.
- Mutual benefit or gain is not the goal, control is, and the Target wants none of it.

- The undermining, scheming bully's tactics are so unwelcome, inappropriate, and undeserved that in no way can the Target be held responsible, even partially responsible.
- It is impossible to rationalize that the Target benefits.
- Bullies need Targets to thrive; Targets find it hard to thrive when bullies intrude upon their lives.

*The people have always some champion whom they set over them and nurse into greatness…. This and no other is the root from which a tyrant springs.*
—Plato

# Why Bullies Bully

Explanation 1: Because they CAN!

Explanation 2: Work Environment-Driven Three-Factor Model

Our model sandwiches the role of the bully's personality—and its toxic combination with a well-intentioned, apolitical Target—between two factors that are entirely in the employer's control. This means that employers can stop bullying by tweaking the environment. With our model, solutions are possible. The emphasis is on *what* to change, rather than *who* to change.

## A. *Opportunities for Worker-on-Worker Aggression Created*

The employer designs work—deliberately or accidentally—that creates cutthroat competition between workers. Employees are pitted against each other in positions or tasks that allow only one winner to emerge, creating many losers. *Zero-sum competition* is another name for winner-take-all outcomes. Wins come at the expense of the losers; victory is carved out of the hides of the vanquished. This is obvious in sales organizations, but anyone can be induced to be cutthroat when rewards, status, or resources are scarce. There's not enough pay or promotions available in government or education; hence, those workplaces are especially prone to bullying.

## B. Mix of People—Exploiters and a Pool of Easily Exploited Targets

Only a small percentage of those who see and seize the opportunities to bully others are cruel manipulators. They must simply be willing to harm others. You might think you are immune, but we all have a dark side. Under threatening circumstances, we ordinary people are capable of incredible cruelty to other humans if we think we have to do so to survive.

Exploiters need be nothing more than Machiavellian. They are ambitious, not cruel. They just want to get ahead and are willing to use others to help achieve their selfish goals. It's the American way of doing business. They are not necessarily disturbed or psychopathic. They look good when viewed from the top.

Targets, as you will learn throughout this book, are blessed/cursed with a strong work ethic. They just want to be "left alone" to do their work. In the most bullying-prone industries, we've found that many employees share a prosocial orientation. They are the "do-gooders." They want to heal the sick, teach and develop the young, care for the elderly, work with the addicted and abused in society. They are ripe for exploitation. While they focus on doing good and noble things and wait to be rewarded for their quality work, they expose their backs for the bully to sink her or his claws into.

## C. The Wrong Employer Response

There are three possible responses to bullying when cases are reported to the employer, either formally or informally.

- It is unequivocally condemned as unacceptable and the perpetrator is punished.

- It is ignored—a form of tacit, informal approval that sends a message seen by all.
- It is rewarded, the perpetrator is promoted or triumphantly showcased as a winner.

Our national 2007 WBI-Zogby Survey showed that employers tend to ignore bullying in 44 percent of cases and actually worsen it in an additional 18 percent of cases.

For Labor Day 2008, WBI conducted a smaller online survey of 400 individuals (an unscientific sample because the respondents visited the website and volunteered to complete the short survey) in which we delved more deeply. As reported by bullied Targets, when the employer was told about the bullying, here is what they did:

- 1.7 percent conducted a fair investigation and protected the Target from further bullying with negative consequences for the bully
- 6.2 percent conducted a fair investigation with negative consequences for the bully but no safety for the Target
- 8.7 percent conducted an inadequate/unfair investigation with no consequences for the bully or Target
- 31 percent conducted an inadequate/unfair investigation with no consequences for the bully while the Target was retaliated against
- 12.8 percent of employers did nothing or ignored the complaint, with no consequences for the bully or Target
- 15.7 percent of employers did nothing; the Target was retaliated against for reporting the bullying but kept her job

- 24 percent of employers did nothing; the Target was retaliated against and eventually lost her job

You can see that employers predominantly did nothing (53 percent) and actually retaliated against the Target in 71 percent of cases who dared to report it.

Consider how workers interpret the employer's response. When positive consequences follow bullying, the bullies are emboldened. Promotions and rewards are explicitly positive. But it is also positive when they are not punished. Bullies who bully others with impunity become convinced they can get away with it forever. Bullying becomes part of the culture, the "way things are done around here."

Factors A and C are completely in the employer's control. Employers determine which work is assigned and how it is to be done. Employers shape the work environment. They also hire people who become part of the mix. However, bullies sneak in disguised as high performers and

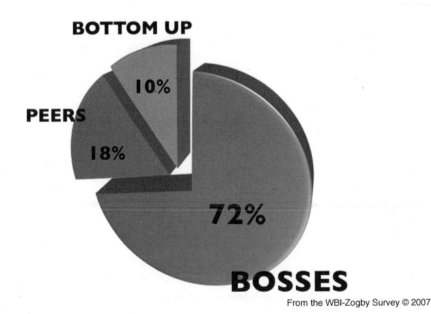

From the WBI-Zogby Survey © 2007

desirably ambitious go-getters. Targets get hired for their qualifications. Never is there a discussion about how abusive the aggressive performer is likely to become when given the chance. Nor is there a discussion about how likely it is that a worker will be traumatized if she or he is exposed to an abusive work environment.

*Bully bosses.* The stereotype rings in our ears. It feels so right. The press loves the alliteration, too. According to the WBI-Zogby Survey, it's real. Most bullies are bosses.

It makes sense that if bullies threaten the economic livelihood of their Targets, they do so only with the title power and authority to make good on their combative promise. Petty tyrants need the title power of supervisor, manager, or executive to operate.

It is also true that most bullying flows downhill. Workers who do not manage others comprise the majority of bullied Targets. However, when all levels of managers are grouped together—first-line supervisors, middle managers, and senior managers—they reported being bullied, too.

Naturally, executives live relatively free of bullying by others. The

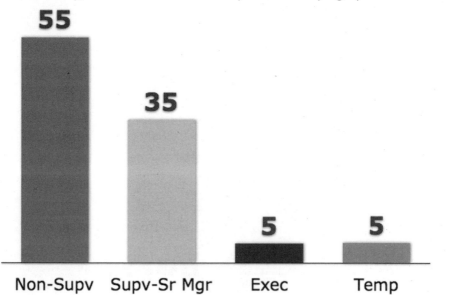

From the WBI-Zogby Survey © 2007 WBI

prominent stress researcher, Robert Sapolsky (*Why Zebras Don't Get Ulcers*, 3rd edition, 2004: Holt), based on years of work with baboons, states that the most stress-free life is lived at the top of the hierarchy. Ask CEOs. And the fact that temporary workers are so rarely bullied speaks volumes about how the "employee" status that we all seek in order to enjoy a semblance of financial predictability (and in the United States, about the only way to acquire affordable health insurance) is a double-edged sword. In exchange for the (often lousy) paycheck, we sacrifice our freedom to simply leave when stress overwhelms us.

# Bullies: Types, Tactics, and Tips for Handling

## WBI 2003 Research Says...

### The Top Ten Bullying Tactics

1. Blame for "errors"
2. Unreasonable job demands
3. Criticism of ability
4. Inconsistent compliance with rules
5. Threatens job loss
6. Insults and put-downs
7. Discounting/denial of accomplishments
8. Exclusion, "icing out"
9. Yelling, screaming
10. Stealing credit

Bullies are workplace politicians. Their goal is simple—to control the people they target. To do this, they engage in a variety of tactics. Regardless of the tactics adopted, they all serve to shame, humiliate, and treat the Target like a powerless person. In a bully's mind, Targets are powerless. This distorted thinking is the only way bullies know how to survive the work world: at someone else's expense.

- **Verbal abuse: 53%**

- **Threats, intimidation, humiliation: 53%**

- **Interference with performance: 45%**

- **Abuse of authority: 47%**

- **Destruction of relationships: 30%**

From the WBI-Zogby Survey © 2007 WBI

## Bullies Start All Conflict and Trouble.
## Targets React.

Bullies can be categorized, but individuals who choose to bully can adopt any tactic at any time to accomplish their goal. They are not restricted to neat categories. They adopt one or more styles, as needed. A short list of illustrative tactics accompanies each type of bully. The list is not meant to be exhaustive. The first three types—Screaming Mimi, Constant Critic, Two-Headed Snake—commit acts of commission. That is, they do things to people to disrupt their worklives. The Gatekeeper bullies others by withholding things people need to succeed, thus setting them up to fail and to take the blame for the mess.

## Screaming Mimi

Stereotypical, but statistically rare. Chooses a public setting to showcase her or his attacks. Controls through fear and intimidation. Emotionally out of control. Impulsive. Volatile. Explosive. Threat of physical violence becomes issue. Wants to instill sense of dread. Overbearing. Self-centered, insensitive to needs of others. Very worried

© 2008, WBI

about being detected as imposter. Bombast masks incompetence. Satisfies need for control by dictating the emotional climate in front of audiences who are expected to tremble as a result.

- yells, screams, curses
- barks out loud that "I AM THE BOSS!!!" and to "DO WHAT I TELL YOU!!!"
- poisons workplace with angry outbursts, tantrums
- intimidates through gestures: points fingers, slams things down, throws objects
- crowds the Target's personal space, moves close to threaten or to make the Target anxious, hovers over, sneaks up from behind to startle
- constantly interrupts the Target during meetings and conversations
- discounts and denies the Target's thoughts or feelings
- threatens job loss or punitive transfer
- traps the Target by insisting that complaints go "up the chain of command," starting with her

## Handling Tips

The Screaming Mimi can launch at any time. You immediately feel scolded or judged, as if you were a child. When you attempt to ignore or avoid conflict with a Screaming Mimi, she only sees your passivity as a welcome mat. The more you try to avoid her wrath, the more she will target you. Physical reactions are common in those who work with the Screaming Mimi. Complaints include:

- stomachaches
- back spasms
- headaches
- skin reactions

These symptoms frequently increase with prolonged exposure.

Your productivity decreases and costly mistakes occur more often when an angry person is breathing down your neck. The Screaming Mimi can make you hate your job, make you dread even going to work. A job you love can become a source of depression and this may lead to thoughts of career change. Work frustrations might carry over to your family life.

Protect yourself if someone attacks you personally. Convert feelings of powerlessness into a source of inner strength.

Here are some protection techniques to try:

*The Silent Mantra:* In meditation, the mantra is one of the most powerful ways to relax and stay centered in the midst of chaos. Find a yoga group or start your own meditation program. Then, as soon as the angry person starts to speak, repeat this mantra:

> *Hear the valuable stuff.*
> *Ignore the anger. It's not yours.*

This takes a little practice. Repeating this phrase silently to yourself when confronted by a verbal attack helps you to deflect the anger and maintain your inner strength. Each time you repeat the silent mantra, you will feel a little less affected by the Screaming Mimi.

*Find the Vulnerable Spot:* A second way to protect yourself and regain your composure is to find the vulnerable spot. Find and focus your attention on the most humorous spot of this person's appearance. Without letting the Screaming Mimi know what you are doing, simply think about the one feature of the bully's physical appearance you find most awkward. Remember to do this silently. Thus, instead of feeling intimidated or afraid of the bully's outburst, you can feel a renewed sense of inner strength because you are not taking her too seriously.

*Keep a Journal:* Whether or not anyone sees what you write, keep a journal. You need to get your anger out by writing phrases such as:

1. I hate you! You bitch!
2. You have no right to talk to me like that!
3. I am a team player. I'm not a sick workaholic like you.
4. Don't ever talk to me that way again in front of my colleagues.

## Constant Critic

Operates behind closed doors so that later she or he can deny what was said or done to you. Extremely negative. Nitpicker. Perfectionist. Whiner. Complainer. Faultfinder. Liar. Masks personal insecurity with public bravado. Loved by senior management because of her ability to "get those people to produce." Plays parent to your child (as she sees it). Aims to destroy confidence in your competence, encourages self-doubt. Satisfies her need to control with obsession over others' performance. When the bully is a boss, the performance evaluation system is misused to manufacture incompetence where none existed before the new boss.

- put-downs, insults, belittling comments, name-calling

© 2008, WBI

- constant haranguing about the Target's "incompetence"
- makes aggressive eye contact, glaring at the Target; demands eye contact when she speaks but deliberately avoids eye contact when the Target speaks
- negatively reacts to Target contributions with sighs, frowns, peering over top of eyeglasses to condescend, sour face (the "just sucked a lemon" look)
- accuses Target of wrongdoing, blames Target for fabricated errors (doctored documents, compromised databases, fake witness accounts)
- makes unreasonable demands for work with impossible deadlines, applies disproportionate pressure, expects perfection
- sends signals of disrespect through over-confident

body language—sitting at a desk with feet up, showing Target bottom of shoes and talking to Target through feet, grooms self (hair, nails) while ignoring the Target; making Target sit while bully stands, hovering over, staying above

- overuses memos, emails, messages to bury Target in correspondence requiring replies
- personally criticizes aspects of the Target's life that are irrelevant to work—appearance, family, friends
- excessively or harshly criticizes Target's work or abilities
- engages Target in intense cross-examination to belittle and confuse

## Why the Constant Critic Acts As She Does

Many of us work with someone who is extremely negative and nitpicking, someone who never seems satisfied. It might be a perfectionist who relentlessly finds fault or an insecure colleague who criticizes your work with the intention of making you feel small. She uses whining, complaints, and criticism to make everyone else feel insecure. How do you deal with someone whose faultfinding is hard to take and stop them from undermining your own sense of competence?

To improve your situation with the Critic at work, it is critical to uncover and understand why she acts this way. Then it will be easier to stand up to her and not get destroyed by her negativity.

Four things most often seen in the Constant Critic are:

1. The person who deliberately sees that they have an obligation, a reason for living, that states they must find something wrong with everything everyone else does. You will find that

this person once had someone in their life who was extremely critical and demanding. This may have been a father, mentor, or boss. From these experiences, the Constant Critic has the impression that an intelligent person naturally acts this way. Perhaps this Critic once was humiliated or lost a job or business because they were too tolerant of other people's mistakes. In either case, the Critic then made a conscious decision to be sure they are always on top of things in the future.

2.  It is essential to remember that no matter what originally made this person so finicky and unpleasant, she cannot rest or relax until her probing uncovers something for her to complain or worry about.

3.  The Critic has a tone of voice or a way of speaking that is hard to take. When she finds fault with your work for the umpteenth time, it is not just the words that hurt, it is the tone of voice or way of speaking that cuts to the bone, whether it is a whiny tone, a flat monotone, or a staccato way of snapping out criticisms.

4.  Because the Critic constantly struggles to stay in control of every situation, it is almost impossible for her to feel that someone else might also be right. It is more important for her to defend her position than to sit down and brainstorm about solutions to the immediate problem. A constant state of worry and dissatisfaction feels normal to her. She is extremely resistant to change and you will never be able to satisfy her.

## Handling Tips

*Humor:* Using humor can work wonders for you as you go head-to-head with the Constant Critic. As soon as she starts to ask probing, faultfinding questions or begins to make critical remarks, take a deep breath and let it out as you say to yourself, "Thank goodness! My life would not be complete without this person's criticism." Don't say it out loud, only several times to yourself.

This simple phrase can prove to be a tool to take the sting out of potentially invalidating remarks. Using your own wit and sarcasm—in a safe and unspoken way, of course—gives you a protective distance that can't be taken away. Using your sense of humor also prevents the launch of your biochemical "fight or flight" stress response. Most importantly, this allows you to remain in control, to remain intelligent, and to preserve the dignity she desperately wants to take away.

*Get a Second Opinion:* When confronted by a Constant Critic who picks apart both your work and your worthiness, it's hard to not believe she is right. She seems to know exactly how to make you feel small, incompetent, or unworthy.

The most important thing for handling a nitpicker is to get a reliable second opinion to assess the Critic's criticisms and to identify:

- What part of her feedback is accurate and what is just her negative way of complaining about everything?
- What part of her feedback is useful to your work and what part is incorrect, misinformed, or just plain whiny?

Some possible sources for quick and useful second opinions are:

- a good friend or respected ally at work who could help you determine if any of the criticism is useful

- someone you work with whom you can call in a
  crisis to give you reliable information about the
  accuracy of the Critic's comments and suggestions
- a close friend, family member, counselor, or
  therapist who can help you regain your sense of
  self-confidence and professionalism even when
  you have just been torn apart.

When soliciting help from others, it is critical to identify the situation and ask exactly what you are looking for. As soon as possible after a Critic has belittled you or your work, call this supportive individual and explain, "I just left a meeting where I had a boom dropped on my head by (the bully). Would you please remind me that I have the qualifications to be doing this work, and that I am an adult, and I deserve to hold my head up even though (the bully) thinks I am an idiot?"

Don't be afraid to ask for support. Whether looking for a second opinion or an emotional boost, be sure to make the phone call and get the support you need. People usually like to be asked for their expertise and their guidance. If the person you call is too busy at that moment to listen to your situation, find a more convenient time to talk or call another person who can give you the information you require.

## Two-Headed Snake

Passive-aggressive, indirect, dishonest style of dealing with people and issues. Pretends to be nice while sabotaging you. "Friendliness" serves only to decrease resistance to giving information she may later use against you. Smile hides naked aggression. Assassinates reputation with higher-ups. Plays favorites. Satisfies need for control by managing the image of the Target in other people's minds.

- ensures that the Target does not have the
  resources (time, supplies, help) to do work

© 2008, WBI

- demands that co-workers provide damning "evidence" against Target, uses lies or half-truths, threatens noncooperators (the "divide and conquer" technique)
- discriminates against smokers by requiring they gather trash from the parking lot while taking a smoke break
- assigns meaningless or "dirty" tasks as punishment
- makes nasty, rude, hostile remarks directly to Target while putting on a rational "face" for others
- breaches confidentiality; shares private information about the Target with co-workers or other bosses
- discriminates against nonsmoking Target by permitting breaks only for smokers
- creates a special personnel file kept in bully's car or locked in her office full of defamatory information to sabotage Target's career inside or outside the organization
- steals credit for work done by the Target

Snakes pretend to be nice, but actually work against you. Beware! She is selfish and needs to be handled very carefully. Not at all a friend or mentor, the Snake's "friendliness" masks her attempts to gain control.

Two-Headed Snakes come in three varieties:

1. *The "Backstabber" Snake:* Quite simply, this person tells you one thing and then says something entirely different behind your back. They kiss up the ladder and attack those below. She tells you you're wonderful while telling her boss that she needs help getting rid of you because you cannot perform.

2. *The "Jekyll and Hyde" Snake:* This Snake's sweetness mask alternates with her mean streak. She tends to be vicious one minute, human and encouraging the next. Unfortunately, you may be the only one who sees both sides of this controller. Others who only see the sweet side are unsympathetic to your complaints.

3. *The "No Problem, Don't Bother" Snake:* These words, spoken by certain individuals, are often a warning that trouble follows. Snakes tell you "no problem" after they have violated the rules and they want to cover it up. They are unethical creatures and expect help carrying out their unethical plans.

## Handling Tips

*Enlist Supporters:* Don't feel alone and unsupported when someone mistreats you at work. Don't dismiss everyone around you as dishonest. However, take time to talk with a trusted friend or counselor to help you sort out your feelings. When talking to your supporters at work (the ones you know you can trust and the ones you have decided you can talk to), you will probably find you are not the only one who has been mistreated by the Two-Headed Snake. Carefully identify a supporter by asking:

- Have they ever experienced any similar problems with this Snake?
- Are they willing to brainstorm with you on ways to improve the situation without anyone having to take on the Two-Headed Snake alone?
- Would they be willing to back you up if you stood up to the Snake? Be clear about what supportive action you expect.
- Would they be willing to join you in a meeting to confront the situation directly?

*Do's and Don'ts When Jousting with the Snake:* Resist lowering yourself into a dirty, nasty street fight. Snakes are obsessed with appearances—they want to appear cool and collected most of the time. Staying emotionally in control is easier with Snakes than with other bully types.

Be clear that you will not tolerate or cooperate with misleading or dishonest statements to help the Snake lie.

Be prepared for this person to argue, threaten, lie, or try most anything to coerce you into cooperating with her. Keep repeating what you consider unacceptable behavior and what you will and will not do.

Avoid waiting too long to bring up the problem or trying to transform or "fix" this bully.

The right words to say to a Snake often require practice. By practicing, you appear less defensive and are more likely to prevent yourself from verbally attacking the Snake (although it might feel good). Some discussion starters that allow you to maintain control:

"I want us to work together. Here's what we can do to make that happen…"

"There's a specific problem you and I can solve if we remember to…"

"There's something you do that I need to ask you to try to do a little differently next time…"

"There's a way you and I can improve our work situation. Are you interested?"

Though the above statements are rational and do not attack or criticize, don't be surprised when the Snake slips into denial. Snakes are bullies. Bullies are illogical. At least you tried.

When working with a Snake, you need to act the minute you suspect that she might be manipulating you. Ask for clarification regarding the specific procedures and results she is after. Your demand for clarity will frustrate the person who relies on clouding every interaction to feel in control. Clarity cuts through confusion. Others will respect you for it. In the process, the Snake's deviousness can be revealed to her supporters as well as her enemies.

## Gatekeeper

© 2008, WBI

Most transparent of the controllers. They need to establish themselves as "one up" on you, to order you around, or to control your circumstances. They control all resources you need to succeed—sufficient time to complete projects, training to prepare for a new assignment, supplies, praise, approval, money, staffing, or collaboration with peers. She satis-fies her need for control by putting herself in the middle of everything, making her feel important.

- deliberately cuts the Target out of the communication loop—stops mail, email, memo distribution, doesn't return calls
- refuses to make "reasonable accommodation" for a Target returning to work with a disability
- refuses to follow internal policies and government-mandated employee protections for Target
- denies privileges and rights to Targets who file complaints against the bully, either an internal complaint or a lawsuit or with the EEOC
- ignores the Target; gives the "silent treatment" and models isolation/exclusion for others
- sets office clocks fifteen minutes ahead of "real" time, then punishes Target for being late at start of day, while not allowing her to leave before quitting time according to "real" time
- makes up new rules on a whim that the Target is expected to follow while the bully is exempt

## Handling Tips

There will be times in every job when you are ignored. One of the games people play at work is the game of exclusion. Not inviting you to an important meeting, not sending a copy of an important memo, not letting you know about ongoing work in progress, or not including you in an important social gathering. This treatment is designed to make you feel invalidated and worthless.

This situation is quite different than dealing with a specific person-ality style who is difficult to work with. The Gatekeeper is not always a boss, but she might be someone you once considered a friend. By some change of circumstance, you and this person used to see eye-to-eye but now you are being treated with coldness or disrespect.

*Why has this person changed?*

Try to recall:

- What was it like when you initially met this person? How did you get along then?
- What changed?
- Did something change in the other person's workload or status at work, thus making her more cold and rigid?
- Did something change in the bully's personal life—perhaps a financial situation making her more secretive or unapproachable?
- Was there an incident between you that left bad feelings?
- In what ways have your needs begun to clash with hers?
- Why does this bully feel the need to put up a wall or keep you at a distance?

Try to take her perspective:

- Were there clues early on that this individual was going to put up barriers toward you or others?
- Is this bully threatened by you being rewarded at work and is shutting you out of the loop?
- If you were in her shoes, would you have any reason to exclude others at work?
- Could you possibly remind this individual of someone else—a parent, sibling, spouse, ex-spouse, boss, or ex-boss—who gave this individual a hard time?

- In what way did you also put up a wall and feel the need to keep the other person at a distance?

In most cases it is not just the bully who has changed. Her actions could have caused you to put up your own wall:

- Does this bully irritate you or cause you to feel cold or distant?
- Does this person remind you of someone else— a parent, sibling, spouse, ex-spouse, boss, or ex-boss—who gives you a hard time?
- Has something happened in your life that has made you a little more rigid or judgmental toward others?
- Is there something about the other person's style of doing things that you find frustrating, building tension between you?

To answer these questions, you will need to do more than just feel hurt. Talk to friends and co-workers about how they see your actions. If your first reaction is that this person doesn't like you or doesn't respect you, try and find out from colleagues if she has been under pressure lately. Maybe she is putting up a wall for reasons that have nothing to do with you. The more you find out about the way you are being treated, the more clarity you will have about the situation. Use a personal journal to detail your feelings.

Once you have a good handle on your feelings, find a way to actually discuss your feelings with the Gatekeeper. This heart-to-heart discussion may be hard to do, but it is the clearest way to find out what is happening. Plan where you want to stage this talk. The best place usually isn't at work. Try to plan a quiet time away from the office.

When you finally get to the point of staging this meeting, don't be discouraged if the Gatekeeper puts up resistance. Remember, this is a person you need to work with on a daily basis, and conflicts need to be resolved. Don't be discouraged if it takes more than one try to set up a meeting.

Expect the beginning of the meeting to be awkward. This is why you are here. Once the ice is broken, address the problems you are having with the coldness you feel between the two of you. The success of this meeting will depend on your honesty and sincerity. Stating the issues simply and calmly will allow the Gatekeeper to listen to your words without becoming antagonistic and feeling the need to defend herself.

If the Gatekeeper will never agree to meet with you, much less listen to your feelings or needs, you will need to enlist the aid of someone in the office who will tell you when the Gatekeeper leaves you out of the loop. A co-worker who has good rapport with the Gatekeeper can act as a conduit or mediator. Don't be afraid or ashamed to ask this person to help you. Consider using a phrase such as, "I need a favor, (the bully) is giving me the cold shoulder and you seem to be on good terms with both of us. Can you help me arrange a meeting for the three of us to get together and clear this up?"

Dealing with a Gatekeeper can trigger feelings left from your past experiences—monitor your own reactions when you feel left out. Even if you think these old wounds are long forgotten and in your past, a frustrating situation can trigger emotions from long ago. You might need to work through the emotional issues in your personal journal, with a close friend, or with a therapist. What did you do in the past at work when you have encountered a Gatekeeper? In the past, how did you get a Gatekeeper to take you seriously and stop excluding you? Thinking about and answering these questions should give you some good insight about your situation.

Remember that timing is everything and the situation can be resolved, but there are seldom overnight changes.

# Origins of Bullies

It is absolutely critical that you, the Target, not ruminate about the bully's motivation. It's not easy when flooded with emotions, all negative, that beg the answer to the question *Why did he do what he did?* You can't believe someone can be that cruel. In fact, they can and are often so cruel.

Searching for the answer can prove elusive. It's a waste of your time. You are postponing taking steps to make yourself safe. So shelve your curiosity about the bully and read on to understand why you were most likely the chosen one. Because you are a Target, you may actually have empathy for the bully. You may be tempted to make allowances for the bully's deficient upbringing, the previous night's fight with the spouse, being driven crazy by her or his kids, pressures from senior management to produce more with less staff. Forget the rational explanations for the irrational and despicable mistreatment you have had to endure. It is unconscionable that you are expected to endure the assaults and suffer in silence.

It's the bully's behaviors that are wrong, regardless of who the bully is as a human being. To partly satisfy your curiosity, here's a partial explanation of bullies' motivation based on socialization and personality. Remember, knowing *why* does absolutely nothing to stop the misconduct in the workplace. To stop it, you will need the employer to change, not the bully. The stress will kill you before the bully will likely reform.

People arrive at bullyhood by at least three different paths: through personality development; by reading cues in a competitive, political workplace; and by accident.

## Chronic Bullies

Chronic bullies try to dominate people in nearly every encounter— at work and away from work. They bully waitstaff at restaurants as well as workplace Targets. They say, "I can't help who I am. Don't like it? Leave," always believing that they do not have to change. Who could argue with their "success"?

The motivation for chronic bullies is their own failure to confront their deepest feelings of personal inadequacy, their self-loathing. Unfortunately, they lack the insight to analyze themselves critically. Their lives are out of their control in some way. So, they control others to compensate. Though they are aware they are intimidating others, they do not necessarily see the connection between personal flaws and their actions. They invent flaws in others (which are mirror images of their own), then irrationally attack others to feel good about themselves.

## Bullies Are Inadequate, Defective, and Poorly Developed People.

## Targets Are Empathetic, Just, and Fair People.

Most bullies were probably brash, bratty kids at school. Schoolyard bullies who were never stopped in childhood grow up to bully others in the workplace. Because people react to them either with fear or indifference, they are used to getting their own way in every situation in which they exert themselves. It's a self-reinforcing cycle. They dominate, others submit or turn away in silence, so they dominate more.

In companies that promote cutthroat competition, chronic bullies are overrepresented. They are seen as "leaders."

Chronic bullies are trapped by a personality they've honed over a lifetime. At this stage of their lives, they couldn't change who they are even if they wanted to. It is true that some chronic bullies have certifiable character disorders—either Antisocial or Narcissistic Personality Disorders. In the general population, these types of people are statistically rare, hovering around 2 to 3 percent, according to the DSM-IV, the classification guide to mental disorders published by the American Psychiatric Association.

These are the most malevolent, mean-spirited, and nasty people at work. They manipulate everyone on some level. They inflict harm on others. Chronic bullies end careers and shatter the emotional lives of their Targets. And Targets tell us frequently that staring into the face of their bully, they swear they are looking at the devil personified. Some bullies delight in humbling other people into subservience. Their cruelty is so satisfying, they cannot stop their evil smirk when they sense public victory. A small number of bullies are undeniably sadistic. They love torturing others.

Targets should know that simply labeling the bully a sociopath or psychopath does not change the situation or excuse the bully. Most important, dwelling on the bully's relatively permanent personality distracts Targets and those who want to help them from changing the work environment. Except for the rare personality disordered types, all bullies can be made to respond to workplace rewards and punishments.

## Opportunistic Bullies

Opportunistic bullies are the one you're most likely to encounter at work. They are masters at reading cues from the workplace. If competition is encouraged, they know that beating up other people will lead to winning. Only "wimps" would stand in the way of competitors and have them slow down to pay attention to how people might be injured. Opportunists are the "climbers."

The opportunists differ from the chronic bullies in that, when they are away from work, they are able to suspend their competitive nature. They are capable of being charming and supportive—they might even host youth groups in their homes. They are great mothers, churchgoers, neighborhood activists, and good citizens.

At work, when the opportunity presents itself to compete to move ahead, they step over Targets who they think might be a contender for the same prize or a person blocking their success. They justify their behavior to themselves as survival. They believe "it's all part of the game." But to the opportunist bully, games are serious business. Careers are built with political gamesmanship.

Most bullies work to make themselves well-connected to senior management, executives, or owners. While Targets focus on prideful work, bullies are busy kissing up to the big bosses. They firmly plant their lips on the behinds of people who have the power to grant favors, promotions, and status in the future. Kissin' ass is called *ingratiation* by the academics. It works too well. It precludes accountability for wrong-doing. They have allies—we call them *executive sponsors*—willing to block punishment for malicious behavior if they are ever exposed. The big bosses think the bullies can do no wrong. Targets have a hard time

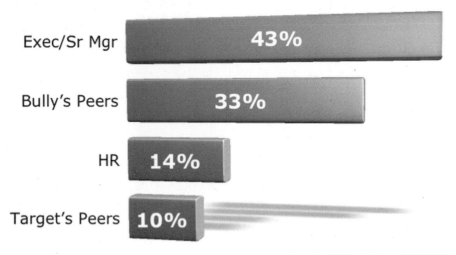

From the WBI-Zogby Survey © 2007 WBI

being believed for this reason. After all, bullies are the personification of the aggressive American doing what it takes to win.

According to the WBI-Zogby Survey, bullies enjoy lots of support from executives, peers (who are mostly managers), human resources (HR), and some turncoats among the Target's peers.

Though companies preach cooperation and teamwork, opportunists know that cutthroat competition is what is actually rewarded. Like chronic bullies, their behavior is governed by reinforcement. Unlike chronic bullies, they will stop hassling others when the organization begins to punish mistreatment. Opportunists are keen readers of signals in the work environment. By changing the workplace culture, opportunistic bullies can be stopped.

When companies lay off ten thousand employees to maintain their profit margins to satisfy Wall Street investors—a deliberate act of malice—how do they justify it? With the belief that "it's just business, nothing personal." Those moments of seizing market opportunities without regard to consequences for humans make organizations just like opportunistic, exploitive bullies.

## Substance-Abusing Bullies

Substance-abusing bullies are very dangerous and threatening because they may not be in control of their decisions at all. According to experts, 74 percent of substance abusers are employed. They do not all live on sewer grates or in homeless shelters. They go to cubicles, stores, and factory floors just as people without chemical dependencies do.

When drugs enter the picture, all assumptions about rationality and logic are tossed out the window. Most substances that hook people are disinhibiting. That means the control mechanism that monitors social politeness and responsibility is shut off. Anything goes for the person under the influence. Unpredictable mood swings become commonplace. Marijuana and alcohol are depressing and induce lethargy and paranoia. Has your bully been a bit too morose, too bug-eyed? Stimulants like methamphetamines create psychotic-like episodes, true craziness, with a healthy dose of paranoia. Cocaine habits are expensive. It's not the rank-and-file Suzy Six-pack that drives from the burbs into the ghetto in a Beamer or Mercedes to buy her supplies. Rank, which begets higher salaries, enables higher-ups to maintain a life of using.

We know that 72 percent of bullies are bosses. Drug testing is ordered by management for their subordinates. Therefore, most drug-using bosses whose altered states may account for much of the chaos and madness Targets endure remain undetected, free from the privacy-robbing experience of peeing in a cup.

## Abusers Who Were Abused

It's true that an unknown percentage of abusive adults were abused as children. It's the cycle of violence. Much adult aggression would be reduced if the cycle could be disrupted in childhood. Children who witness violence directed at one parent have had violence modeled for them. Knowing that a bully has a history of familial abuse, whether directly or vicariously experienced, matters little in the workplace. There is no way to change the experience now. And the bully as an adult has to be held responsible for her or his conduct at work, regardless of the deep-seated origins of the aggression.

# Neurological Brain Structure

There are fascinating advances in neurology that shed light on aggressive behavior. Some people, such as serial killers, may have a prefrontal cortex that differs in size from the normal brain. Differences account for reduced ability to control impulses and to understand the consequences of one's own actions. Thus, serial killers have little control over their violent tendencies and little to no conscience or remorse over harming others. Even if this sounds like your bully, what can you do? What can your employer do? A lobotomy? Nice to know. Fun to imagine, but worthless when considering what to do on a daily basis with your abuser.

# Reactionary Defense of High-Level Bullies

Stanford University management professor Rod Kramer, in an article titled "The Great Intimidators" in the *Harvard Business Review* in 2006, has tired of the promotion of social intelligence (defined by the soft skills of empathy and interpersonal skills to influence others) as desirable traits and wants us to appreciate the harder side of people responsible for change in organizations and society—"political intelligence." Politically intelligent leaders use hard skills to exploit the anxieties and vulnerabilities they see in others. They appreciate the power of fear. And yes, they do a little bullying in the process. It's intellectual combat for the sake of realizing the leader's vision.

There is a sort of Darwinian logic to intimidation because it works. It can mean the difference between success and failure. Kramer thinks this is especially true in highly competitive, contentious, or political environments like Hollywood, the high-tech world, and Washington DC. He believes the "great intimidators" are not typical bullies, who humiliate to make themselves feel good. For the great ones, exercising their political intelligence is motivated by their vision. They see a path and are impatient to clear that path even when the impediments are human. They disdain constraints on their vision or tactics. Kramer discovered this when interviewing people who worked with abusive bosses and who actually liked them. Thus, Kramer's advice to those working with a "great intimidator" is to not quit but to stay in place.

Hey, Rod (and Gary can call him that because long ago they attended graduate school together), it's unbridled narcissism, requisite fealty to the almighty creative genius at the top. You've been too long in the CEO glorification biz and too close to Silicon Valley–types who think the universe revolves around them. This seems to be what contemporary American business school education is all about. Just

51

remember, George W. Bush was a Harvard Business School MBA! He had political intelligence, but...

## They're Assholes

By contrast, another Stanford University management professor, Bob Sutton, said it best in his *New York Times* bestselling book *The No Asshole Rule*—bullies are assholes. And there is no excusing that!

# Chapter Three:

# Targethood: An Undeserved Burden

*That's what it takes to be a hero, a little gem of innocence inside you that makes you want to believe that there still exists a right and wrong, that decency will somehow triumph in the end.*
—Lise Hand

Bullies don't usually torment everyone. Recall the factors in our Why Bullies Bully explanation (page 22). The presence or absence of negative consequences after bullying is what either discourages or encourages the bully. It's learning theory at work.

Now apply this to the interpersonal, bully-on-Target level. Consider the response of different individuals to being targeted by a bully. Some will naturally counter the aggression directed at them with aggression. And for reasons too twisted to review here, the bully respects those people. Bullies employ disrespect, bravado, and bluster. When it is reciprocated, they recognize it as coming from someone like them. And we are all more comfortable around people like us, those who share our worldview. Aggressors are BullyProof.

What makes someone a Target is when the bully is testing her or his humiliating tactics on several people at work, the Target who does not fight back or confront the bully immediately. That yielding opens the door to future mistreatment because the Target failed the test of being a jerk just like the bully. In fact, the Target turns her or his cheek, a morally superior act according to several religions. The Target may also delay action, hoping that with the passage of time, the bully will stop. Unfortunately, the bully interprets all inaction as submission.

Thus, Targets are individuals who will not or cannot defend themselves when assaulted by bullies. This is not a weakness, only reality.

At no time does a Target ever invite the misery inflicted on him or her. Never does a Target tell her new supervisor to pull her into weekly closed-door meetings for a verbal bashing. Never does a Target demand that the bully assign undoable work with an impossible deadline. Never does a Target invite humiliation in front of peers. No, bullying is always an unwanted assault.

Neither are Targets ever responsible for the bully's unilateral decision as to who to bully, what method to use, when to turn it on or off, or the location of the mistreatment.

## Are You Being Bullied?

Remarkably, you could have been bullied for a long time without recognizing it. Your desire to "tough it out" or your strong work ethic or your personal shame can prevent you from admitting what is happening despite it not being your fault.

Family members notice before you do. And sometimes it is the family physician who discovers it, when during a routine visit your blood pressure soars sky high. Inevitably, the physician tells you to leave the job that might kill you because he understands the health costs associated with staying too long, of enduring unremitting stress.

You Might Be Bullied When...

- you feel like throwing up the night before the start of your work week
- your frustrated family demands that you stop obsessing about work at home

- you feel too ashamed of being controlled by another person at work to tell your spouse or partner
- all your paid time off is used for "mental health breaks" from the misery
- days off are spent exhausted and lifeless, your desire to do anything gone
- your favorite activities and fun with family are no longer appealing
- you begin to believe that you provoked the work-place cruelty
- you attempt the obviously impossible task of doing a new job without training or time to learn new skills, but that work is never good enough for the boss
- surprise meetings are called by your boss with no results other than further humiliation
- everything your tormenter does to you is arbi-trary and capricious, working a personal agenda that undermines the employer's legitimate busi-ness interests
- others at work have been told to stop working, talking, or socializing with you
- you constantly feel agitated and anxious, experi-encing a sense of doom, waiting for bad things to happen
- no matter what you do, you are never left alone to do your job without interference
- people feel justified screaming or yelling at you in front of others, but you are punished if you scream back
- HR tells you that your harassment isn't illegal, that you have to "work it out between yourselves"

- you finally, firmly confront your tormentor to stop the abusive conduct, only to be accused of harassment by him or her
- you are shocked when accused of incompetence despite a history of objective excellence, typically by someone who cannot do your job
- everyone—co-workers, senior bosses, HR—agrees (in person and orally) that your tormentor is a jerk but there is nothing they will do about it (and deny saying what they said later when asked to support you)
- your request to transfer to an open position under another boss is mysteriously denied

As bad as being bullied feels, it is natural to downplay its impact on your life for many reasons.

From the thousands of Targets' tales we've heard by telephone at WBI, it is clear that surprise plays a large role in worsening the impact of bullying on Targets' lives. They always feel bushwhacked; they didn't see it coming. Every bullying situation starts with either the bully or Target being new to the other person. The Target can be a new hire or a transfer to a new work unit and run into the bully from hell (72 percent of the time it is a boss, 18 percent of the time a co-worker, and 10 percent of the time the bully bullies from a lower position). The bully may come to your established workplace as a boss or new co-worker. It also is a new situation when the bully is a recently promoted supervisor from within your group, a former peer. Being "new" creates the opportunity to exploit.

# Who Gets Bullied

According to WBI research from 2003, the top reasons bullied individuals gave for being bullied (in order of frequency) were:

1. The Target's refusal to be subservient, to not go along with being controlled (reported by 58 percent of survey respondents)

If the bully is the boss of the independent and skilled Target, the boss has only to constrain the Target's creativity, pile on impossible burdens, or steal credit for accomplishments. These Target types will leave the job or stay to outwit the bully because, thanks to their self-confidence, they have a low threshold for the lies bullies dish out.

If the bright Target chooses not to compete with the bully, he or she could be thrown off track and walk away from a job in disbelief about the banishment. All Targets want "to be left alone to do the job I was hired to do, as best as I could do it." There is a naïveté about these Targets. They are highly proficient in the work to be done but oblivious to office politics (the sole reason to exist, according to the bully's world view).

2. The Target's superior competence or technical skill (reported by 56 percent of survey respondents)

The Target in many cases is a veteran in the organization, the "go-to" employee trusted by everyone else to know the answers to difficult questions. The bully, new to the organization, could learn much from the Target. Instead, the skill poses a threat to the insecure bully. All efforts are directed toward tearing down the Target and her or his reputation and status.

3. The Target's social skills: being liked, positive attitude (reported by 49 percent of survey respondents)

Bullies eat "nice" people alive. Bullies are competitors and live for the opportunity to work with a bunch of cooperators—people who can willingly be bossed around. Imagine the glee of a sadistic supervisor who inherits a group of positive, nonconfrontational people to manage.

In light of all the talk about "team-ness" being central to successful work performance in most contemporary American workplaces, it is ironic that the people with a more advanced stage of human development (the ability to cooperate) fall prey to the primitive, Neanderthal bullies.

Research shows that when everyone cooperates, groups maximize benefits to each person. They get more goodies, whatever goodies there are. But the human tendency to grab the most for oneself prevails in studies with groups that have chances to build a collective cash pool. The rules typically call for a doubling of the amount of cash in a bowl if no one person withdraws money from the bowl during a round of a game.

Unfortunately, groups in U.S. psychological studies break the bank and rarely play more than one round. This happens because greedy individuals (from a random group of people sitting around the table) snatch the money bowl for themselves, ruining the game for others. They do this despite being free to talk out loud, to formulate a strategy, to agree to keep doubling money that could be split.

The reality of the workplace is no different. The formal, written rules call for teamwork, dangling the biggest prizes to groups that cooperate with each other. Operating rules, however, undermine cooperation. Bullies, as strong competitors, know that if they grab "goodies" at the expense of Targets, they win. The cooperators are left to watch the competitor dictate the outcomes (gains or losses) they will experience.

It is clear in the competitive workplace populated with bullies, cooperators are second-class citizens. Americans hate being second. In the face of a winner-take-all world, cooperators don't stand a chance without a concerted institutional effort to wrest control of the rules away from greedy bullies.

Cooperators are not weak; they are simply over-optimistic that good will naturally and automatically prevail. Bullies interpret "nice" as the unlikelihood of being confronted or stopped.

*Nice* is not such a positive trait when you consult the *Oxford English Dictionary*. When *nice* is an adjective describing a person, it means the person is wanton or lascivious (lustful, bawdy), according to its Middle English origins. Its Anglo-French origins are even worse: silly and simple. And its derivation from Latin, *nescus*, means ignorant, from *nescire*, not to know! Yikes! And you thought it was a great personal description. *Nice* gets people in trouble in the contemporary workplace.

4. Ethical, honest reporting of fraud and abuse (whistleblower-type behavior) (reported by 46 percent of survey respondents)

Targets don't have an integrity problem. Hypocrisy is a workplace and societal problem. Institutions fill their hallways with framed testaments spouting noble notions about "respect for individuals" and "courtesy and dignity for all." Yet most ring hollow when employees pass daily and can snicker under their breath "nice frame." People working in the culture can tell anyone who bothers to ask if there is a fit between what really happens and the glowing phrases crafted at an expensive off-site retreat for executives and consultants. Employees know that integrity is about fit, of not having to falsify.

Targets who work in schools, in medical centers, in research university labs, in churches, and in nonprofit organizations dedicated to improving public health seem to expect their employers to both proclaim and act in accordance with higher moral goals than an auto shop. Of course, they are routinely disappointed. The school district may be honored with a presidential award for excellence based on the work of a man who was chased away. The man's health was damaged and his career tossed to the rocks, but the tormenting district superintendent accepted the plaudits anyway. Bullies have no shame.

Nurses call the Institute helpline regularly. The same people tasked with saving lives of strangers turn on their own if they don't like someone's makeup or the car she drives.

The ethics gap deserves a fancy name, but there is none. It is the primary malady from which Targets suffer. It is clear that no workplace is immune to bullying. It happens in the "best" companies and in the ones where we might expect it for some stereotypical reason.

Targets have nonpolitical, and therefore impractical, expectations about how organizations and people should treat each other with integrity. Whistleblowers take seriously the responsibility to see that schools funded to care for special needs kids not misuse the money. Tobacco industry insiders go public with information that belies the falsehoods the industry wanted the public to believe. Integrity is a very personal decision. Organizations get involved when someone in power wants to silence the one with integrity. The bullying starts small, between two people. The entire organization enlists its goon squad when the morally superior whistleblower refuses to back down. Character assassination begins; the Target loses her job, family, friends, and health. Was the Target's decision worth it? Whistleblowers would tell you they'd do it all again, given a chance. The truth compels them.

Targets also prize equity and justice. They believe that rewards should be proportional to talent. That's why it's so irksome when incompetent bullies steal ideas and get promoted. As you'll read in the following pages, Targets are almost always smarter than their bullies. It's not fair.

Justice is a principle that causes Targets limitless pain. The entire complaint-response system disappoints the person hoping to see justice done. When bullies are confronted about their misconduct, they lie. This outrages the Target, who may have taken great risks to have the bullying surface in public. Targets make difficult clients for attorneys. Though it is the law that does not provide protection, Targets hold attorneys accountable for not being able to do more.

Targets driven by a strong sense of equity, justice, and integrity make life challenging for those who wish they simply would disappear. Maybe they make us uncomfortable because they remind us of how we all should be, of what we should aspire to become. It is that guilt that allows witnesses to the bullying to abandon the principled, passionate, and driven Target.

# Do Targets Communicate Vulnerability?

Bullies scan groups for those least likely to counter their aggression with aggression. Maybe it is an evolutionary remnant of our place in the animal kingdom. All predatory species select and attack the weakest prey. It's done for survival, not sport. Humans, on the other hand, sometimes enact violence for the pure pleasure of harming another human being. They wound Targets but keep them around to inflict more harm, as a cat plays with a wounded mouse.

Bullies test the field, especially with new employees. They look for the Targets who put up no resistance to attacks. The bully backs off when resisted. Behavioral researchers speak of an aggressor's mental calculation of an effort/benefit ratio. The people who require more effort to harass than is considered worth it to the aggressor are no longer seen as Targets. That is to say, bullies are lazy. They want an easy mark.

Many of us hate conflict and confrontation. We want peace and quiet. Being nonconfrontational when provoked makes Targets look and sound nonthreatening. This is done with both words and nonverbal messages communicated to the bully.

## *Vulnerability through Words*

Self-effacing statements can be a sign of humility or civility. In those instances, we hear lots of praise heaped on others from the Target, a genuine desire to deflect credit that she herself deserves. "I could not have done this alone. There are many others to thank. My co-workers made it impossible for anyone to fail." "I owe my success to everyone around me." The person may not intentionally be choosing to defame herself, she may simply be choosing to not draw any attention to herself.

However, self-denigrating, self-defeating statements are telltale signs of a deeper insecurity. There is evidence that the seed of self-doubt was planted long ago, in one's childhood, and has reared its ugly head through conflict with a bully. All of us have doubts at one time or another, but most believe that we are inherently capable of overcoming obstacles. Those with a history of doubt are always more susceptible to spiraling into despair whenever confronted by powerful people who only criticize and demean them.

It's one thing for the maniacal bully to put down Targets, but when Targets do it to themselves, it's painful to witness. For instance, it hurts to hear someone say:

- "I only slow the others down."
- "I never was good at this sort of thing."
- "You all should go on, I can't help. I'd only make it worse for you all."
- "I never learned how to work computers. My kids are much smarter than me. I'm such a dolt."
- "You may be right that I screw up a lot, but I'll try harder next time."

In addition, there are aspects of speech that provide nonverbal clues to a hovering predator. Relevant paralinguistic cues (all aspects of speech except the words themselves) include tone of voice (mousy, timid), rate of speech (either slow enough to be interrupted or too fast and flurried, masking a fear of being detected as less than competent), and showing a tolerance for interruptions by the bully, all of which combine to convey a general lack of confidence.

## Vulnerability through Actions

The way Targets walk, carry themselves, sit, stand, use their hands, and use interpersonal space is scrutinized by the bully, perhaps without the Targets' awareness. Fear or intimidation can be signaled by a hesitant walking pace, short stride, or actually walking backwards to attend to what the more powerful person is saying. Confident people typically gesture with their hands to punctuate speech. The absence of gestures does not necessarily indicate poor confidence. It does, however, convey a reticence either learned in a family that discouraged free expression or a deliberate delay in taking action. In either case, the bully pounces on the quiet, non-expressive person, assuming that he or she will not fight back when attacked.

Finally, bullies exploit personal space to their advantage. They stand too close, hover over your shoulder in your cubicle when your back is turned, and touch you to signify control rather than compassion. Whenever a Target fails to back the bully off, to reestablish a comfortable distance, that person risks having the invasion of her personal space wreak havoc over her sense of control. Cowering or tolerance of invasion often indicates submission to the bully.

## A Private Vulnerability

Some Targets carry a private burden inside. Somehow and by someone they have been previously traumatized. Though years may have passed, the memory never dies. At WBI, we have talked with many victims who have shared horrific stories of such traumatization. For many, the cycle is hard to break. For instance, when she was a child, her parents may have undergone a divorce that caused deep feelings of resentment, abandonment, or loss. She may have been sexually abused as a child, and as an adult, told to keep secrets about embezzlement by a bank manager. A female Target may have seen her young daughter killed by a reckless driver as she crossed the street and spent years healing, only to have her gay male boss demand that she "make a beautiful baby" for him and his partner. A man who was shamed into tears daily as a child by a domineering father may jump from one demeaning boss to another. Approximately 38 percent of respondents to the WBI 2003 survey indicated that they had been previously traumatized.

We have learned that previously traumatized Targets:
- are more reluctant to tell others about their torment

- lack confidence that the bully is the reason for the harsh treatment
- tolerate much more craziness and instability at work because they are accustomed to chaos
- experience so much shame that it is especially hard to ask for help or to talk about it, even to spouses
- appear angry to co-workers and management when finally speaking up about the bullying— pent-up resentment toward the bully comes spewing out angrily and unfiltered
- are more susceptible to the uninvited assaults by a bully because of the retraumatization effect
- experience an emotional setback from reliving deep memories at each step of the fighting back process—with each repeating of the story to a bureaucrat, a psychologist, a lawyer.

We offer this knowledge about previously traumatized Targets to help you and your families understand why the healing process takes so long. Healing cannot begin until there is separation from the bully and supporters. If a lawsuit is begun, it postpones indefinitely the end of the bullying situation. Sometimes, well-intentioned family members get frustrated that the Target doesn't simply "let it go." It is not that easy. Spouses may not know about the Target's early-life experiences.

The bullying episode provides a chance for starting that intimate, private discussion.

In no way does an increased susceptibility excuse the bully's unconscionable, despicable behavior. Prior traumas are none of the bully's or employer's business, but often they will use that information against the Target. In that case, he or she will need the unconditional support of family more than ever.

Some common forms of denial surrounding bullying are:

## Simple Denial

Maintaining that bullying is not happening despite evidence that it is and that it is also perceived by others. This is the "see, hear, and speak no evil" approach. When the group discusses what the bully does, you leave the room, believing that when it is out of sight, it will be out of mind.

## Minimizing

Admitting to bullying, but downplaying it in such a way that it appears to be much less serious than it is. The lines "tough times build character" and "I have to grow a thicker skin, that's all" run through your mind.

## Rationalizing

Offering other reasons or justifications for the behavior of the bully. To make the insane appear normal, you convince yourself that the bully's tactics are somehow justified. This leaves the Target with no one to blame but herself. "I must have done something to cause her to launch on me."

## Intellectualizing

Avoiding the hurtful effects of the bully by dealing with it on the basis of generalization, intellectual analysis, or theorizing. This is the "macro" approach. The justification sounds like: "Worldwide competition has driven my company offshore," or, "I'm lucky to have a job at all," "The pressure the poor CEO feels is more than a person should bear," "She has no choice, she's merely going with the flow," or finally, "I have to accept a lean and mean environment so the company can remain competitive, because this is an economic necessity."

## Healthy Self-Denial

When we are hurting from the effects of bullying and we feel vulnerable, we want the pain to stop. When we feel threatened or vulnerable after yet another round of bullying, it is sometimes important to deny the situation. It is too much to comprehend all at once. It's as if we are wearing a blindfold. We refuse to take it off to see what has happened.

This often works in the short term so we can finish what we need to do. It helps you limp to the planned vacation, to time off. When you are ripped by the boss, you use denial to get through the afternoon until you can get home and verify his craziness to your family and friends.

Without denial, the trauma from bullying could overwhelm you and render you inactive and immobile. Losing a job or constant harassment from a boss or co-worker can lead to shock. Denial is the defense we use to avoid the flooding of emotions after the initial shock wears off.

Everyone uses some sort of denial when in pain. If you come from a background of a lot of pain, you may have learned to use denial often to escape that pain.

# Origins of Self-Denial

In the Target's family-of-origin, no one calls bullying what it is. The bully, the abusive family member, encourages and sustains denial by everyone.

In childhood, you may have often heard the words, "You have nothing to cry about." This teaches the Target to not trust genuinely deep feelings. When someone denies your right to feel and express a genuine emotion that you feel, it is called discounting. Having one's personal perspective disregarded while growing up explains why Targets would accept similar verbal taunts from the bully. Adult Targets simply do not trust or value their own version of events. Bullies always try to invalidate what you know to be true.

When the bully is confronted about unacceptable behavior, he or she may say it never happened or that the Target "provoked" it. The Target who thinks she has no right to dispute those lies may instinctively search for a rational explanation, believing the bully has a logical reason for acting as he did. The Target thinks, "There must be some reason she is mad at me," or, "If she thinks my work isn't good, it probably isn't."

The Target spirals into a trap of self-defeat, acting on a script rehearsed since childhood. The bully's work is perpetuated by the Target's internal script.

The Target's belief that the bully is behaving logically is one of the main sources of confusion. The bully may calmly assign an important work project one minute, only to scream when it is not done in ten minutes. This rapid change from rational to irrational behavior increases the Target's confusion, driving the logic-hungry Target to look for sanity in an insane world. Denial minimizes pain from the confusion, from the double-bind, crazymaking communication style of the bully.

The Target may never have asked the question, "Am I being bullied?"

Many people have never heard of bullying and they do not know what it is. In many cases, the concept is totally new to them. It is amazing how many people have said to us that just having a name, a label, for what they were going through helped them start to do something about it. It helps pierce the veil of secrecy and shame imposed by bullies.

Daily torment from a bully also encourages self-denial by Targets. They are told by bullies and their apologist allies that they are too sensitive, too competitive, and trying constantly to have their own way. It is akin to brainwashing and can even extend beyond work to encompass family and friends outside work.

# Bullying Is NOT the Target's Fault!

## Denial Cycles

Denial can come and go after bullying as a way to avoid acknowledging pain. This is demonstrated by psychologist Lenore Walker, who has researched domestic violence. Her model of the cycle of abuse from domestic violence fits well with the concept of bullying.

Applying Dr. Walker's model to the work world goes like this: first, everything seems to be going well at work. Then, tensions begin to rise as the Target experiences stress from the bully's undermining tactics. This is followed by a verbal, destructive incident of bullying, causing the Target confusion. She wonders how she can change herself to make her boss or co-worker happy. The Target's attempts to change (to meet the bully's standards) to appease the bully are at first met with approval. Things around the office are quiet for a while—until the bully feels out of control, and then the cycle begins again.

For the cycle of bullying to stop, denial must be broken. Targets must recognize the bullying and begin to intervene on their own behalf. Taking control of your life and your destiny is the only way to stop bullying.

## Prolonged Denial Worsens Situations

Denial is only acceptable as a short-term survival strategy. While Targets are in denial, they remain stuck in circumstances of their own invented perceptions that prevent a realistic assessment of the situation. Without taking that first appraisal step, no action to restore dignity at work can or will be started. Prolonged denial is a dead end.

Retired organizational psychologist Jerry Harvey, author of *The Abilene Paradox and Other Meditations on Management*, blames the overreliance on denial on people's overblown negative fantasies. That is, they imagine the worst possible, albeit unlikely, outcome from confronting the bully—they would lose their jobs, the bully would turn on them, they would have a heart attack, the bully would kill their children, and so on. With a mind full of negative thoughts like these (mostly about events that would never occur) individuals act very conservatively. People want to take no risk.

Our aversion to risk coupled with an exaggerated imagination limits thinking about possibilities and healthy alternatives.

Further, the longer a confrontation with the source of your pain at work is postponed, the less likely that action will ever be taken to stop the bully. Prolonged denial is a form of distraction which, over time, actually loses its only usefulness—the power to mask depression and self-doubt.

## *Ironic Reality*: Failing to Confront Costs a Procrastinating Target and Family More Than the Worst Imagined Consequence.

## *It's Always about Control*

Control is the central underlying theme, the ultimate basis of bullying. Dealing with the chaotic co-worker or boss, the out-of-control corporate environment, and the rigid rules of the business world are all closely linked to the theme of control. The need for control is always there. Worries about losing control are the core issue for both Targets and bullies.

For the Target, the need for control is great. The fear of appearing too open, too needy, too aggressive, or too angry is linked to every aspect of work. Seen from the other side, control means being dominant, demanding, aggressive, and totalitarian. Targets believe that the only way to protect themselves is to maintain control. The issue becomes black-or-white. This emphasis on control leaves the Target vulnerable to bullies who start the entire bullying melodrama in order to satisfy their own lust for control.

Stephanie Brown, in her book *Safe Passage: Recovery for Adult Children of Alcoholics*, draws a distinction between coping and being defensive. She states that coping creates problems in that situations (with bullies) are never resolved. Thus, using denial as a coping strategy only leads to escalating problems—it never solves the problem. Without resolution of some sort, Targets find their pain prolonged indefinitely.

Targets are trapped by bullies in a web of lies. The gravest danger comes when self-doubt begins to overwhelm the good employee. Over time, even the strongest person is worn down by constant verbal and tactical assaults.

Some Targets are surprised that another person, a fellow human being, could treat them so cruelly. These are people just wanting to do their jobs. The shock of having to react constantly to the uncompromising bully drains a great deal of their energy. Exhausted and disbelieving, they are unlikely to assert their rights effectively and renounce the bully.

In a way, bullies have much of the work done for them by veteran Targets. After the initial bully assault plants the seeds of doubt, many Targets become their own worst enemies by staying wounded. The failure to mount a counteroffensive, to put the bully back in her place, sustains the suffering.

## Procrastinating

Targets may be too shocked or surprised to respond at first, but eventually fear freezes them. They don't seem to be able to take action to protect themselves. When friends and family ask why they are immobilized, several different reasons are offered, but fear is common to them all.

- "I love my job. It's the manager I can't stand. I will just stay away from her."
- "I need major surgery in six months and have to have insurance benefits to pay for it."
- "Some days are better than others. I can make myself invisible for a couple of weeks at a time."
- "We are putting two kids through college and my wife doesn't work. I have to bring home a paycheck."
- "I can tough it out. At least he's not as bad as the supervisor who left."
- "No one in my family would understand my quitting. We've had only winners for generations. I can't quit."

Each of these people is more afraid of an unknown future in a different place, of doing different work, than they are of the certain misery faced daily at the hands of their tormentors. If these people would draw two columns, labeled Personal Costs of Doing Nothing and Benefits of Doing Nothing, they would see that the costs far outweigh the benefits. Unfortunately, like an alcoholic who has to hit bottom before finding the motivation to change, Targets wait an incredibly long time before taking steps to purge bullies from their lives.

## Catastrophizing

Targets also freeze themselves by getting caught up in worst-case thinking. Targets play disaster movies in their heads. The script for this melancholy movie may play out as follows:

- Target complaints are met with indifference or rejection
- She feels no one listens to her or takes her seriously anymore

- The bully is made a hero by the company for her toughness and for squeezing every ounce of productivity out of her staff
- Family and friends threaten to abandon the Target
- The dog and cat sniff her and run, sensing a foul odor oozing from a day of clawing and fighting with the bully
- The bully steals her husband in the final scene, leaving the Target homeless, unemployed, and disabled with an appeal of a denied workers' comp stress claim pending as the sun sets. The End.

This type of thinking is an illustration of how deep inside a Target's life a bully can get. The Target is the star, but the bully is the film's director.

## Action Is the Antidote

*Whatever you do, you need courage. Whatever course you decide upon, there is always someone to tell you you are wrong. There are always difficulties arising which tempt you to believe that your critics are right. To map out a course of action and follow it to the end, requires some of the same courage which a soldier needs.*
—Ralph Waldo Emerson

Ask yourself: how can it be any worse than it already is? You answer, "By being retaliated against by acting out." This is harassment heaped on top of harassment.

The point is that continued crap is guaranteed if nothing is done to stop the bully. Even if complaining is unlikely to stop the bully, you cannot be certain of retaliation until you try. What have you got to lose? The job you once loved changed the day you were targeted.

To summarize, the worst risks you imagine would accompany outing the bully and fighting for your own justice pale in comparison to the actual health risks you face from daily exposure to this stress-inducing terror machine, your bully. You have little to lose by trying the approach we advocate in this book in later chapters. But we're not going to ask you to confront the bully yourself. You'll prod the employer to do it for you.

## Chapter Four:
# The Irreconcilable Difference

*There is exploitation when an owner considers workers not as his associates or auxiliaries but as instruments from whom to obtain the most service at the least possible cost. The exploitation of man by man is slavery.*
—Antoine Frédéric Ozanam

Many people who find themselves the target of a bully wonder *why*. Why is this happening to me? We discussed earlier the potential role of bullies' personalities in governing their actions. More central to bullying is the concept of control. Whether you are a Target or a bully, you have to deal with control. The problem lies with the definition of "control." Bullies and Targets see control in two different ways.

Newborns start with an openness, a readiness to be shaped by their social environment. During infancy, we all are under the complete control of our parents. We benefit from this control to learn how to talk, walk, and function in society. Different parenting and socialization experiences determine our path to develop as either Targets or bullies.

If you were raised with unconditional love and reasonable levels of independence acquired as you moved from childhood through adolescence to adulthood, a healthy sense of self-control, or reflexive control, developed. Being in charge of our own lives satisfies most people.

Adult Targets continue to operate as if surrounded by a world characterized by cooperation, benevolence, and safety. Their world view, the lens through which all perception is filtered, is mostly positive.

The bully never experienced the security of self-acceptance and cooperation in childhood that allows for adult cooperation. Because this was lacking, the bully grew up less secure. With little self-acceptance, bullies develop intense feelings of powerlessness and worthlessness.

There is an Oz-like quality to a bully. The bully requires the smoke and mirrors presentation that the wizard used in the emerald palace of Oz. Remember the wizard's debunking? Toto pulled back a curtain that revealed a little shriveled-up man working the levers of his great-man illusion machine.

Bullies are illusion artists. It's all appearance, no genuine substance.

Bullies lack insight about their deficiencies, coupled with a denial of the consequences of their actions on others. They deny abusing or attempting to control others. They are never personally responsible. In their minds, Targets "provoked and deserved" a verbal tirade.

Bullies are:

- unpredictable
- angry
- intense
- sullen

- critical
- jealous
- manipulative
- explosive

## The Controller

Bullies live, eat, and sleep to control others. They never really experience life any other way. Living, for them, is to control others with power. Power, real or imagined, is vested in both status, which accompanies job titles, and in the ability to generate fear and chaos for a work group.

The bully is desperate to dominate. The bully feels powerless unless he or she is in control. The bully's reality depends on being in control by controlling others.

Bullies have no intention of being in a "relationship" with their Targets. Normal relationships at work require give and take by both parties. The bully never admits to such humble interdependency. She or he may lie to the Target, saying that the two are peers, equals. This only lulls the Target into sharing secrets, habits, and other private information that can be used later during vicious, below-the-belt attacks.

To be equal suggests inferiority to a bully. Equals have the right to reject one another. The bully hides a vulnerability to rejection, something very much feared. Also in a relationship of equals, the bully would have to show feelings and ask for what she wanted. She would eventually ask of others a question that could be answered "no." Bullies abhor being on a level playing field.

Finally, there is a rebound effect that fiercely independent Targets experience. When that type of Target pushes the bully, the bully escalates her cruelty because the challenge to control is so threatening. Remember, resistance to the bully's control was the No. 1 reason Targets believed they were bullied.

## The Cooperator

The Target unknowingly smacks right into the wall of power and control projected by the bully. The most important moment for the Target is when she begins to question the rightness of the bully's behavior toward her. Depending on the difference in styles, it takes time for Targets to acknowledge that "something just isn't right." By then, family and friends question what seems like a tolerance for the bully's disrespectful mistreatment.

The Target and bully have opposing perceptions about control. The difference can be traced to their respective families-of-origin.

The family-of-origin is the biological family you were born into. The combination of heredity and parenting style within the family determines to a great extent how we behave as adults. Parenting styles affect the child's disposition (whether we become passive, respectful, hostile, or assertive) and our ways of relating to the world.

There are two main parenting styles relevant to Targethood: passive and autocratic. Passive parents make few rules and tend to overprotect their children. Autocratic parents have strict and fast rules and allow little, if any, input from their children. Egalitarian parents, however, use a more democratic approach, combining rule-making with input from their children. This approach is the least likely to foster Targethood.

Children who grow up in passive and overprotective families exhibit the shyness, reticence, and quietness that make for an anxious adult in social situations. These same qualities make children from these families unsure of their abilities, and thus, easy prey for bullies. Parents who are overprotective keep their children socially naïve because their overindulgent loving never allows their children to develop a realistic view of the world.

Autocratic parents never allow their children to behave in a way that differs from the parents. These children have an unrealistic view of the world, too. Because children of authoritative parents repeatedly are told what to do and how to do it, they become shy and quiet and show signs of withdrawal. These children are less spontaneous and lack confidence in social situations. This sets them farther apart from other children and makes them susceptible to bullies.

One's family-of-origin affects the adult ability to solve problems. Through the daily routine of family life and the celebration of family events, the family is the place where we first learn to be social, to get along with others. If you are raised in a family where there is constant upheaval and there are no predictable rituals (such as meals or large family gatherings), you never develop the ability to have a normal interaction with others. The disruption of daily rituals in a child's life has profound impact because without the daily exposure to normal conversation, the child has little chance to begin learning the first steps of problem solving. Without the ability to problem solve, the child is easy prey.

Research from the area of addictions provides an alternative explanation. It is clear that there are differences in children from alcoholic homes that allow some to grow up with more resilience than others. It is possible that this resilience is also what allows Targets to be able to learn to cooperate.

Targets as children are those who learn through the first two years of life that they don't have to use control to get what they need. Like the resilient children, they are given much attention, no prolonged separation from a parent or caregiver, and they experience no overt parental conflict. (They may have problems, but these problems do not overwhelm the rest of their lives.)

They learn to use cooperation in a way that doesn't require winners or losers. They don't need to control anyone. They live and function by collaboration. At work as an adult, they prefer an atmosphere that will foster teamwork, cooperation, and creativity.

Bullying is made possible by the failure of the Cooperator to realize the world is peopled by Controllers who do not have the Cooperator's best interests in mind. The Target's naïveté determines the size of the surprise when she finally realizes the bully's cutthroat nature.

Into the snake pit steps a Target who believes that colleagues at work will express freely their feelings and ideas and actively seek collaborative relationships. Because the job and good relationships define her work world, she assumes this is true for everyone else, including bullies. She loves her job, meaning the tasks that push her to employ her skills. Office politics are either ignored or considered of minimal importance.

Unfortunately, bullies see the workplace as a battlefield, a site to plunder others, home to the carnage that they consider unworthy adversaries who populate their workday and interfere with their divine right to unchallenged control over minions. Getting along is the farthest thing from a bully's mind. Politics is the sport of competitors. The spoils, literally the body count of those successfully dominated and devastated over the years, go to the bully.

## The Inevitable Collision

It is disingenuous to characterize the clash between two such fundamentally different people a mere "personality conflict" or "miscommunication" or "misunderstanding." All of those labels suggest that the Controller is willing to meet the Cooperator at least halfway. This is not true.

As long as Targets keep functioning under the rules of cooperation, they may believe that they are doing something "wrong." They turn themselves inside out to please the bully who never will be appeased. A Target's healing cannot begin until she realizes that her relationship with the bully is not normal. Only after beginning to doubt the bully instead of herself can the Target take a turn toward safety and improved personal health.

Our portrait of a bully is sad. It turns horrific when we look at the pathological dance with an unsuspecting Target. How could a Target fall into such a trap?

The answer is that Targets rarely see bullies coming. They simply see the world through a completely different lens.

> *Jill is a supervisor at a glass factory. She came to work at the factory after serving ten years in the Navy. She prides herself on running a "tight ship" and has received commendations for her work as a supervisor. Sandy decided in high school that she wanted to work as an artist. She started her job in the glass factory immediately after graduation. After three months working under Jill, Sandy is ready to quit and give up her dreams.*

What happened? Sandy walked right into a relationship with a Controller. The following is an example of the relationship between the two women.

> Jill comes walking into the break room and flops down in a chair at the same table with Sandy and casually says to her, "Boy, are you a troublemaker."
>
> Sandy, looking up, replies, "Why do you say that?" (Although she is surprised, she responds as though they are both operating under the same rules, a shared reality.)
>
> Jill is now ready to begin the battle for control. To her, Sandy needs to understand that Jill is the SUPERVISOR. "The boss just vetoed your crazy idea to simplify the paint line." Jill says this with a touch of anger and a discernible note of triumph.
>
> Sandy then feels she must defend herself. She says, "When I talked to you yesterday, I was just discussing some ideas that I thought might help us work faster."
>
> "Well, I thought you wanted the boss to hear your idea. He did and he feels my way is better." In her mind, Jill has won. She has used her control over Sandy to attack Sandy's basic perception of her abilities and herself.
>
> Sandy is hurt and confused. She cannot seem to get Jill to understand that she only wants to help in their department. She is frustrated and doesn't seem to understand what Jill expected of her. She doesn't perceive Jill's need for control at all—because Jill often tells her that new ideas are important, this to Sandy, means mutual empowerment, not the control over others.
>
> If Sandy had said, "I felt hurt when you said I was a troublemaker," Jill, as a confirmed bully would have discounted her feeling by saying, "You're really blowing this out of proportion!" or (sarcastically), "Well, aren't you the poor thing."

*Sandy would still be left feeling hurt and confused.*

*If Jill were in the reality of cooperation (Sandy's reality), she would have said, "Oh, I'm so sorry, I guess I should have talked more to you before I talked to the boss." In this case, Jill could be accused of being crabby but she would then acknowledge her irritability.*

*Although Sandy operates under the reality of cooperation, she has no idea that Jill will never consult her about anything. Sandy has no idea that Jill functions with an entirely different mind-set. Unfortunately, Sandy might never realize that Jill is not a Cooperator, but functions in a hostile world of control.*

# What's Yours Is Mine, Too

There is another way to represent the contrast between Controller and Cooperator. It is a way of describing relationships that involves keeping score for the things that matter most to people. It's a model of social exchange that turns into exploitation.

Consider the Cooperator's world view with respect to keeping score in a game. Do you remember Mark McGwire's stated wish during the 1998 baseball season as he and Sammy Sosa eclipsed the all-time home run record? McGwire said he wished they could end the season in a tie. That statement was rare coming from a professional athlete whose world is defined by competition, dominated by competitors. For a brief moment, the world watched as competitors at the highest level of sports chased the record as friends, each wishing the other the best.

The ideal outcome for a Cooperator is to achieve a 50/50 split of the "goodies" (resources) that employees play for at work. Some Cooperators have angelic souls and act the altruist. Altruists prefer to give to others. They would settle for giving the other person 100 percent of the resources, taking nothing for themselves. No one has spotted an altruist in the workplace in years. They are an endangered species in the competitive arena of business. Call if you spot one.

In the following diagram, the two endpoints on the horizontal line depict the altruist on the left, the Cooperator in the middle seeking common ground, and the Controller at the right end of the line seeking an absolute payoff.

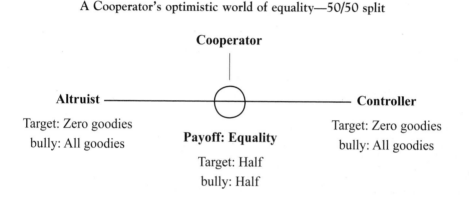

A Cooperator's optimistic world of equality—50/50 split

Cooperator

Altruist ———————————————————— Controller

Target: Zero goodies
bully: All goodies

**Payoff: Equality**
Target: Half
bully: Half

Target: Zero goodies
bully: All goodies

Controllers are strict competitors, zero-sum game players. Their winnings come at the expense of others' losses. The ideal outcome for a Controller is 100 percent for herself and nothing for the Target. Their logic: what's mine is mine and what's yours is mine, too. Note how in the second diagram, the Controller cuts into the Cooperator's half of the "goodies."

The Target–bully tango in this exchange–exploitation model is a struggle between the two about where the goal should lie. The bully pushes from her side, trying to flatten the line, to achieve domination. The Target is pushing back (once she realizes the exploitation she is suffering) just to get to the halfway mark. The Target does not think about pushing past the 50/50 boundary into the Controller's turf. If and

**Bully exploitation of the Target's split on the way to domination**

when she did go beyond the restoration of self-respect, beyond getting back to neutral, she would then see herself as a bully.

Resources over which Controllers seek domination:

- Approval
- Credit for accomplishment
- Time (hours worked, free time)
- Supplies to do the job
- Authority on the job
- Respect
- Reputation with co-workers
- Target's competence

*Chapter Five:*

# Witness Paralysis

*You gain strength, courage, and confidence by every experience in
which you really stop to look fear in the face....
You must do the thing you think you cannot do.*
—Eleanor Roosevelt

## Why Team Members Do Not Help

The bully typically singles out one Target at a time. However, there
are witnesses. Why do they watch and do nothing?

---

## TO THRIVE, BULLIES REQUIRE
### Secrecy • Shame • Silent Witnesses

### You Can Stop Them.
### Cut Off Their Life Support!

---

If groups (call them work teams) are powerful enough to bend
individuals to their will, to get inside individuals' heads and make
them doubt their own competence, to make them do things that hurt
themselves, then logic would dictate that fellow workers who see a
bully hurting someone would run to the rescue. Right? Wrong!

The strange tale of people acting in groups and influencing individuals now gets stranger. For many reasons, people witnessing the injustice of workplace bullying rarely act. They either will not act, by choice, or cannot act, for reasons often unknown to them and to the Target, who could certainly use their help.

Let's take a look at five common things that affect co-workers and witnesses of bullying, which discourage them from intervening or helping.

## Abilene Paradox

Social psychologist and noted author Jerry Harvey honored his Texas roots when he named this phenomenon. The group dynamic is perhaps the most relevant to understanding why bullies can be witnessed by so many people and still get away with it.

The Texas city is the namesake for the paradox. It refers to the story (retold by Harvey) of a lousy decision by his family. On a hot summer day, the family piled into a car without air conditioning and drove too many miles to Abilene to try a new diner. The heat was oppressive and the food was lousy. But no one dared to speak in those terms until later that night back home.

Finally, the matriarch of the family broke the silence by complaining about the food. Then everyone chimed in with their complaint—the car was hot, it was stupid to try an unknown restaurant. It turns out that no one wanted to go in the first place, but no one said so when it mattered. Eventually, they all blamed the father for suggesting the drive.

To Harvey, whenever a group is about to do the wrong thing, despite knowing it's the wrong thing, it is a group "on the road to Abilene."

Imagine a committee of bright people making a stupid decision. We know from talking with each person alone that every one of them thinks it's a stupid thing they are about to do. When the committee votes, however, they choose to do the stupid thing anyway! Later, usually much later, when the decision backfires, the committee tears itself apart in its search for a culprit. The group desperately needs someone or something to blame, long after the decision could easily have been prevented.

This describes a group in agreement, not in conflict. They all agree privately and individually about the true state of affairs. They do not communicate their feelings to one another, however. Then publicly, in the presence of each other, they all deny the agreement that they don't know exists among them.

The paradox is that both the private and public versions of reality coexist. In fact, this is the mismanagement of agreement, not disagreement. It is all made possible by a public silence regarding what each individual knows to be true. Sound like where you work?

Take a bullying example.

> *All of the Target's co-workers know what is happening. If interviewed alone and free from retaliation, each would deplore the obvious pain the Target is experiencing. However, in group settings, even without the bully present, they don't do the right thing.*
>
> *When together, they don't plan how to use their group power to overcome a lone bully. Instead, they ignore the rampant mistreatment by not communicating their positions or feelings publicly. If the Target later pursues legal action and investigators on her behalf interview the team that made up the hostile environment, the finger pointing begins.*

Why does this happen? Harvey traces it to people's overblown negative fantasies. That is, they imagine the worst possible, riskiest outcome from confronting the bully—they would lose their jobs, the bully would turn on them, they would have a heart attack, the bully would kill their children, and so on. We called this catastrophizing. With a mind full of negative thoughts like these, mostly about events that will never occur, the individuals act very conservatively as a group. As a group, they want to take no risk. So they do the wrong thing, all for lack of talking about it openly. They let bad things happen to the Target that they believe, as individuals, should not happen.

Sick? No, simply a natural human aversion to risk, thanks to an exaggerated imagination that limits thinking about possibilities.

Silent, inactive witnesses to the bullying of others is a group "on the road to Abilene."

## Groupthink

Groupthink is the second group dynamic that inhibits witnesses of bullying to intervene or help Targets.

This also involves groups making poor decisions, such as allowing the bully to hurt people in the work team. In groupthink, the wrong thing is done by the group, but they are not aware that the action is wrong, as they were in the Abilene paradox.

Groupthink is George Orwell's term from *1984*, the dark futuristic novel. Psychologists borrowed the term to describe a group incapable of critically assessing the pros and cons of a decision. Because the group members feel so tightly connected, so cohesive, they prefer to see only one side of an issue. They are easily led by a forceful leader and busy themselves by falling in line behind the boss and kissing up to stay in good favor. They become a mindless, overprotective clique when assembled as a group, putting the political goal of squashing dissent above all other matters.

Groupthink is relevant to bullying if we imagine a management committee on which the bully sits. She is in the club, so to speak. The Target tries to find an ally among the bully's peers. If and when the Target approaches group members, she will be given the cold shoulder.

The management group will not be open to hearing complaints about one of their own. The bully is safe in her cocoon; the wagons are circled to protect a club member.

Little wonder that appeals for help to the bully's peers so frequently fail, from executive suite clubbies to shop-floor buddies. Groupthink is designed to protect club members from hearing anything that contradicts their comfortable view of the world. It's the wall that separates the in-group from all others. It carries with it a code of silence that plays into the bully's strategy.

## Dissonance

Cognitive dissonance is the third dynamic that inhibits witnesses. Leon Festinger is the psychologist closely associated with cognitive dissonance theory.

Dissonance about cognitions, beliefs held by the potential helper, freeze the group members as individuals. Let's get inside Sally's head and try to understand her thought process.

> Chris and Sally were Helen's best friends during her short stay in the department. All were psychotherapists. Sally was the first to offer her friendship. Sally spent many lunch hours telling Helen horror stories about Zoe, Helen's terrifying boss. Zoe had chased out a man from Helen's position a year before and he was rumored to not have recovered from the stress Zoe caused.
>
> Sally herself had transferred to another supervisor to escape Zoe's unpredictable rages and admired Helen's ability to get along with her. Chris had once held Zoe's position as boss, but gave it up after Zoe was hired as a staff therapist. Chris's life was made completely miserable trying to counter Zoe's political tricks and sabotage. So she abdicated and Zoe got her job, the one she wanted.

*Chris confided in Helen that she was terrified of Zoe and managed to avoid contact with her as much as possible. She even took to hiding in her office until Zoe passed so she wouldn't have to face her in the hall.*

*Helen was later driven from the department by Zoe. Despite the similar experiences with Zoe by Chris and Sally, both refused to meet to comfort Helen after she left. Both left unanswered Helen's telephone messages. Later, when Helen sued the corporation, Helen's attorneys interviewed Chris and Sally and concluded that their testimony would damage Helen's case, as they both chose to support Zoe's position.*

The most common way to reduce dissonance after choosing sides is to exaggerate the positive aspects of the side chosen and the negatives associated with the side not chosen. For example, Sally could focus on the unfairness of Helen's banishment, but that could lead her to support Helen in court, risking good relations with Zoe, the tyrant.

However, Sally, like most people, chose the path of least resistance. She decided to downplay Helen's plight and conclude that where she works isn't so miserable after all. She rationalizes to herself that she would have to be stupid to stay in such a place and she is not stupid. Therefore, Zoe's world with Zoe in it must not be so bad; Helen was wrong.

As with all of these phenomena, we're simply trying to explain why people do not help more. Dissonance is not about morality. Once people rationalize away internal conflicts to make themselves feel good, the likelihood of them taking the humane, but more difficult, action decreases.

You can probably see how dissonance is related to siding with the bully. Since the survivor and bully are both still there, the survivor engages in a mental calculus of sorts to justify staying. She concludes, like Sally, that Zoe is more important than Helen, who is gone anyway.

## Co-workers Side with the Bully, the Aggressor

The fourth reason that the team fails to use its power to stop a bully is that team members side with the bully. The origin of the principle of identification with the aggressor is in psychoanalysis, but let's not get too Freudian here.

What's important is that this explains how the Target's best friend or the person who once stood as the Target's strongest ally can turn against her.

Most bullies want to torment the Target out of the job. Loyalties typically switch after the Target leaves. Without the painful daily reminders of the bully's devastating effect on the Target, co-workers are free in the aftermath to act as if the Target was never there. They may buddy up to the bully in a way obvious to observers, but without a personal awareness of what they are doing. The newfound loyalty to the bully may be borne out of fear to protect themselves, but to all observers, it looks like a choice made freely.

Sadly, after the Target is gone, former co-workers will dump on the Target, blaming her for her fate, for simply not understanding office politics, or for having a "personality clash" with the bully. This rationalization protects those left behind at the expense of the departed Target.

Of course, bullies can explicitly demand fealty from the Target's co-workers. While the Target was still on-site, the bully forbade co-workers from socializing with him or her. Another cruel tactic is to forbid the Target from getting help with tasks from co-workers. Isolating a person in attempt to control their perception of reality is a tactic used by torturers, too.

## Winners Take All—Targets Are Losers

Without the book *The Winner Take-All Society* by Robert Frank and Philip Cook, we would have called this explanation "Americans' love of competition." We revere winners and have no "mental shelf space" left for the losers.

It is a pervasive marketplace mind-set that has invaded our social relationships. The vast majority of riches go to the privileged few at the top of any profession, sport, or hierarchy. In a way, the classic American competitive zeal encourages us to denigrate luckless Targets and elevate the bully. After all, if the workplace is war, the conqueror (even if she's a bully) gets the post-game interview while the vanquished retreats unnoticed and unloved.

To win at the expense of other competitors is called zero-sum competition. In a zero-sum world, there are no shared victories, no proportional payouts. There is only one grand prize for the winner. Losers get nothing.

Competition is driven by the perception of scarcity. There has to be a limited pool of possible rewards—monetary and social—over which workers have to fight. At work, social goodies can be as simple as civilized conversation, decent humane treatment, empathy for another's pain, and personal time given to someone who needs nothing more than the validation that companionship or an open mind can provide. These "resources" are not scarce. They are limitless.

Yet the bully and her accomplices, by virtue of witnessing but taking no action, hoard them. By doling out praise and kindness in a miserly way, the bully controls the competition.

We naïvely refer to "free market" competition as if the game is fair. In fact, the distribution of opportunities always tilts toward the powerful. In organizations, bullies control those who are opportunists; those whom they designate as Targets don't have a chance.

It is unthinkable that we treat bullies decently at work, while ignoring the deliberate harm they cause to others. What we score as success doesn't make sense either. We place a high value on the size of a person's workstation, type of chair, type of benefits for which she's eligible, window or interior cubicle, basement or penthouse office, day or graveyard shift, expense account or out of pocket, and so on.

Success is defined by relative standing rather than absolute performance. Companies blithely credit bullies with winning and treat Targets like losers. Hey, the game is rigged!

## Who Does Support Targets?

As part of the WBI 2003 Survey, Targets were asked if they reported their mistreatment to others and what actions those persons took. The possible actions were:

- Positive actions (maintaining the Target's perspective, testifying, keeping the relationship)
- Doing nothing, even though by virtue of telling the person a request for help was made
- Negative actions (abandonment of Target, turning into an enemy, siding with the bully)

Potential supporters were: co-workers, bully's boss, Human Resources, spouse/partner, and friends from outside of work. The results below summarize who knew about the bullying and what they did in terms of helping or hurting.

|  | Co-workers | Boss | Human Resources |
| --- | --- | --- | --- |
| Positive actions: | 15% | 18% | 17% |
| Did nothing: | 28% | 40% | 51% |
| Negative actions: | 57% | 42% | 32% |

It is clear that workplace "insiders"—co-workers, the bully's boss, and HR—were destructive, not supportive. Positive support came only from spouses (85 percent positive actions) and friends outside of work (79 percent positive actions).

The 2008 WBI Survey explored in-depth co-workers' responses to workplace bullying. Survey respondents (95 percent of whom were bullied Targets) said that 95 percent of co-workers saw the mistreatment and that 97 percent were aware of what was going on. But here's what co-workers actually did:

- 0.8 percent banded together, confronted the bully, and stopped the bullying
- 7.1 percent offered specific advice to the Target about what she should do to stop it
- 28.4 percent gave only moral, social support
- 15.7 percent did and said nothing, not helping either the Target or the bully
- 13.2 percent voluntarily distanced themselves from the Target, isolating him or her
- 4.8 percent followed the bully's orders to stay away from the target
- 12.9 percent betrayed the Target to the bully while appearing to still be friends
- 14.7 percent publicly sided with the bully and acted aggressively toward the Target
- 2.5 percent of actions weren't clear

Co-workers were nearly as unhelpful as employers. In 46 percent of bullying cases, co-workers abandoned their bullied colleagues, to the extent that 15 percent aggressed against the Target along with the bully. Co-workers did nothing in 16 percent of cases.

Some co-workers did do positive things in 36 percent of cases—mainly limited to offering moral support. The rarest outcome (less than 1 percent) was for co-workers to band together to stop the bullying through confrontation. Co-workers' personal fears were the preferred explanation by bullied targets (55 percent) for the actions taken or not taken by witnesses.

In conclusion, co-workers are not bad people. You are one yourself. However, fear suppresses action. Bullying leads to a fear-plagued workplace where nearly everyone is paralyzed. Do not count on them.

Despite all this bad news, there is real-world evidence that groups do confront bullies as a group—and it works! A shining example is the "Code Pink" technique used by surgical nurses. These highly skilled professionals are often berated and belittled by pompous surgeons, both men and women. In some hospitals, whenever a bullying surgeon steps over the line into mistreatment, "Code Pink" is called by the targeted nurse. Immediately, supportive nurses form a circle around the physician. Together, they declare their unwillingness to assist that person with current and future patients, if an apology is not given with a promise to behave in a civil manner.

The interdependent nature of surgery makes the surgeon powerless without the help of the team in the operating room. All work stops and the physician is accountable for her or his bullying. It is the physician who is responsible for the patient's life. "Code Pink" is the group displaying its power to the bully, demanding cooperation instead of controlling games. According to reports to WBI, every bullying surgeon confronted in this way yields to the group. The nonsense can be stopped!

## Chapter Six:

# Help from Family and Professionals

*Freedom is the will to be responsible to ourselves.*
—Friedrich Nietzsche

With understanding and the support of loved ones, the stress reactions of Targets usually pass more quickly. Occasionally, the traumatic event is so painful that professional help may be necessary. This does not mean the person is weak. It simply indicates that the particular traumatic event was too powerful for that person or any reasonable person to manage alone. Isolation is the enemy. Asking for help is essential.

Listen patiently and carefully, spend time with the person, offer unsolicited help with daily tasks, reassure the person about being safe, don't take expressed anger personally, don't tell her that she is "lucky" it wasn't worse (say that you are sorry that the bullying ever occurred and that you want to understand and help).

As mentioned earlier, when Targets call for help, there is a good chance that much time has passed. Targets often wait too long to seek help, thinking the problems are their fault. It is extremely important that Targets are not isolated. They should rely on, not distance themselves from, friends and family during these stressful times. Caring friends can help. Here's how.

# How Family and Friends Can Help

- Targets did not cause the bully to assault them. (If you think Targets invited harm from the bully, stop now. You will do more harm than good. Do NOT volunteer. You can't help!)
- "Bullying" is the name for what they experienced.
- They are likely not the only Target of that bully's unreasonable behavior (they are probably not alone).
- There are witnesses, perhaps silent at first, who may eventually help combat the bully.
- Shame and guilt are what the bully wants the Target to feel. Both are natural, but are useless. They delay recovery and healing.
- Their perceptions are valid and OK. Being kind, bright, or cooperative still matters most.
- They are not imposing on others by seeking help. People do want to right wrongs and help others.
- Bullying is common at work. (Half of all adult Americans either had it happen to them or witnessed it.)
- The bully's way of viewing the work world is perverted, not the Target's.

## *Giving Support*

### LISTEN without judging or evaluating

- Avoid criticism.
- Affirm, be positive.

- Avoid asking why the Target did what she or he reported. This puts the Target on the defensive and makes you seem an investigator, virtually an accomplice of the bully.
- Be patient. Let the Target talk at her or his own pace. Do not interrupt or fill silent time with your talk. Do not finish sentences for the Target. Take a breath before you speak so you can be calm and deliberate. Put care into your voice. The floor belongs to the Target. You are to follow the lead.

## CONFIRM/VALIDATE the Target's reality

- Assume the Target's perspective completely. Do not try to be "balanced" by stating both sides of the conflict between the Target and bully.
- Use only as much information as necessary, based on a strict "need to know" basis. Sometimes simply putting a name to the experience is enough to start the healing process.

## SHOW EMPATHY

Empathy is the ability to walk in someone's shoes and to feel what they feel. See the situation from her perspective. If you have had similar feelings, say so. If you have not, don't lie. Simply try to understand what it must feel like and convey that understanding.

## SHARE PERSONAL EXPERIENCES

When appropriate, without imposing, try to tell your story. Make sure you emphasize your success in moving on with your life. You have the chance to be a source of hope. Seize it.

## EDUCATE

- Be current on the topic. Turn to the WBI website (www.bullyinginstitute.org) and this book for information.
- Suggest actions to take—call the labor commissioner, ask co-workers about their experiences, visit www.nela.org for an attorney referral, help build the business case for the employer, visit a physician to document impact on health. Be an idea generator for the Target.

Remember, you are *not* required to fix the problem for the Target.

# Consumer Guide to Professional "Helpers"

## *Therapist Selection*

Until we train and certify mental health professionals who clearly understand workplace bullying, we cannot refer you to anyone. The professional mental health help you need is a local service. We cannot attest to the quality of telephone counseling, though we do strategic coaching by phone and it seems to be sufficient. We suggest using your health insurance, if you have it still, to meet with a counselor.

Counselors can be Masters-prepared (MA in clinical psychology) or LCSW clinical social workers. Psychologists have either a PhD in clinical psychology or a PsyD also in clinical psychology. Psychiatrists are physicians (MD) who are able to prescribe medications for psychological distress. In most states, only psychiatrists can order medication. In some states psychiatric nurse practitioners or physician assistants (ARNP, PA) can also order medication. Most counselors work collaboratively with a professional who can prescribe medications in cases where the need arises.

Your current or former employer may offer employee assistance (EAP). However, many EAP counselors have trouble honoring confidentiality or feel sympathetic to the employer who pays their contract. It is preferred that you find an independent mental health professional.

## Types of Counselors to Avoid

- One who says that you're the problem and does not believe that anyone could do what the bully did.
- One who is curious about your relationship with your mother, but doesn't want to hear what happened at work.
- One who specializes in family relationships or teenagers.

## Types of Counselors to Hire

- A specialist in trauma, post-traumatic stress disorder (PTSD), or one who leads groups of PTSD sufferers.
- A specialist in domestic violence.
- A specialist in anxiety disorders.
- A therapist who advertises certification in EMDR (a technique to reduce anxiety)

You may be reluctant to quiz prospective therapists on the phone prior to an initial appointment. Remember, you are the client. You are paying or directing insurance dollars to their pockets. Shopping for therapy is a consumer task. Therapists are in business. If he or she makes you uncomfortable when you ask the questions we suggest you ask, do not use him or her as a therapist. If during the initial session a therapist makes you uncomfortable, feel free to leave that session.

You probably tolerated bullying too long. That's why you're seeking a therapist now. So don't let a therapist bully you and worsen your emotional health.

## Questions to Ask When Shopping for Therapists

- Have you heard of the term "workplace bullying"? If not, would you be willing to learn about it? (You can download articles from the WBI website and direct the therapist to this book.)
- Do you understand how a work environment can elicit or cause dysfunctional behavior at work?
- Do you emphasize present issues over early life experiences?
- Do you have a conflict of interest regarding any matters related to company X (my current or past employer)?
- Is there an ideal number of sessions that you prefer? How would you characterize your therapeutic technique?

Try to interview three or more therapists (or their receptionists) before scheduling the initial session. If it doesn't work out with one, you will be able to call on another.

If the therapist resists the concept of workplace bullying and is not open to learning, do not hire that person. If they underestimate the role of a work environment that includes having a bullying boss and an unsupportive HR, this type of therapist is likely to blame you for your fate. You cannot work with a therapist who has a conflict. He or she will defend the employer and be biased. Most contemporary counselors use "cognitive-behavioral" approaches that would include desensitization techniques that work well to decrease anxiety. Nearly any therapeutic philosophy works to reduce work-induced anxiety, stress, and trauma except psychoanalytic or psychodynamic (Freudian) approaches.

The task of finding a therapist cannot be passive. You must be a questioning, active consumer. If this threatens any therapists that you screen, avoid them.

Your experience with bullying validates years of research. Bullying clearly affects the psychological health of targeted people.

You might want to read some of the scientific articles at the Workplace Bullying Institute (WBI) website to acquaint yourself with the literature.

## Union Representatives

Unions, like employers, are organizations. They have agendas and goals that may or may not meet your needs. It saddens us to say that unions are not necessarily good at giving unconditional employee support. Unions have appropriated the name "labor," but their influence extends to only about 10 percent of the American workforce today.

### Excerpted Cases from Our Files:

*Clara was a Teamsters union member and schoolbus driver. Her boss was an old-fashioned sexual harasser who sabotaged her bus so that she lost her brakes with a load of children on board. Because the national union publishes guidelines clearly defining how the local union is supposed to defend harassed employee members, she called the union for help. But when she called, her rep called her a "fat, ugly broad not worth fighting for" and refused to see her.*

*Susan is the only female meat packer at a grocery store. She belongs to a union. Troubles with her immediate boss and the store manager led her to the union. In preparation, she wrote eighteen questions she wanted answered about the reprehensible behavior of both bosses. The union rep scheduled only thirty minutes to hear her complaint. Halfway through the meeting, after rolling his eyes in disbelief, he terminated the session. Susan protested so much that he scheduled a follow-up session the next day. Her husband accompanied her to that meeting. The rep was formally cordial and did start the formal grievance paperwork. When asked when they would get answers to Susan's eighteen questions, the rep yawned and said, "Maybe never, there isn't time." Could they fax the list for him so he could find answers at his own pace, they queried. He refused. Only after Susan called the local union president, whose election she helped win, did the rep consent to read her questions.*

*Gary works for a steel mill with a local union. Recently, his company decided to do away with all employee breaks, despite the fact that most employees work eight hours a day for a forty-hour week. The company says they are becoming a continuous operation, and not only have they extended the time worked, but they have removed people from Gary's department. Now, two people are expected to do the work of three people. Gary asked his union rep about laws that say an employer has to give breaks after an employee works so many hours. His union refuses to help. They are letting the company do what they want to do.*

*Tara was bullied by a sexual harasser. She ran to the union and simultaneously to an independent employment lawyer. Her legal claim was postponed until the union grievance procedure was completed. She expected it to be weeks. Her case was a clear-cut example of illegal sexual harassment. Once a month for a year, she called the union checking on the status of her grievance. They always put her off. Her lawyer could do nothing. Two years later, a union rep called Tara to announce her hearing had been scheduled the next week. But she had returned to college and could not attend at the scheduled time. The rep said this jeopardized her claim. She called the local union president at home explaining her dilemma. He assured her that a new time could be set taking into account her class times. He told her to fax him her schedule. She did so. Weeks passed with no word of a new time for the hearing. Then, nearly two months after she first contacted the president, he called her to formally announce that her grievance had been dropped because she failed to appear at the hearing two months ago! He denied receiving her faxed schedule and the conversation they had about rescheduling.*

It is a shame that young employees are ignorant of the positive role unions can play in improving working conditions. However, to reverse the rapid decline of unions' popularity, unions will have to improve service to existing members. There is no excuse for the only official employee advocates to be too busy to help employees who seek relief from horrendous workplaces.

Several corporate-sponsored foundations and groups have large fund reserves and pose as friends of employees. Most are imposters. One such group is the National Right to Work Legal Aid Foundation. In 1997, they had four hundred cases active in the courts to fight "union abuses" on behalf of employees. In reality, the only "abuses" they challenge are compulsory union dues of which a portion is earmarked for political action committees. The NRTW, a union-busting organization, is hardly the type of helper you need to get better service from your union.

If you feel that your union fails to protect your union rights for arbitrary, malicious, bad faith, or discriminatory reasons, you can sue under the National Labor Relations Act.

# Is It Discrimination?

You'll recall that in 20 percent of bullying cases, discrimination played a role. Cruelty is heaped on top of discrimination. In most cases, there is no discrimination; it's plain cruelty and there is no law against nonphysical human-on-human cruelty at work in the United States.

If you are the target of harassment, in most situations, the bully will not have broken the law. That is one of the most frustrating aspects about workplace bullying. Federal laws dictate under what limited circumstances you are protected. We are not lawyers and cannot interpret the law for you. The National Employee Rights Institute published *Job Rights and Survival Strategies* by attorneys Paul Tobias and Susan Sauter. The following brief summary of the anti-discrimination acts was taken from that book.

Title VII of the Civil Rights Act protects employees from workplace discrimination if they are members of one of the "protected classes": according to race, color, religion, national origin, or sex—this includes discrimination based on pregnancy.

Employees are protected from age discrimination under the Age Discrimination in Employment Act (ADEA) for workers age forty years or older. However, beginning in 1997, the courts have begun to allow employers to claim "economic reasons" to cut loose older workers who just happen to earn the higher salaries, thus eroding federal safeguards.

It is also against federal law to discriminate based on disability (defined as a physical or mental condition that substantially limits a person in a major life function or functions). Only permanent, chronic, or long-term conditions apply, according to the Americans with Disabilities Act (ADA).

# How to Find a Good Attorney, Your Legal Advocate

We can make referrals only to attorneys with whom we have experience or when a bullied Target recommends them. See the *Success Stories* section of the WBI website to get the names of the few attorneys who have done great things for clients.

Let's be clear. We are not attorneys nor do we purport to be giving legal advice. Only licensed legal professionals—paralegals and attorneys—may do this. Nor do we have a legal defense fund to help bullied targets with no money. Legal help is expensive!

There are three points we have to make before guiding you through the process of selecting a lawyer.

1. There is no law in any U.S. state against workplace bullying. Lawyers interpret existing laws. Therefore, no lawyers specialize in workplace bullying. There are few laws against cruelty against humans in general. At work, nearly anything goes. There are stronger protections in place against abuse of animals in this country! America is an aggressive place and the legal attitude is that only "disadvantaged" people deserve protection.

2. Filing a lawsuit leads to predictable retaliation, tremendous financial expense, and the risk of worsening the emotional damage caused by bullying. Despite some laws that prohibit retaliation for filing formal complaints, nearly all employers ignore the rule and retaliate. They hate being exposed. Attorneys are expensive; they read documents very slowly and charge in six-minute intervals. Chances are high that you will have to pay a significant retainer ($10,000 or more) and deplete

your savings before a trial date is set. Many bullied Targets report that being deposed is akin to rape. The anxieties triggered are strong and repeat the worst feelings experienced during the original bullying. If you were traumatized at work, your involvement in a lawsuit that requires you to repeat your story to the other side puts you at risk of being retraumatized.

3. The justice you seek to reverse the unfairness experienced in your bullying workplace can rarely be achieved in a courtroom. We know Targets who have won more than $1 million in a settlement and were still not satisfied. The bully still had his job and was telling lies years after the lawsuit. Fairness comes in small, unexpected ways—the bully is caught committing criminal activity and goes to jail, the bully is finally fired and you get to wave good-bye from the front office door.

4. Do not be offended by a callous lawyer who has too little "bedside manner." Lawyers, just like humans, differ in their style of telling you bad news. Knowing that there is no law should help you accept the judgment coming from attorneys. They may have to let you down. It's just that some are better than others at doing this.

## Types of Lawyers to Hire and to Avoid

### Plaintiffs vs. Defense Attorneys

Most attorneys specializing in employment law represent employers. So, when calling attorneys' offices, ask if the person represents primarily plaintiffs (the little guy or gal in the office willing to fight the corporation) or mostly defends corporations and employers. There is an organization of attorneys who are primarily plaintiffs' attorneys: the NELA (National Employment Lawyers Association). NELA members must have 51 percent of their clients be individual plaintiffs. Consult the NELA website (www.nela.org) for members in your area.

## Employment Law Specialists

You want a specialist in employment law—consult NELA or the local bar association for a list. The most popular area of employment law is civil rights. There are state and federal laws that make harassment and discrimination illegal. In one-fifth of bullying incidents, discrimination plays a role. Employment attorneys listen carefully to prospective clients for evidence of illegal discrimination. They want to hear that discrimination is present; they hear the sound of coins. Discrimination can be based on gender, race, ethnicity, age, or disability. You must be a member of a "protected status group" to claim damages. But if your harasser is similarly protected, you could be out of luck. Same-gender or same-race bullying rarely qualifies as a violation of existing civil rights laws. Without discrimination, it is hard to get an attorney to take your case.

The bad news is that bullying is much more prevalent than illegal forms of mistreatment. And attorneys are deaf to cases that don't include discrimination as part of the mistreatment. It's not just their fault; blame the law. If you can claim discrimination, you have to get permission from the federal EEOC before you can hire a private attorney. Sometimes it is mere formality, but it can delay your taking action. You have to tell the federal government that you have a discrimination complaint against the employer first, then get a "right to sue" letter. The current (highly politicized and pro-employer) EEOC has no interest in pursuing cases on behalf of individuals. The EEOC is reluctant to punish employers. And their cases can take ten years to finish!

Another type of bullying-related case that could be illegal is when the conduct is so outrageous and the impact on you so severe that you could claim "intentional infliction of emotional distress." Courts have nearly impossible standards to reach to win emotional distress claims. And your entire life's medical record can be reviewed by your employer when you sue for emotional distress.

There are some other, equally unsuccessful legal avenues to pursue. You can read a summary of relevant laws written by law professor David Yamada at the WBI website and at the New Workplace Institute (www.newworkplaceinstitute.org).

In short, U.S. employment law—at both the federal and state level—is weak. Employers have the upper hand. If you have a union, you have more rights and can slow down the employer's drive to fire you (if the union is supportive). Without a union, the doctrine of "employment at will" prevails in the United States. You can kiss your job goodbye if any employer representative wants to take it away from you on a whim. All rights belong to the employer except in rare instances.

## Conflict of Interest Avoidance

Whenever you call a legal office to schedule a preliminary appointment (sometimes complimentary), ask if anyone there represents the employer you are considering suing. When there is conflict of interest in the office, your side of the case will get scant attention. On the other hand, you want to inquire if any attorney in a given office has experience fighting your bullying employer (search public court records to identify which attorneys have fought them in other cases—they will be more effective than a rookie who has never dealt with that employer and its defense counsel before).

## Paying Attorneys

First of all, the best use of an attorney's time is to rent them to write you a demand letter to your bullying employer. Only an attorney could or should threaten legal action. You should not threaten; you will scare no one and it will backfire. Attorneys are also ideal to help you negotiate favorable separation agreement terms. In all other matters, you are probably looking at a longer-term relationship with an attorney. There are three payment methods: (1) contingency—in cases where the attorney accepts the case and does not charge her or his fee until a victory is won and a percentage of those winnings go to the attorney (you may have to pay the smaller court costs as they are incurred); (2) retainer—a large chunk of money is advanced and regular payments are expected as the case progresses; (3) pay-as-you-go—hourly rates vary from $250 to $400 per hour. It always makes sense to volunteer to help your case by doing as many small things as you can to keep costs low. For instance, you should not give your attorney voluminous documentation about your case. Shorten descriptions to save reading time. He or she can always ask for elaboration when it's time.

## Attorneys Who Pay Attention

This case is probably your first and only case. Attorneys are fond of saying that they have many cases that need their attention. Therefore, recognize the following trade-offs. In a small firm (a solo private practice is the smallest possible), you will get attention, but that person may not have the resources/money to fight a big employer with many defense lawyers. Large firms may have the resources to fight the big employers, but their caseload is so high they will take weeks to return your phone calls or email questions. Ask when you are screening attorneys about their caseload during the period anticipated to work on your case. Also ask how they want to be contacted—phone, email—and stick to what they request. Then, when they ignore you, you have the right to state that you were following their rules.

Remember that you are a consumer of a very expensive service. You have the right to shop around and to ask tough questions. Attorneys offended by your assertiveness will not be good legal partners for you. Demand experience, ask for their success rate, and ask for referrals from satisfied clients. Call the referrals before signing contracts.

Eventually, when there is an anti-bullying law in your state, certain attorneys will emerge as experts. After a law is in place, we can begin to train attorneys to better understand the phenomenon of bullying and the special type of clients who are bullied Targets. Until then, this is the best advice we can offer. Whether or not you eventually file a lawsuit can only be determined in concert with a licensed legal expert in your state or city.

## The WBI Lawyer Interview

Here's our condensed guide to what to look for when selecting an employment lawyer. Ask direct questions if the attorney does not offer this information during the initial telephone call. No attorney is likely to answer all of these questions or demonstrate all the desired principles, but you are the customer and you have the right to know.

Desirable principles to see in an attorney:
- a fighting spirit
- an ability to be empathetic, to share outrage at your plight
- wisdom based on direct experience in court
- the realism to tell you whether or not you have a legal leg to stand on (and you, in turn, have to know that the law frequently offers bullied people no remedy; it's not the attorney's fault)

Ask for:
- telephone numbers of satisfied clients (and then ask them many of the questions that follow)
- experience with similar cases brought against similar defendants
- a record (or fear) of going up against the organiza-

tion that supported the bullying

- an itinerary of how and when will you be prepared for your deposition (or will you be left to devise your own strategy?)
- your assigned primary contact person
- a frequency of regular case updates about upcoming deadlines, defendant stalling, etc.
- an assessment of time available for your case, given the current caseload
- results:
  - overall percentage of claims settled (and at what stage?)
  - percentage of cases gone to trial and the results
  - average monetary award won for clients with similar cases
- a willingness to accept case on contingency (court costs paid by firm or by you) vs. retainer and fees as you go
- a recommendation of another attorney if any of the questions are not answered to your satisfaction or the attorney doesn't want you as a client.

Our simple reminder to you is that if you must engage an attorney, you will still have to carry the majority of the burden for winning your case. You, and only you, will provide much of the information and be the steadiest source of new angles and approaches they could take when they get discouraged. And if you expect them to prop you up emotionally, forget it. You must have a support network in place to help you keep your balance.

Remember, lawyers differ in their abilities and interpersonal skills.

But the law should govern most of the choices they make. Even the lawyer blessed with the most empathic ability cannot manufacture a law. She or he is stuck with what the legislatures have written and how courts interpret those laws. Limits in the law most often account for the abrupt refusal to take your case, though it feels like another in a long string of personal attacks. We don't defend tactless lawyers; more important that we work to create laws that give even the least skilled attorney a fighting chance to win your case.

Screen several lawyers until you sense a comfortable fit. Then, lower your expectations for riches and justice. See all of the previous warnings. And call us if your attorney may be interested in our forensic services as an expert witness.

## Chapter Seven:

# Getting Ready to Confront

*What counts is not necessarily the size of the dog in the fight,*
*but the size of the fight in the dog.*
—Dwight D. Eisenhower

We have found that the effects of bullying on Targets follow a very predictable pattern. There are ups and downs and lots of switching directions in mood and energy.

There are two reasons for being aware of your post-bullying emotional cycles. First, you will be less surprised. In a Target's chaotic world, any predictability is useful to begin to regain the control that was stolen from you. Second, you will not be able to take the necessary steps to extricate yourself from the mess and get to safety if you are in certain stages.

Here's the sequence of stages we've discovered most Targets pass through.

## Stage 1: Victimhood

The immediate pain of harassment dominates all thinking. Too easily forgotten are the twenty years of experience you brought to the job. We guess that the harassing manager was new to the job or your unit. "How could this have happened to me?" you think. It's easy to feel beaten as you research your options and learn the destructiveness of the effects of bullying. People who don't have experience with this issue are incredibly naïve about their rights and procedures. The adversarial employer offers no information that gives you an advantage. Oddly, those who have gone before you rarely offer advice, somehow thinking it best for you to discover everything by yourself.

*Cure:* Know it is the system that creates or sustains a creepy, malicious person like the abusive bully. You were not singled out based on any real flaw or weakness. You were simply nonconfrontational at the time of the initial assault. Attackers prefer less combative, more cooperative victims.

## Stage 2: Power Surge

Help is found! The workers' compensation/disability/EEO-complaint systems are discovered. Tales of favorable jury awards or large settlements in cases like yours suddenly appear. Attorneys are identified. With friends and advocates, you actually feel sorry for the wrongdoing employer. You are all-powerful. Sure, you hear warnings about how long justice takes, but at this early stage, the future looks rosy.

*Cure:* Hold on to these feelings. You'll need the strength. As you repeatedly hear the merits of your case and how much you deserve to win, let the rationale sink in. You'll need to hear the echo to get you through stages three and four.

## Stage 3: Vulnerability

The counterattack begins by the employer. Their deep pockets become apparent as their legal spinmeisters paint you as a fraudulent, greedy, professional lout. Their resources are limitless compared to your puny contingency-based lawyer's office. Your lawyer stops returning your calls because, after all, she has paying clients. There is a steady stream of interrogatories (questions from the company counsel) leading up to the dreaded deposition. If your case goes that far, your lawyer's percentage also rises.

Depositions are institutionalized assassinations. You're never quite ready for the experience. Just remember corporate lawyers believe in a "scorched earth, no survivors" strategy. Your lawyer probably didn't have the time to rehearse with you for the inquisition. To listen to the employer's defense arguments, you begin to feel like you should apologize for working for twenty years and hampering their productivity for so long.

Of course, if you are not suing in a court of law, the bureaucrat in charge of minimizing workers' compensation claims for the employer—someone you probably knew as an acquaintance while working there—becomes the enemy. Your needs directly conflict with that person's job security. These auditing types have few friends at work because distrusting others ("they all file fraudulent claims") is central to doing their job well. Yucky people. They populate the typical Personnel or Human Resources (HR) department.

It finally dawns on you that HR works for management. Because you have an injury, you begin to learn firsthand how much access employers have to your medical records. They review your prescriptions. Had a temporary bout with depression after your father's death? They've got records that will be misconstrued to impale you. They'll spin their records to show that you are a worthless piece of dung hooked on doctors and drugs. Pain? You'll be labeled a "chronic pain patient"— code for illegitimate pain. Now the descriptions by physicians come to be used against you: spinal disc enlargement, not uncommon for a person your age, soft tissue damage is undetectable, pain is subjective, no treatment exists, you'll just have to work through it, and surgery is not advised. Stress is a mental fiction. Stress is for wimps. Stress builds character. And the daily torment the employer exposed you to was applied for motivation's sake.

*Cure:* Keep telling yourself it is the other side's job to fight back. Keep your mind on the justice you seek. Watch legal shows on television to see how adept defense lawyers are at rationalizing what they do on behalf of corporations. Also, you might get an idea or two for your lawyer on strategy. Read Ralph Nader's book *No Contest* to validate your fight. Your cause is noble, but the courts don't recognize it.

# Stage 4: Isolation and Abandonment

Now you feel alone. The other side has shown its muscle; it is scary. Your white knight attorney is always unavailable and fades into the background. Colleagues from work, former friends, find it hard to keep in contact. They fear being in your place someday and treat you like you have the plague. It is ironic that it was they who encouraged you so strongly to stand up against the cruel bully. Of course, they did not take their own advice. You imagine them on the stand testifying against you at trial.

*Cure:* Refuse to be alone. Fight isolation; it magnifies stress. Social support is lifesaving. Force friends to maintain contact. Stay involved with life outside your case. Volunteer to help a group do something you've always wanted to do. Start the at-home business you've longed for. Be your own boss. Don't let the dispute become your life's defining moment—shove it into the background. Don't lose the passion for your case, simply throw your day-to-day energy into constructive activity. Build or make something. Get involved with something or someone.

Don't let all your family discussions drift toward progress, or lack thereof, in your case.

Tell your story to a reporter. Renew old relationships with friends who knew you before this fiasco and who did not work with you. You deserve validation that you indeed had a life before. The current dispute does not define who you are as a person. Write down the case details and your feelings. Get therapy to deal with the downside of challenging a big bad employer.

# Stage 5: Anger

It is usually aimed at everyone, primarily yourself, but even at supporters. Partly because you are no longer in your regular work routine, with time on your hands and isolated, the vengeful arguments directed at you from the other side erode your confidence. This is very dangerous. Don't let the "kernel of truth" in. Self-doubt feeds on itself, relying on the script written by your enemies. If you must be mad, be mad at them. We've found that anger over the circumstances seems to be a requisite to healing.

*Cure:* Reread the "Anger and Shame" chapter in this book (page 217). Read books about how to defuse anger. It is too destructive to turn it inward. It is antisocial to rage at others. Trust your sense of self; be defined by those who love you rather than focusing on garbage slung by opponents in a legal fight.

# Stage 6: Resolution

You find a way to move on. In victory, you can become a forgiver of enemies more quickly than in defeat. At the end, partly to make sense of the stressful process just endured, you could become a crusader. You fought for a cause and find that many others have the same plight. You want to help. There may not be a business in it for you, but you feel fulfilled doing meaningful work. You forget that you ever worked for that crummy employer.

*Cure:* Moving on while allowing resentment to fade is the most certain path to your positive mental health and feelings of self-worth. Winning a lawsuit does not necessarily give the sense of closure to this dark chapter in your life. What seems to matter most is registering your disgust at the bully's conduct and letting her, the company, and the world know that you found it outrageous and intolerable.

One woman who suffered under a bully for years decided to complain, to fight Goliath. She passed through all six phases. Her very

private resolution was the delight she felt the day she waved goodbye to her tormenter as the bully left work forever, preferring to take
early retirement rather than stay and fight. No headlines, just a long-
postponed, quiet, victorious moment as the bully was banished.

Our favorite behavioral researcher, Pam Lutgen-Sandvik, PhD,
professor at the University of New Mexico, captured Target stages in
another useful way. Bullying assaults your sense of self, your identity.
That identity must be repaired and restored. (The chapters in Section
Two are all about this process.)

1. *The Pre-Bullying Phase* is characterized by the
   disruption of your psychological comfort and
   day-to-day predictability. The first assault
   challenges your mental perceptions of yourself.
   It is crazy-making. Your identity repair goals
   include reestablishing a sense of security and
   safety, identifying causes of the abuse, and
   validating your sense of self.

2. *The Bullying Phase* is about the extreme
   dissonance between who the bully says you
   are and who you know yourself to be. There
   is stigma attached to being targeted. You are
   now a pariah in the work team. Your image is
   seriously damaged when you are not believed by
   senior management. You are actually blamed for
   being abused. Your identity repair goals include
   countering the lies and accusations, highlighting
   the truth about past successes, and convincing
   others of your value and truthfulness. Perhaps
   the most important aspect of this phase is the
   destruction, or at least shaking up, of your values
   and beliefs about the world. (You once thought
   it to be safe, secure, and benevolent.) This is the

toughest identity work to undertake. You have to come to grips with the reality that it can be an unfair world. Shock and surprise are the basis of the trauma you experience. You have to regain a sense of equilibrium and prepare to convert the beliefs that you brought from childhood.

3. *The Post-Bullying Phase* is consumed by dealing with losses. As our research shows, most Targets lose the jobs they once loved through no fault of their own. This entails a loss of not only a job and often a career, but the personal identity you invested in that job. Targets suffer the most when they make paying work their sole means of identity. When jobs are lost, it feels like your soul is lost. Grieving must necessarily take place. The loss must be accepted and incorporated into your life narrative going forward. The principal identity repair goal is to heal from the trauma, to "put oneself back together again," stronger and remade as the result of learning from this transformative experience. It's a matter of converting evil to good.

## Your Readiness to Confront

The second advantage you get from knowing predictable stages of Targethood is so you can accurately determine your "readiness to confront." When you do finally decide to stop the rationalization (for whatever reason—perhaps at the insistence of your physician or clinical psychologist), it is critical that you have enough stamina to see the fight through to the end.

If you commit too early, at the early Power Surge stage, you will come crashing down, relatively unprotected, while your case languishes over time.

Little children cannot be potty-trained until their biological clock says all the organs are ready. In a similar fashion, no confrontation should be undertaken until you are psychologically stable. Because self-doubt plays such a major role in bullying, it is important to be genuinely confident that there is nothing wrong with you before you begin the fight.

You can't effectively fight alone nor be motivated to win unless you are angry. Anger follows being hurt. Stop the hurt first. Then, fight if you want to.

We believe our method of fighting back, the three actions steps in chapter 17, represent your best approach for more than one reason outlined there.

# Should You Fight Back?

Be warned. Fighting back through internal complaint channels and through our suggested informal system without reliance on lawyers both carry a low chance of success. It is an uphill battle; it is your choice.

## Reasons to Not Fight Back

The disadvantages all revolve around the price martyrs pay when challenging institutions that can outgun, delay, lie, distort, and outlast any lone individual's campaign for the truth to come out. They include: (a) costs to your health; (b) the toll vicious defensive employers can impose; and (c) economic losses.

### Health Costs

You know that Targets pay for being bullied with their personal health—emotional and physical. They also pay a social toll. They are excluded and isolated at work by once loyal co-workers who now cower in fear about being associated with the "troublemaker." Worse yet is when the abandonment becomes betrayal: they now side with and aid the terrorizing tyrant against the Target. Though this is somehow understandable through the lens of an intellectual, high-brow, dispassionate analyst, it sickens us all to witness when it happens. It's enough to drive a sane person to look like a raving, paranoid lunatic. And this is in fact what the employers do.

PTSD (post-traumatic stress disorder) is common among Targets traumatized at work by cumulative assaults on their competence, confidence, self-image, and job security. Work Trauma, a special form of PTSD, is recognized by experts as complicated and it doesn't go away easily or quickly. A prolonged fight through the endless steps of internal grievances and appeals, or through the legal system with years of delays built in, ensures that the anxieties, listlessness, nightmares, and phobias that comprise PTSD will linger. It also can be relived at each meeting, retelling of the story, or receipt of mailed determination letters. Fighting back prolongs the agony. Healing by grieving over the losses is postponed until the stressor—the fighting back itself—has ended.

## Defensive Employers Exact a Toll

It is the nature of the workers' compensation system (misnamed for suggesting that it benefits injured workers at all) and all internal complaint systems that the Target (the complainant) be treated as a fraud, a malingerer, and a thief trying to get something for nothing. Complaining threatens the appearance of organizational calm. Corporations revere their image. People and processes that uncover bullying face incredible pressure to silence them.

When an employer responds to your complaint, denial begins. Several people, departments, and institutions both inside and out get involved. Denial occurs in two ways: (1) ridiculous official pronouncements that the company has no problem with bullies; and (2) justification for the cruelty because it leads to something positive for the employer (productivity, meeting deadlines, "motivating" staff with toughness).

When faced with such bold lies and illogical excuse-making, Targets initially get "perception shock." They can't believe what is being said to and about them. Because they have strong beliefs in equity and justice, they think the lies will eventually wither when contrasted with the truth they are prepared to tell. Don't believe it. Getting the truth to a public, safe, and impartial forum on the employer's turf is nearly impossible. Even when you do, there is no guarantee that truth will triumph. Courts tend to be hostile by defining employers as masters and employees as servants. The assumption is that servants should be grateful for their paycheck.

The truth is that the Target has been placed in harm's way by the employer. It is the workplace that enabled the unwitting Target to expose herself to a cruel, control-driven bully. All the resources at the employer's disposal will be used to dodge responsibility and accountability for the bully. They will try to paint you, the Target, as the problem.

When Targets dare to fight back, the bully's allies materialize out of thin air. Co-workers take sides against you. The Personnel department role of bully and employer-protector becomes clear.

If you dare to actually file a lawsuit, the employer goes berserk. Its defense attorneys pull your medical records, searching for a clue to convince the court that you were always crazy. This defense strategy drives them to discover or invent personality flaws. (If you also claim sexual harassment, they accuse you of being a slut—the "nuts 'n' sluts" defense.) According to Targets whose cases move to the deposition stage, the process feels like "intellectual rape." Depositions and other steps in the battle can retraumatize you. Before filing suit, Targets should ask their attorneys to explain every ugly activity they could face. Target lawsuits should be undertaken only when you are emotionally strong. The risks of prolonged traumatization and delayed healing are great.

## Economic Losses

Once a Target's health is compromised and her or his social support network torn apart, what more could go wrong? Economic devastation, that's what! After sick leave, vacation pay, and other paid time off days are exhausted, Targets are pressured by employers to take unpaid time off under the FMLA (Family Medical Leave Act). In the short-run, a physician's off-work order for job stress and disability pay are a better alternative to unpaid time off. If your fight is not resolved quickly (which it never is), long-term disability pays only a fraction of normal pay. Workers' compensation claims, if successful, also replace only a portion of your full pay. Employers have their physicians and insurers ready to deny your claim of suffering psychological injury at the hands of a harassing bully. You will have to fight long and hard to win an award. You suffer financially while the fight drags on.

The ultimate outcome is termination. When a bully zeroes in on a Target, job security is lost. According to the WBI-Zogby Survey, 64 percent of Targets were either fired or quit. Another 13 percent were forced to transfer, to leave the job they loved, in order to retain a paycheck.

Appeasing the bully never makes the Target's job more secure.

Staying under the bully's thumb only increases risks. Risk of declining health, self-defeat, and abandonment. Appeasement back-fires. It did for Europe trying to postpone Hitler; it works similarly between a Target and the bully.

Getting out on one's own terms should be a goal of every Target.

A sad consequence of bullying is that the great paying, challenging work that you once enjoyed can be stolen from you. Remarkably, some bullies are not satisfied driving the Target out. They hound the banished person into the next job, killing chances with a defamatory job reference or actually contacting management at the next place to poison the impression they have of the newly hired Target. This is illegal. There are ways to combat both practices. A reference-checking firm may help stop the first type of attack and a lawyer familiar with defamation cases can address the tricky part of how to use your bullying employer as a reference.

Without a job, while living on savings, Targets turn to lawyers to seek justice on their behalf and they are told to pay a several thousand dollar retainer on good faith with no promises of results. In a short time, if the Target was the sole wage earner, the home has to be sold. The familiar saying that middle-class American families are two paychecks away from homelessness becomes a reality.

Our legal system, the alternative to an internal complaint mechanism for Targets, rarely does the right thing. See the discussion in chapters 19 and 20 about the shortcomings of "protections" in current employment law.

To summarize the case against fighting back, it can prolong health problems, costs friends, and is expensive. It is little wonder that Targets stay in horrific, destructive workplaces because they "have to have" their paychecks. No one has the right to blame them for making what appears to outsiders as a self-destructive choice.

## Why You Should Fight Back

Fighting back should not be undertaken until the Target is safe. At some stage, the Target gets over being hurt and gets mad. That's the signal that BullyBusting can begin. Two major reasons to fight back, despite all the potential setbacks, are: (a) to satisfy your need for fairness and doing the right thing; and (b) being able to move on with your personal dignity intact.

### Equity and Justice for All

BullyBusting also depends on how violated the Target feels. Targets believe the world should be fair. Payoffs and outcomes should be proportional to effort and skill invested in work. That would dictate the greatest rewards for the most competent among us. Reality rarely meets this idealistic standard, however. Incompetent boobs who dominate their more competent peers, thanks to organizational politics, utter the familiar refrain: "Life is not fair. Live with it."

Feelings of inequity and injustice seem to drive most BullyBusting, even though the odds are stacked against bullied Targets. Whistleblowers are extreme examples of bullied Targets who risk everything to fight back. They do so because they cannot imagine accepting what was done to them. They live according to a higher level of moral decision-making than most of us who play the political game, deluding ourselves that we have to "pick the right fight worth fighting for." Then, we let others chip away at our integrity in small doses over long periods of time. Before we know it, we've lost sense of what, if anything, we stand for. If we dare to fight, then our opponents can rightly claim that we have little reason to fight back now when so many earlier compromises went unchallenged.

Whistleblowers claim the moral high ground early and often, shaming the rest of us who are too cowardly to demand equity and justice. It is sad when bold American principles are dismissed as "idealistic" or "radical" when discussion turns to the workplace. We salute whistleblowers and other principled Targets for demonstrating the courage the rest of us should admire and emulate.

Inequity and injustice disgust Targets; they want to do something to right the wrong. Some Targets fight back because they know no other way.

## Moving on with Dignity

The most important reason to go BullyBusting is to close a dark episode in the Target's life. Naïve co-workers, family, and friends admonish Targets for not "just moving on" with their lives. Bullying is not so easily put aside. Bullying is an invasion of the Target's sanctuary of how she sees herself. The damage to the psyche and the confidence to move on is more harmful than physical abuse.

In WBI surveys, Targets repeatedly told us that their greatest regret was to leave without confronting the bully, without telling the employer what was done behind closed doors, or without letting everyone know how they were driven out. In the absence of identifying the bully as culprit, staff are frequently told that the departed Target left for "personal reasons," or for bad performance, which allows employers to blame Targets and never be held accountable for the bullying. When the Target does not provide information about the bullying, the bully and employer spin the story in a way that serves to cover up the dirty deeds.

By fighting back, word soon spreads through the grapevine that the Target was harassed by the bully and key people in the company caved in to the bully's demands and supported the wrong person. For the purposes of BullyBusting, we care less about the impact of knowledge on the bully and employer than the restorative effect it has for the Target.

BullyBusting restores self-respect and lost dignity. You owe it to yourself to go out on your own terms.

We've found that the nature of your (nearly inevitable) departure from the bullying workplace determines whether you rebound and land the next job relatively quickly or skulk between the sheets, too traumatized to leave your house. Try not to leave with your experience shrouded in shame and secrecy. Leave kicking and screaming about the injustice done to you. Name names. Identify the bullies. And, as you'll see in our approach, you will shout it from the highest peak in the organization, not allowing your story to die in a lowly HR office behind closed doors.

Despite the odds against success, because the employer and bully collaborate to serve as prosecutor, judge, jury, and executioner, BullyBusting sends a message to witnesses that at least one Target did not accept the lies, distortions, and career-threatening tactics intended to humiliate her. She serves as a model of courage. With luck, witnesses and future Targets will stand firm and defeat the bully, shaming the employer who supports the perpetrator of psychological violence.

# Advice from Veterans of the Bullying Wars

Here is wisdom, in their own words, from survey respondents who were asked to say what would they have done differently when bullied:

- *Take a stand and get the help you need to confront the bully, because you wouldn't have a bully on your back if there were more people on your side.*
- *Fight back from the beginning.*
- *Realize that the bully is really a coward. Also realize that you should not back down, but don't become a bully yourself.*
- *Tell others that you trust what is happening. Build support and get ready to confront. It is not OK! Reflect on your past work experiences and realize that this is related to the bully and not a truth about you. Constantly do reality checks with others.*
- *Don't take any kind of crap from anybody. Stand up to them.*
- *I think I did the best thing by confronting him. I also provided support to others who were being annoyed by his behaviors and encouraged them to speak up. I also informed my senior colleagues of his behavior and its effects on me... that was a tremendous help... they had been putting up with it and sloughing it off... when they realized that he was hurting me and [they] even heard some of the comments and thought them "stupid," they intervened by giving friendly advice to him.*
- *I would have challenged the bully more and stood up for my own beliefs instead of backing down.*

- *I would have confronted the situation earlier, taken legal action, and been less passive and forgiving.*
- *I would have gone to the operations of our corporate office or the district manager with my complaint instead of our immediate manager.*
- *I would have kept a better record of bullying incidents.*

As you can see, the message from those who have been there is to confront rather than to face certain ongoing humiliation. You may have to mount the campaign to out the bully alone, but before you prepare yourself to accomplish the three action steps (outlined in a subsequent chapter), consider that maybe, just maybe, others can be enlisted to help.

# Do Not Attempt BullyBusting Unless and Until You Are BullyProof.

......................................................................

# After the Assault, Restoring the Lost You

*Chapter Eight:*

# Work Trauma: Understand the Injuries Done to You

*The soul of man is immortal and imperishable.*
—Plato

Targets bear the brunt of job stress in America. Our society still questions psychological pain. At times, we seem enlightened. We joke about Prozac and the growing family of anti-depressants, but its familiarity is testament to the prevalence of depression and the numbers of people who seek help for it. Then, we act stupid about psychological processes when we callously discount those asking for help as being "weak" or "needing a crutch." Despite the extensive body of pharmacological research about brain chemistry and the biological bases of diseases like depression, we still expect people to "tough it out."

Personal experience breeds tolerance, however. The concept of bullying is immediately recognized by anyone who has been through it or knows someone who has—there are no more than two degrees of separation.

There are several diseases or disgraceful habits once accepted as "the way things are done" that are no longer taboo. We've learned to talk freely about impotence, incontinence, sexual harassment, domestic violence, child abuse, drunk driving, and a host of cancers— breast, prostrate, colorectal. We at WBI predict an end to taboo status for workplace bullying.

## Work Shouldn't Hurt

The first step is to raise public and lawmaker awareness of the damage bullies inflict on the quality of the Target's life. Americans should be intolerant of such unwanted, harmful invasions of a worker's life. Its constituency is diverse and large, including people of all races, income levels, and political persuasions. Bullying unites its veterans. There is an untapped reservoir of American support for public policy and law reform concerning this subject.

Only corporate defense lawyers believe that employees deserve a traumatizing workplace, if that's what ownership wants. We have federal and state laws ensuring physical workplace safety; shouldn't there be freedom from psychological injury, too?

For workplace bullying to be taken seriously by policymakers and people who naturally repel bullies, Targets must be able to demonstrate that harm has occurred. For any law proposed, the employer lobby will demand documentation of extensive damage. The current tort most closely related to bullying is *Intentional Infliction of Emotional Distress* (IIED). In order for a Target to sue and win a legal case, he must prove to the court that the injury has been severe. Courts mirror the "get tough" public judgment, underestimating the severity of emotional distress claimed by Targets in lawsuits.

Not everyone at work is targeted for mistreatment by bullies. Of those targeted, the harm they suffer ranges from mild to severe. Same bully, same tactics, different Targets, different types and severity of damage. Individual differences determine whether the Target loses sleep or spirals down into a deep depression, reduced to an essentially traumatized life.

As a more severe example, the Swedish ordinance outlawing "victimization" at work requires the employee to be "placed outside the workplace community." In other words, the worker has to lose her job to have been damaged.

## The Many Faces of Hurt

### Emotional-Psychological Health Damage

- Poor concentration, forgetfulness
- Loss of sleep, fatigue
- Stress, irritability
- PTSD (detailed later)
- Mood swings, bursts of anger
- Spontaneous crying, lost sense of humor
- Indecisiveness
- Panic attacks, anxiety
- Clinical depression
- Feelings of insecurity, being out of control
- Nightmares about the bully
- Obsessive thinking about the bully
- Always anticipating the next attack (hypervigilance)
- Shattered faith in self, feelings of worthlessness
- Shame, embarrassment, and guilt
- Self-destructive habits: substance abuse, workaholism
- Altered personality, unrecognizable to family and friends
- Suicidal thoughts

## Bullying Can Be Hazardous to Your Health! It Causes Psychological INJURY. Targets Are Not Mentally Ill.

Psychological pain should not be minimized or denied by Targets themselves or by others. Stoic bravery and toughness are no match for suicidal thoughts or feelings of terror when you turn in to the company parking lot in the morning. Seek help. You owe it to yourself and the people who love you. They recognize the very real pain you endure from bullying and want it to stop.

The greater the severity of psychological pain, the more dangerous the effects and the longer they seem to last. It is a fact that those exposed to domestic violence are hurt more by the verbal abuse than the physical wounds, which heal easily.

### Physical Stress-Related Health Damage

- Cardiovascular problems, from hypertension to heart attack
- Reduced immunity to infection: more colds, flu
- Menstrual difficulties
- Itching, skin disorders
- Stress headaches and migraines
- Increased allergies, asthma
- Indigestion, colitis, irritable bowel syndrome
- Rheumatoid arthritis, fibromyalgia, chronic fatigue
- Hair loss
- Weight swings
- Hyperthyroidism: overactive thyroid gland
- Diabetes mellitus

- Neurological changes in brain structures and neurotransmitters

## Damage to Social Relations

- Co-worker isolation from personal fear
- Parents encourage compromise with bully
- Co-worker resentment, attempts to silence you
- Spouse questions your role in dispute with bully
- Children and friends outside work show strain
- Wavering support from family
- Abandonment/betrayal by co-workers
- Separation/divorce by immediate family
- Abandonment by friends outside work

## Economic-Financial Damage

- Sympathetic medical provider recommends halted work hours for job stress
- Paid time off (PTO) accounts begin to be used
- Sick leave exhausted, switch to short-term disability
- Employer encourages unpaid leave under FMLA (Family Medical Leave Act)
- Employer orders you to choose between termination and workers' compensation (WC)
- PTO accounts exhausted, no days left
- Placed on long-term disability, income cut
- Personal savings tapped
- Creditors renegotiate payment structure
- File for WC, potentially lose the right to sue
- Formally terminated in a way so employer can deny unemployment compensation
- Disability payments run out

- House and property sold
- Personal savings depleted

In a matter of a few months, it is possible that a vibrant, healthy, competent employee can be driven to ruin—economic, physical, and emotional. And this is all due to the unilateral decisions made by an incompetent, insecure, vicious individual backed by the power of an employer who did not want to get involved in what they see as a "personality conflict" between two people.

## Stages of Stress

The bully is the source of the Target's stress—she and the havoc she produces are the stressor. The responses of your body and mind to stressors determine the extent of damage inflicted. The sequence of biological stress is well known. There are three stages, as described by Hans Selye:

1. Alarm—the turning on of the entire body's defense systems, designed to be brief; it enables the "flight or fight" response in the face of danger, physical or psychological. Unfortunately, the body reacts to fright from the impending pounce of a tiger the same way it does to an insult from the bully. Alarm triggers the sympathetic nervous system that releases adrenaline to deal with the stressor.

2. Resistance—the maintenance of an alert stage that usually stops after the alarm. The body expects, and needs, this reaction to be turned off so that normal functions can resume. Resistance to the bully, however, is continuous, and that depletes the body's defenses. If you stay in resistance too long, the body rebounds and the actual damage occurs even when the stressor is gone.

3. Exhaustion—a full system breakdown, mental and physical. It demands that the stressor be removed or it will claim your life. To get to exhaustion, you have to ignore all the warning signs that your body gives. These can lead to death if the stressor never disappears and the body and mind continue to fight indefinitely.

## Stress Is Real

According to the American Institute of Stress:

✓ Job stress is far and away the leading source of stress for adult Americans. Seventy-eight percent of Americans describe their jobs as stressful.

✓ Seventy-five to 90 percent of visits to primary care physicians are for stress-related problems.

✓ The National Safety Council estimates that one million employees are absent on any average workday because of stress-related problems.

✓ Job stress is estimated to cost American industry $200 to $300 billion annually, as assessed by absenteeism; diminished productivity; employee turnover; accidents; direct medical, legal, and insurance fees; workers' compensation awards; etc. Put into perspective, that's more than the price for all strikes combined or the total net profits of the *Fortune* 500 companies.

✓ Sixty to 80 percent of accidents on the job are related to stress.

✓ Forty percent of worker turnover is due to job stress.

✓ Workers' compensation claims for job stress have skyrocketed—California employers shelled out almost $1 billion for medical and legal fees alone.

One reporter asked us why we take Targets at their word. "Aren't you concerned that they are making it up?" was her concern. Why would they? People lie about beauty, wealth, and health. There is no reason to fabricate a tale about strokes, heart attacks, and immobilizing anxiety.

## Symptoms of Stress

Here are some very common signs of a stress reaction in a traumatized person.

### Physical Indicators

- Nausea, tremors of the lips, hands
- Feeling uncoordinated
- Profuse sweating
- Chills
- Diarrhea
- Dizziness
- Rapid heart beat
- Chest pain (have a physician examine you)
- Rapid breathing
- Increased blood pressure
- Muscle aches
- Uncontrollable crying
- Headaches

### Thinking-Cognitive Indicators

- Mental slowness or confusion
- Indecisiveness
- Trouble with problem solving
- Time/place disorientation
- Poor concentration
- Memory problems
- Difficulty naming objects

- Nightmares
- Self-blame
- Minimizing the experience
- Sense of an unfair world

## Emotions as Indicators

- Anxiety
- Fear
- Anger
- Grief
- Depression
- Sadness
- Shame
- Feeling lost, abandoned, or isolated
- Guilt
- Feeling shocked
- Numbness
- Wild mood swings
- Wanting to hide

# *The 2003 WBI Survey Found...*

## Top 12 Health Consequences for Bullied Targets

1. Severe anxiety (94 percent)
2. Sleep disruption (84 percent)
3. Loss of concentration (82 percent)
4. Feeling edgy, easily startled (80 percent) [Hypervigilance/PTSD]
5. Obsession over bully's motives and tactics (76 percent)
6. Stress headaches (64 percent)
7. Avoidance of feelings, places (49 percent) [Avoidance/PTSD]
8. Shame or embarrassment that changed lifestyle/ routines (49 percent)
9. Racing heart rate (48 percent)
10. Recurrent memories (46 percent) [Thought Intrusion/PTSD]

11. New body aches—muscles or joints (43 percent)
12. Diagnosed depression (41 percent)

Harvey Hornstein, author of *Brutal Bosses and Their Prey*, surveyed nearly a thousand people for his book. Especially interesting were the health consequences for people subjected to disrespect. There were meaningful and statistically significant correlations between disrespect and depression (r = .64), anxiety (r = .58), and the loss of self-esteem (self-respect) (r = .45).

## Post-Traumatic Stress Disorder (PTSD)

The American Psychiatric Association recognizes a condition called acute stress disorder with symptoms that include disorientation, confusion, intense agitation, and dazed detachment, sometimes followed by amnesia. This reaction apparently makes the development of PTSD more likely. The risk is also high when the stress is sudden and severe, prolonged and repetitive, humiliates the victim, or destroys the victim's community and support system. Bullying does this!

PTSD is the injury that results from an overwhelming assault on the mind and emotions. A trauma is an event beyond the range of ordinary human experience—something that would be overwhelmingly terrifying for almost anyone. Even hearing about the suffering of another person is sometimes enough. Bullying often qualifies as a trauma, repeated over time.

The immediate response to a trauma can be intense fear, helplessness, or horror. The reaction may be delayed by days, weeks, months, or even years, and can last for a long time. There are three classes of symptoms:

*Hyper-alertness:* People often are edgy, irritable, easily startled, and constantly on guard. They sleep poorly, become easily agitated, have trouble concentrating, are aggressive, and are easily startled. Eighty percent of Institute survey respondents reported this symptom.

*Thought Obsessions:* An involuntary reliving of the traumatic event in the form of memories, nightmares, and flashbacks that may recreate the responses and feelings of the actual event. Sufferers may act as though the event were recurring (these episodes may or may not be recalled), and may display anxiety symptoms when exposed to anything that resembles some aspect of the trauma. Forty-six percent of Institute survey respondents reported this symptom.

*Emotional Flatness:* A need to avoid feelings, thoughts, and situations reminiscent of the trauma, a loss of normal emotional responses, feelings that seem unreal. Forty-nine percent of Institute survey respondents reported this symptom.

- Not caring about the ordinary business of life, feeling cut off from the concerns of others, an inability to trust others.
- Sensing that there is no future, anger at those responsible for the traumatic experience while feeling ashamed of their own helplessness, or guilty about what they did or what they failed to do. Sufferers feel demoralized and isolated.
- Suppressing anger that might lead to an explosion of violence. They no longer are able to use their feelings as cues to pay attention to their needs. Trauma victims habitually respond either too intensely or not at all.

The three PTSD symptom categories were included in the health checklist in the WBI 2003 Survey. For each individual, a trauma cluster score was computed with a score range of 0 to 3, corresponding to the number of symptoms reported. Thirty-one percent of participating women and 21 percent of participating men exhibited all three trauma symptoms. The bully's gender was not related to the generation of Work Trauma. The maximum trauma cluster score of

3 could be equally attributed to female bullies (51 percent) and male bullies (49 percent).

Average trauma scores for women were significantly higher than for men (1.80 vs. 1.51, respectively). Naturally, previously traumatized Targets experienced more Work Trauma than those with no prior experience (2.07 vs. 1.63).

Female Targets with partners had a slightly higher average trauma score (1.81) than women without partners (1.77); whereas male Targets with partners had a much lower average trauma score (1.46) than men without partners (1.76). This means that partners can mitigate the Work Trauma experience. However, it is primarily the men's partners who provide the helpful support and not the women's partners.

There was a significant positive correlation between education and traumatization. That is, as education level rose, the number of trauma symptoms rose. This can be explained by assuming that education leads to greater skill or greater commitment to work. In turn, that skill threatens the bully and increases the intensity of the abuse. Also, the people most vulnerable to abuse could be the most competent if they also believe that the workplace will treat them fairly and reward their skill. In a sense, the bright Target is apolitical. He underestimates the importance of political manipulation to others. This ensures surprise when assaults come his way. Trauma is partly the result of a violation of one's expectations, of idealistic assumptions shattered by a cruel reality.

It is important to know that PTSD was first introduced to the medical community in 1980. Its purpose was to provide a diagnosis and treatment for Vietnam veterans and those who had suffered a great trauma (seeing a child killed, surviving a fire, etc.). However, for most cases of workplace bullying, the Target's experience is different. The Target usually experiences the symptoms described above, but the one-time, traumatizing stressor is usually not present.

The symptoms however, result from the last in a series of cumulative bullying events. Most bullies assault their Targets over a long period with no single episode seemingly harsh enough to disrupt the Target's life. The damage comes from the accumulation of hurtful assaults.

What is most important to remember is that the resulting symptoms are similar to PTSD and need to be treated by a professional who is knowledgeable about the effects of stress and PTSD. A mental health practitioner with an understanding of the possibilities for harm by prolonged exposure to verbal attacks and this type of trauma is most important for treatment of this type of workplace bullying.

You might suggest that your therapist get a copy of the 1994 Donald Meichenbaum, PhD, book, *A Clinical Handbook/Practical Therapist Manual for Assessing and Treating Adults with PTSD*.

# Treating Work Trauma

Borrowing from the suggestions of William Wilkie, MD, in the Australian book *Bullying from Backyard to Boardroom*, we propose treating PTSD using the following method.

1. The foremost thing to do is to reassure the Target that she did nothing to cause her own victimization. She is not to blame. The most severe damage a bully can cause is to undermine the individual's confidence in her competence. Targets often blame themselves for the bullying, for lacking courage, for being weak, or for feeling defective when hurt by criticisms (however unwanted, unprovoked, and undeserved). Above all, the Target is to be held blameless.

2. Assure the person that she is an injured person, not a mentally ill one. She should receive treatment for the injury just as certainly as if she had fallen and broken an arm at work. She's not crazy.

3. Targets do not have to find a rational meaning for the bully's inane actions. If no reason can be

found, she might have to come to grips with the
reality that the bully's behavior is unwarranted
and irrational.

Meichenbaum and his colleagues have provided information about
how most people react when suffering from PTSD. There are predictable reactions and some stages you may go through.

People who have been exposed to a traumatic event, or a series
of traumatic events, have a difficult time letting go of the memories.
Hence the apparent obsessiveness of Targets that taxes the patience of
family and friends. This is not unusual, because bullying is meant to be
degrading and mean. This trauma not only attacks your work but questions your very existence, and can become the only thing you think
about. It hurts when someone sets out to destroy you both at work and
at home.

*Bev is a forty-four-year-old medical assistant who has
worked for more than twenty years. She is in a stable personal
relationship of eleven years with a supportive partner. She is a
gentle, nice woman who truly believes that if you work hard at
a job you will be liked and your talents will be acknowledged.*

*When Bev began working, she was eager to learn and
in her career has worked for many different doctors. She has
always sought out new experiences and new information.
She also has done temp work that attests to her ability to
come into an office and quickly adjust to differing needs of
different doctors.*

*Last year, after a series of temp positions, she decided
to look for a permanent job. She received several offers and
decided to accept a job in an office where the last assistant
had stayed for seventeen years. Bev welcomed the chance to
use her skills in this new setting.*

Bev quickly learned the office procedure—but that wasn't good enough. Within the first week, the physician began to find fault with her work. At first it was simple things. He told her she didn't work fast enough. She didn't perform certain procedures "his" way. He would trap her in one of the patient rooms during her half hour lunch and she would lose the only time she had for herself. There were no breaks and only severe disapproval if she asked for time to go to the bathroom.

Bev decided that she would work as hard as she could because she felt she must be doing something wrong. No matter how she tried to reinvent herself, the doctor was never satisfied. By the end of ten months, he was openly ridiculing her on a frequent basis. He went so far as to tell her what to do, and when she went to do it, the doctor would push her out of the way and do it himself. He used silence to confuse her and then berated her for not talking to him. He told her that she was "doing well" but her work was only at 90 percent and that "if she really tried, she could do better."

The final straw for Bev was a Friday afternoon. After being told to go to the doctor's office, the doctor told her she was causing him so much stress he had to see a doctor and that she should try to get along with him so he was not stressed.

Stunned and humiliated, Bev left the office in tears. During the weekend, she cried and blamed herself for her failure at work.

Bev was suffering from depression and was showing signs of prolonged trauma. She consulted a therapist and was referred to her physician for an evaluation for depression. She was placed on disability, began therapy, and started attending a women's group. Slowly she began to feel better about *herself, but after two months, she received a letter from the doctor. To her surprise, the letter outlined all her faults, told her once again that she had injured the doctor, and informed her that she had "quit" and had been replaced.*

*This cruel letter threw Bev into a tailspin. She felt like she had been kicked in the stomach. This was followed by many days of crying and obsessing about her job. She continues therapy and her support group is helping her come to terms with what happened. At this time, she continues putting her life back together.*

The more you obsess about the trauma, the more it becomes the focus of your life. This is where emotional numbing can take over. All your time is spent in organizing your life so that you can avoid the emotional feelings that accompany the memories of your trauma. However, when reminders of the trauma present themselves (driving by the worksite, seeing other workers, contacting those working on your disability claim), they may trigger an emotional response just as intense. For you, this will be just as if the trauma has occurred again. Your body can revert back to the fight or flight response, which is, in Meichenbaum's words, "the wisdom of the body" taking over in a survival response, or, if you become too scared, your body will shut down because your very safety and security are threatened. This is a natural and important part of the process.

All trauma should heal with time as long as the Target acknowledges that she is not to blame and starts the road to recovery. Be aware that events and circumstances that prolong trauma and a return to pre-injury functioning include battling interfering physicians, dull lawyers, disbelieving colleagues, doubting family members, and defamatory references that find their way to the next employer.

*Chapter Nine:*

# Assess the Bully's Impact

*A scientist heated a pan of water to a high temperature. Then, she tried to put a live frog into it. The frog jumped out immediately. A second frog was put in a pan of cold water that was gradually heated to boiling. That frog never tried to jump. It was boiled to death.*
—A parable

When exposed to a bully, most people go through three stages of emotions.

1. You are excited about your job and consider it a positive experience.
2. The bullying starts, and you bend over backwards to please the bully. Although your efforts are unsuccessful, you continue to appease the bully.
3. Finally, you can no longer ignore your frustrations and you explode at the bully, leaving you feeling even more terrible than before.

The phases go something like this. You get a new job and you are eager to go to work. You are ready to do all you can, not only for yourself, but for your boss and your company. You come to work ready to move mountains. No task is impossible. Usually, this over-enthusiasm fades within the first month, and you settle down to producing the best work you can.

You become aware that something is wrong. You don't seem to be able to do anything right. Though you continue to do the same good job as before, your good ideas are not recognized. Soon, you are questioning whether or not you have the capability to do your work at all. The more you try and improve, the more your boss or co-worker gets angry at you.

You have run into a bully. Instead of questioning, you imagine that you are not doing something you should do. You then decide you must change in some way. But, regardless of any change you make, the bully still continues to find fault with you or your work. This, in turn, makes you even more determined to find a way to please someone who will never be pleased.

When you have exhausted every avenue (and then some) and you still are not doing it right, you become frustrated. You have done everything to please; why can't the bully understand? Why can't she see how hard you are trying? Why isn't your best effort good enough?

Then comes the explosion. One day when you have been harassed and shamed once too often, you look the bully straight in the eye and you say, "Leave me alone. I'm doing the best I can. Just leave me alone."

Your explosion does not make you feel better, it only makes you feel worse. You begin to think, "What if she's right? What if my work is inferior?" Now you've really done it, you've alienated the one person you need to keep your job.

Sound familiar? That is the reaction most people have when they are faced with continuous bullying. You feel your best just isn't good enough. You are full of self-doubt. Finally, you begin to see the pattern in this sick cycle. You question why this is happening. You decide it is really not you. Now it is time to stop the bully, once and for all.

Getting to the step at which you know it's time to stop the noise, the lies, the venom from the bully is made more complicated because you are immersed in hurt. It's easy to lose track of how deep your troubles are.

Adaptation to a toxic environment carries a price. Only much later, sometimes too late, do people realize the price they have paid for going along with someone else's hurtful plan for their future.

# Assessing Impact Before It's Too Late

We present two exercises to help you when the bully attempts to exert control. It is important that you control the definitions of who you are.

For each exercise, A and B, there are two sets of questions to ask.

## *Exercise A*

You have seen how to recognize bullying. The first exercise is designed to help you counter the bully's false accusations so you can remind yourself of just how competent you are.

There are four areas that will help you begin your recovery from bullying. These are the areas or aspects about yourself that you, friends, family, and co-workers (if any can be trusted) will evaluate.

The four areas are:
- *How I Relate to Others*
  Descriptions of strengths and weaknesses in
  relationships with friends and co-workers.
- *How Other People See Me*
  Do you get along well with others? Are you seen
  as angry? Helpful to others? Shy?
- My *Performance at Work*
  Describe the way you handle job assignments.
  Are you on time? A procrastinator? A "neatnick"?
- My *Ability to Reason and Solve Problems*
  Do you like the freedom to improvise? Are you a
  quick learner? Do you have special knowledge in
  certain areas?

Now take some time to write down as many phrases as you can on the following page to describe yourself. Be candid with yourself. Don't be shy or humble.

*Note:* As with all exercises, we suggest that you create lists and fill in boxes on separate pages so that parts of this book may be shared with friends without the risk of revealing information you'd prefer to keep to yourself.

*How I Relate to Others:*

*How Other People See Me:*

*My Performance at Work:*

*My Ability to Reason and Solve Problems:*

Now, make two blank copies of the series of questions. Give one to a trusted friend or co-worker, and one to a supportive family member. Ask them to jot down how they feel you do in each of the four areas (these are to be shared only with you).

When the sheets are returned, lay them side-by-side. Do you see similarities? What are your strengths. Do you judge yourself too harshly?

## Exercise B

This exercise is another way to evaluate how BullyProof you are in the following three areas. Add any dimensions or aspects that are important to you.

- *Quality of Relationships with Others:* This is an indirect indicator of whether or not the bully has poisoned the good relationships you have with others. First, evaluate how you see the quality of your relationships with family and friends. Then, have family members rate the relationship they each have with you. Repeat for friends (as before, co-workers may be included only if they are trustworthy). The pattern that emerges can send a warning signal of pending trouble.

  FOR COUPLES: We have noticed that many couples are severely strained when one person is bullied. Split-ups and divorces are common. The worst-case scenario is when the bullied Target loses track of the decline in quality and the partner waits too long to tell him how she is impacted. Targets need to talk to their partners as soon as possible about their bullying to get support.

- *Confidence in Personal Competence:* This area taps resilience under duress, the ability to focus on "the work" in a storm, and the firmness of your belief in yourself as being right and not deserving the mistreatment received. All bullies, regardless of the particular tactics used, aim to erode the Target's belief in herself. The erosion of this confidence is perhaps the most devastating effect bullies can have. It is among the toughest setbacks from which Targets have to recover.

- *Emotional Effectiveness:* Bullies play on Targets' emotions heavily in order to push them out of control. Too much or too little emotion can be problematic. Of course, you should add any aspects of your life that the bully has tried to dominate to this short list. Then, complete the four-step process described on the following pages for each aspect or dimension.

## First Set of Questions

Turn a critical eye toward yourself. As honestly as you can, state what you Do Well and what you Could Do Better in a two-column table like the one on the next page. Record observations about yourself, as you see yourself. Answer the question for yourself, strictly from your personal point of view.

After you fill in your answers, you can compare the responses. As you look at the answers, keep in mind that you are not necessarily immune from the bully's attempts to control and influence you. If you find that the list under Do Well is longer than under Could Do Better, remember only you can know if the items in one column are more important than items in the other.

## Example

Let's demonstrate how the exercise works for the first worklife area—Quality of Relationships with Others. You will rate that quality, as you define it, strictly from your point of view. If the good news (Do Well) outweighs the bad (Could Do Better), then it's safe to say that you feel your relationships with others have remained relatively immune from damage.

Box 1

**QUALITY OF MY RELATIONSHIPS WITH ...**

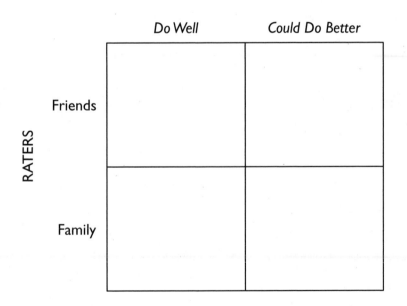

Box 2

**QUALITY OF YOUR RELATIONSHIPS WITH ME**

## Second Set of Questions

Ask trustworthy friends and family to rate, in their opinion, your contribution to the quality of the relationship they have with you. In other words, you will ask them to say what you Do Well and how you Could Do Better, strictly from their point of view. Each person answers for her- or himself only.

There's no need for raters to see the comments of others. Encourage frankness. This tool works only if raters are honest and forthcoming. When raters are truthful, you will discover problems that you often did not see for yourself.

On the other hand, if raters prefer to tell you what they think you want to hear (and minimize the bad news), you and they might stay in denial. Without candor, no changes are possible.

Next, assemble an Impact Table summarizing the observations that you and the others noted.

**Box 3**

### QUALITY OF RELATIONSHIPS

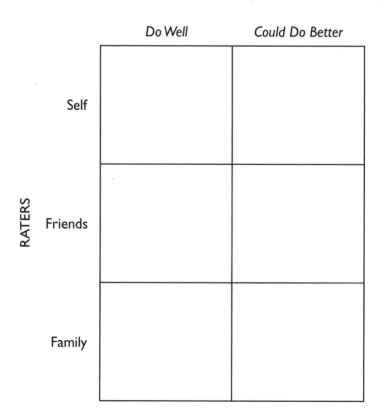

## Interpret the Impact Table

Make the comparisons between columns of opinions that others provided. Compare the rows. Look for patterns.

Who thinks you are relatively BullyProof?

Regarding what aspects?

In what areas are you blind and therefore vulnerable?

Who sees the effects of the bullying experience as you do?

Are they right or are those who disagree with you right?

How are the differences in observations related to the different levels of support you receive?

On whom can you count for a reality check when needed?

Have you lost your sense of perspective? Are you the frog in boiling water?

Repeat this four-step process for each relevant aspect of your worklife.

1. Do your self-rating.
2. Ask others to rate you.
3. Summarize the observations in an Impact Table.
4. Interpret patterns for meaning. Regain perspective.

Box 4

## CONFIDENCE IN PERSONAL COMPETENCE

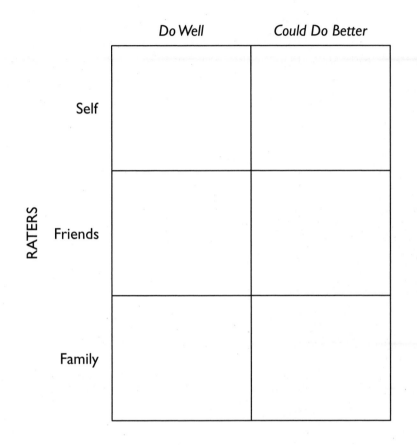

|  | *Do Well* | *Could Do Better* |
|---|---|---|
| Self |  |  |
| Friends |  |  |
| Family |  |  |

RATERS

Box 5

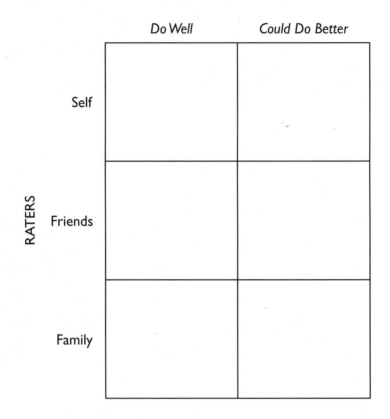

**EMOTIONAL EFFECTIVENESS**

# Changing Your Perspective

After you have decided what things you can do to change the way you act and feel at work, there is a simple tool to help you when you encounter bullying behaviors.

The way you look at situations with the bully will dramatically affect your attitude. Practice dissociating yourself from unpleasant memories. By mentally stepping away from an unpleasant event or a bully, you can adjust your point of view. Remember, you can never change the behaviors of the bully, you can only make changes in yourself.

Try using the following three steps to reevaluate your situation with a bully.

Step 1.

Compare your bully problems to a catastrophic event. Does this compare to losing a leg or a loved one? Do you need a different perspective on this situation?

Step 2.

Mentally edit the memory of your encounter with the bully as if you were editing a film. As you replay your last encounter, view it as if it came from another camera angle. Turn the camera so you can try looking at it in different ways. Go over the memory with a friend to try and get a new perspective on the situation.

Step 3.

Reframe the problem and change the meaning of the experience. Try to look at the experience as a positive event rather than an attack on you. Are there any ways the bullying experience could be positive?

*Chapter Ten:*

# Establish and Protect Personal Boundaries

*No one can make you feel inferior without your consent.*
—Eleanor Roosevelt

Boundaries are central to separating who you are from who the bully wants you to believe you are. Much of what applies to understanding boundaries carries over into other areas that influence Targets.

Much of a person's identity and self-confidence comes from having appropriate boundaries in place for protection against assaults by bullies who seek only to control and hurt their Targets.

## Boundary Characteristics

Two boundary characteristics that affect, and are affected by, bullying are:

- your personally chosen and defined boundaries, established so you can live your life the way you seek and want
- your boundaries' susceptibility to invasion by a bully

In its simplest definition, a boundary is an unseen, unmeasurable limit or barrier that simultaneously creates an inside and an outside. It is an invisible wall with two sides. Inside each individual boundary resides an identity—personal, family, or group. Challenges to those identities are launched by invading bullies from the outside who want to dictate the terms of a Target's identity.

Except for skin, boundaries are psychological. For our purposes here, we speak of psychological boundaries. They can be identified by gauging your tolerance for having them invaded. Invasions of personal boundaries by others causes discomfort and anxiety. When uncomfortable enough, we typically take steps to stop the invader that caused the pain.

People have different thresholds. Some have a higher tolerance for letting others meddle in their lives; some tolerate little to no meddling. Meddling ranges from suggestions about how you should live your life (typically tolerated from close friends) to full-scale verbal assaults by bullies repeatedly telling you how incompetent and worthless you are.

The greatest danger a Target faces in the working world is to have loose or nonexistent boundaries. That person becomes an unprotected Target for all who love to hurt others.

One way to repel invasions by bullies is to use verbal commands to stop the bullying behavior, to announce that a line has been crossed, that you have a policy of zero tolerance for such unacceptable actions and that it will be enforced. This is "tit for tat." Most bully invasions are done with words. Most Target's have little practice dealing with these intrusions.

INVASION ⟶ DISCOMFORT ⟶ REPEL INVASION

The following are categories of boundaries ordered by an orientation toward others. This list builds from the primary boundary of personal identity and widens to include one's social world.

Identity Boundaries
- Physical/Personal Space
- Emotions
- The Self

Family Boundaries
- Unit Solidarity
- Empathy
- Work and Family

Work/Social Boundaries
- Jobs
- Friends, Co-workers, Supporters

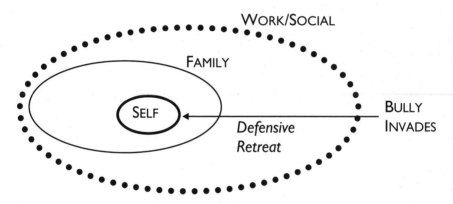

*Depiction of Bully invasion piercing protective boundaries in stages, with the Self serving as the Target's last stand.*

# Identity Boundaries

## *Skin, Touch, and Space*

The knowledge of separateness from the world begins in the crib. Just connecting the act of swinging your little baby foot with moving the mobile begins the journey to Selfhood. Your developing infant brain gets and implants the message that you are not your environment. Though your mind cannot yet fathom philosophy, you know that there is an "out there." Miraculously, you've taken the first step toward an "internal you." The assembly of an Individual begins that early.

For humans, our skin literally becomes the physical boundary between us and the external world. It is through that skin that so much brain and neural development takes place. Touch stimulates and comforts. It is the language of love, nurturing, and acceptance. The absence of touch sets the stage for needy, love-starved adults.

The rules about who you allow to touch your skin develop in childhood. Nearly everyone touches an infant.

As you grow older, based on cultural mores and family tradition, strangers will be forbidden to share the intimate zone of touching skin. When the unwritten rule is violated, you automatically get anxious and take evasive action. That's why inappropriate contact by strangers is a hostile gesture. More will be said about the use of personal space when we discuss traps in nonverbal communication.

## Emotions

Emotions are also learned in childhood and follow family- and peer-specific unwritten norms and rules. Those values learned early in life are:

- expressivity: emotions are publicly displayed
- labeling: names given to internal feelings in response to events.

There are entire textbooks written about the healthy development of human emotions. Growing up with few inhibitions about expressing feelings tends to create adults who readily show their feelings. It's good to grow up free from much of the anxiety that seems to burden those who live scripted lives. An uninhibited spirit is less likely to suffer from stress.

The point most relevant to workplace bullying is that people who naturally show emotions will generally be seen as more vulnerable than those with a closed style.

You have the right to call your emotions what you want. Gut feelings are ambiguous. They are normal reactions to potential stressors in your life. The emotional label you choose determines whether the feeling is positive or negative.

## The Impact of Feelings

Imagine the gut-wrenching, sweaty-palms feeling as you're about to turn in a project you've worked on for six months. If the person you're giving it to is the office tyrant, your sworn enemy, you're likely to call that swirling feeling nausea in anticipation of the undeserved verbal tirade you've come to expect. You're literally sick, knowing that she will bark about how "stupid and incompetent" you are. You condition yourself to recognize the symptoms as those of impending shame. No one should have the right to inflict shame on you or be able to trigger it through fearful anticipation!

On the other hand, if you're submitting the project to the person who promised a promotion and raise when it was done, those are harmless butterflies in anticipation of a new phase of your career. You're dizzy with anticipation of spending the extra money and all the recognition a new job brings.

Same stomach, different names for the feeling that goes with physiological symptoms. Research has shown that we're all somewhat susceptible to labeling of our emotions by others when the feelings are unclear. However, it's dangerous when you are ready to experience a positive emotion and an outsider barges in and defines the feeling for you. In anxious times, we are more susceptible to an invasion of our emotional boundaries.

## *The Self—Putting It All Together*

All the "firsts" in your life begin in early infancy with parental relationships. Besides meeting your needs for food and shelter, parents influence and impact whether we develop into strong or weak selves. When old enough to interact with others besides parents, the Self is further developed by peers who shape you into what you are and will become. The final product called "you" continues to develop through a lifetime. The core—your fundamental approach to how you deal with what life throws you—is predominantly determined at a young age.

With a well-developed Self in place, you can resist all attempts by others to define your identity, to invade your personal space without permission, to exercise control over you, and to define feelings for you. A poorly developed Self seems to doom adults to search outside themselves for answers to inner questions. This renders them more vulnerable to influence by others. It is not a question of goodness or badness, but rather a matter of dependency on others for definitions. This dependency puts such people in the bully's direct line of fire.

The Self is the safe place to which you can retreat when under attack. It is the one boundary that should never be compromised, invaded, or traded away to get along with another person. Think of it as the last box inside several other boxes, each inside the other. You and you alone control access to it. And the reprogramming of the lifetime of scripts stored there will be undertaken only by you, on your terms. Changes are yours to make.

Let's not get bogged down in psychobabble here. Simply put, never discount the importance of Selfhood. All feelings of adult worthiness, entitlement to certain "rights," pride, and competence flow from experiences, many of which were too early to recall.

# Family Boundaries

## *Family-of-Origin Factors*

Our first social group is our family-of-origin, a group of manageable size. The family-of-origin is the place to rehearse behaviors for the larger world of strangers in which we don't always get our way. Families teach us to be social beings, capable of respecting or disregarding others. In a healthy family, a child is taught to develop a self-concept separate and different from other family members.

Healthy families also provide unconditional support for us as blossoming little people. Ideally, parents and older siblings foster independence by teaching us to fend for ourselves while tolerating dependence on the family for comfort in the toughest of times.

## *Family Interactions and Targethood*

Unfortunately, there are families that live with sick "enmeshed patterns," better described as smothering rather than helpful. One for all and all for one sounds like teamwork until the identities of all the children and usually one parent are sacrificed. Distinct personalities rarely emerge from such families. Enmeshed families squash the human need to become an individual, to matter, to be special in some unique way.

"Disengaged" families are equally defeating. They are families where members have little contact with each other and little to no love. Children grow up believing they are worthless, needing to justify in their own minds the neglect they experience.

Adults who grew up with either of these disturbed arrangements are likely to rely too heavily on people at work for support, validation, and even for an identity. Bullies smell neediness and exploit it to their advantage.

## Healthy Families

Healthy families form a protective boundary behind which adults and children can retreat to safety when and if necessary. It's a much looser boundary, woven more by solidarity among family members, than the shell around the Self.

A bully is a person who denies her emotions (low expressivity). She operates from rigid boundaries. In her disengaged family-of-origin, she was not connected with her parents. Because of this, her feelings were not developed or brought to the surface. More importantly, when any feelings do surface for her, she easily becomes overwhelmed and withdraws from all contact with others.

## Empathy

Another gift taught in healthy families is empathy. Empathy is the human capacity to understand, intellectually, what another person is going through when things go poorly and to recognize the emotional state of that person because you've gone through it. Sympathy is cold—that's why pity serves no purpose. Empathy is sympathy with emotions included. It is the basis of compassion. Families are the first teachers of compassion.

Empathy requires the loosening of rigid, personal protective boundaries. It involves letting in the experiences of others. Empathy is always considered one of humankind's higher level traits. Unfortunately, the openness and compassion that characterize empathy render you vulnerable to assaults from a bully who despises positive traits. As a witness to the bullying of another person, it is empathy that will compel you to take action to alleviate the Target's suffering.

In general, bullies are thwarted by independent Targets and don't bother with them. Research in workplace aggression found that bullies are essentially lazy. They prefer easier-to-control, vulnerable Targets.

## Work and Family

When you're the adult and parent, you face the issues of allocating your energy and time across family and work activities. The critical boundary question is how much intrusion by work into your private time will be tolerated. The answer is necessarily personal. Some advisers sketch pie charts slicing an ideal life into several domains: income-generating, physical health, learning, love, and spiritual, to name a few. Their concern is balance.

For BullyProofing yourself, the concern is whether or not you can fight work's intrusive effect on the rest of your life. Targets under fire from bullies may try to keep the torment a secret from everyone at home. However, the strain takes its toll in small, unavoidable ways. There may be loss of sleep, increased moodiness, a shorter fuse for getting angry, and general depression. Astute family members cannot help but notice, but may say nothing until you, the Target, share the cause of your grief or ask for help.

The thing to remember during bullying is that the separation of the work-family boundary fools no one. The family cannot help but be affected by trouble at work. Trying to will away the negative impact of bullying on the family with words ("I won't discuss at home what happens in that hellhole") or the shutting down of discussion about it during family time prevents Targets from getting the support and love they so desperately need to offset the lies and isolation that have become work. The family often cannot solve the problem of bullying. However, they can offer support and comfort when asked. Attempting to go it alone while feigning a calm, collected exterior is foolhardy.

Well-intentioned Targets want to spare their families the hurt, but they are wasting too much energy by covering up. It's better to recruit the family's support right from the start. Isolated Targets are weakened. Targets, backed with a family's love, can shorten the period of vulnerability. Supported Targets can move forward quicker and reestablish a normal work-family barrier when work is more normal.

# Work/Social Boundaries

Social boundaries are looser and less permanent because so many people share in their development and maintenance. Nothing is as personal, nor should be as inviolate, as a person's identity.

## *The Job*

Based on the figure depicting family and personal boundaries embedded with the work/social boundaries, you can see how far from a personal identity the job should lie. That is, your identity was formed long ago and is very distinct from what you do for a living, for economic necessity. At least that's true for the majority of folks. There are a few among us whose work and soul are deliberately fused and inseparable (usually artists).

For the rest of us mere mortals, and nearly everyone who gets bullied, it is critical to separate your identity from the job. Jobs are frequently snatched away without warning, without care for the consequences you and your family face. If every time you change jobs, you had to change the person you are, you'd be exhausted from the task of restructuring a life several times (five to seven changes, according to recent surveys).

Jobs pass and are shared by hundreds, if not thousands, of others. Your identity has to remain relatively permanent to lend stability and purpose to your life. When you can no longer count on a job, you still must be able to count on the uniqueness that is you.

Here is the critical point about job boundaries. Assaults on boundaries force the Target into a defensive position. The question you have to ask yourself is whether or not a job is worth defending—"I have to have this job, there are no others for me," "I can't do anything else," "I have to hold on to this job that tortures me daily because it's easier to get a job when you have a job." It's especially maddening when we at the WBI hear advice seekers defend holding on to a job (thus showing a strong job boundary) immediately after describing the incredible destruction it has brought to their lives.

With this perverted logic, Targets elevate the importance of keeping that specific job at the expense of their self-worth as if they deserve no better (thus yielding to invasions of their identity boundary). This rationalization and compromise make little sense. There will be another job. However, if this job kills you, you won't be around to work it.

## Friends, Co-workers, Supporters

This boundary captures the widest group of nonrelated people in your world. It is not of a uniform size, thickness, or permeability. It is in a constant state of flux. Essentially, this boundary separates those in your "in-group" from those not within your inner circle. In broad societal terms, common grouping variables are profession, race, age, gender, etc. These are broad group identities that may be invoked when you and your peers gather together for breaks and social events.

At work, the co-worker boundary is a good example of how a temporary, constantly changing group identity can hurt Targets of bullying. One day, the group is commiserating about the bully's torment. They may even share stories of misery from when they themselves were the bully's Targets. As a reasonable person, you might assume that you will all stand together to fight the bully in front of her boss.

However, the next day, you, as the Target, may suddenly and inexplicably find yourself out of the group and left to fend for yourself. You stand alone with your plight. It's as if the frank griping sessions never happened. The many reasons for this turnaround are based on fear.

The feelings of abandonment by a group that originally supported you compounds the pain. When a group turns on you, it is easy to doubt that you are right and the bully is wrong. The speed with which a group forms, disbands, and re-forms should send a warning that groups deserve the least trust.

Unions are also a group to which you may belong, whose ostensible purpose is to defend your rights. However, they too are prone to abandon you for various reasons driven by the group's survival priorities rather than the merits of your case. They satisfy their contractual obligation by starting the grievance process but that is long, tortuous, and inefficient for dealing with daily bullying. The courage of a special individual in the group willing to take risks on your behalf is more important than any group identity.

## Boundaries and Defenses

When facing assaults from a bully and retreating to a defensive position, it's natural to first seek validation from your work group for the perception that you're not crazy. If it's a team of turncoats, you will get no support. The response to this rejection is to focus entirely on your job. Targets try to "stick to the job" and ignore all the madness manufactured by the bully, thus, going it alone at work.

Then, when intense concentration to your job fails to serve as a distraction from bullying, the next possible source of comfort is the family. Sadly, even families can tire of the steady stream of workplace horror stories. We wish it were not true, but it is a rare family that gives unconditional support from the beginning to the absolute end of a bully's campaign.

This leaves the final source of comfort as the Self. It's the box within the boxes, the innermost circle, the one thing you have to count on—faith in your identity.

Of course, this model of levels or layers of boundaries that one after another fail to ward off the bully is the worst-case scenario. In the best of all possible worlds (though rarely occurring), your work group stands solidly with you so that you have multiple sources of support, with family and identity providing additional support. With all boundaries intact, a bully has no chance to overcome a Target.

# Boundary Rights

## Cats and Dogs

The writer Mary Bly compares boundaries with cats and dogs. "Dogs," she writes, "come when they are called; cats take a message and get back to you."

Dogs always want to be close to people. They will jump on our laps (no matter what their size), or come on the bed, always trying to get as close as possible. Their boundaries are very close and they expect all other animals to have the same boundaries.

Cats, on the other hand, have very distinct boundaries. They come and go when they want and if they want. When they want to be close, they determine when, how, and where. They are aware of the humans in the room, but human movements do not interrupt what they are doing. Their boundaries are very different from dogs. Cats need more space and their boundaries are more rigid.

Like cats and dogs we all grow up with different boundaries. We learn and tend to practice the boundaries we were taught as children. We tend to see them in black and white and rarely even question them. What we fail to see is that boundaries are not only black and white, but also come in shades of gray.

## Avoiding Spineless Flexibility

The contrast to rigid boundaries is when boundaries are so flexible they can't hold shape. When you encounter someone with loose boundaries you will see that they are like chameleons.

> Lisa is a chameleon. At work she will agree with a co-worker that their boss is unreasonable. Ten minutes later when someone else states that she feels their boss is a great and understanding fellow, Lisa will agree with her. She is unable to let the phone ring at lunch and at the end of the

*day, for fear she will miss something important and get into trouble. Thus, she misses many lunches and spends many hours working after 5 p.m., just to finish the work that was interrupted by phone calls.*

*Because Lisa's boundaries are too flexible, she often feels overwhelmed with balancing life and work. Each new demand distracts her. She has difficulty setting priorities and following them. She gets started on one task only to get side-tracked by something else. She may appear disorganized.*

## Maintaining Your Boundaries in the Face of Power

Certain roles carry rank or power—parent, supervisor, boss, teacher, coach, doctor, police officer. It is important, however, to know that no matter what power a person has in relation to you, there are still boundaries they should not violate.

No matter how understanding your boss seems, you are not his priority. A supervisor who invites confidences, who treats you as a peer, or who leans on you for support is violating a boundary. Your supervisor is not your peer. No matter how much he cares for you and your job, his own job is most important to him. If he has to sacrifice you to keep his position, he will!

Your supervisor's job is to support you as a worker. It is not your job to listen to his problems. If this happens, you become his sympathetic ear and your own loyalty becomes divided. Your energy then is diverted from your actual work and a bond is created between you and your supervisor that causes confusion between loyalty to yourself and to the company.

Good boundaries between workers and supervisors or bosses is like good parenting. It allows for safe communication, security in risking, appropriate meeting of needs, attention to role requirements, and support of subordinates. The goal in any business should be the maximum and finest development of the worker.

There's much talk about "flat organizations," "boss-free work-places," and "egalitarian management." We'd love to believe it, but our experiences with the dark underbelly of the work world has taught us to doubt. Better to err with cynicism and be safe than to let down your guard and be eaten alive.

If you doubt that power differences truly exist, ask who has the power to terminate your livelihood based on a false rumor, vague concept such as "competitiveness," or a whim. Whoever has that clout is NOT your equal. Remember that fact when you are encouraged to "let down your guard, to just be friends." Friends outside; acquaintances inside.

## Recognizing Unhealthy Work Boundaries

It is a fact of life that some bosses and supervisors (and even some co-workers) are very unhealthy and abuse their power to get their needs met. If your boss is unhealthy, bullying behavior will echo throughout your organization. If bullying is part of your organization, you have a choice. You can try to develop a healthy base with your co-workers and promote a healthy relationship with your supervisor or boss. If this is possible, you might find that as you become more healthy, the people around you will become more healthy.

However, if you are asked to cross a boundary that violates your personal space, you will need to assess whether or not this is a healthy place for you to work. You need to ask if you should take yourself out of a work situation where you are being violated. You should do this as soon as you can. If it is with co-workers, you can practice and use the skills you need to preserve your dignity. If it is with a supervisor or boss, decide whether you can repair the damage to your boundaries. If you can't, you need to look for a new position.

## Your Personal Boundary Rights

You have a right to privacy. You have the right to choose what questions you answer. You don't have to tell anyone your thoughts or feelings. You are not overly sensitive if you decline to answer a thoughtless question.

If a boss, supervisor, or co-worker seems nosy and asks inappropriate questions, you can practice these answers: "I don't feel like talking about it." "I want to keep that to myself." "That's my business." "I'm surprised you think you have a right to that information." "Whoops! That's private."

*Chapter Eleven:*

# Avoid Unattainable Standards

*Face your deficiencies and acknowledge them, but do not let them master you. Let them teach you patience, sweetness, insight.... When we do the best we can, we never know what miracle is wrought in our life, or in the life of another.*
—Helen Keller

The internal compass that governs much of our lives is a set of privately held beliefs and values. There are other forces exerting their influence over what we do and say on a daily basis (a bully is an example of an obnoxious external factor). However, the legacy of our parents is the presence or absence of beliefs that are as broad as a philosophy toward life or that can be as narrow as obsessing over uncrossed handwritten letter "t's."

## The Shoulds in Our Lives

A "should" is an internal, private expectation about how the world ought to be. It is our personal standard, the ideal, to which reality is compared. Everything and everyone we encounter is compared to the standard in our head. After a lifetime of judging, the scrutiny is done without deliberate thought. It is automatic.

The teaching of values and beliefs began in infancy. Attention to our cries was an early sign of respect for us as human beings. Attentiveness rather than neglect molded one of the most primitive attitudes toward others. We progressed into learning how to handle anger, mistakes, and pain. We learned rules about what is acceptable conversation. Even life goals and the manner in which we treat others were modeled for us or informally introduced by parents and older siblings.

For most of us, parental evaluation of our behavior played a large part in determining confidence or worthlessness. In turn, our values developed from that scrutiny. Values like commitment, honesty, generosity, dignity, intelligence, and a strong work ethic are the parental legacy that ripples through our adult lives.

Kind and ambitious parents were the types to find ways to keep their children inspired. Here's one such inspiring quote.

> Aim at the sun and you may not reach it, but your arrow will fly farther than if you had aimed at an object on a level with yourself.

Your childhood experience determines whether you read that statement as a challenge to do even better (with the understanding that you always do well, keep striving to do more) or that your history is one of always taking the easy way out (aiming at a low level) therefore you should take a wild shot at the big prize, though you most certainly won't win.

If evaluations meant anxiety-plagued scrutiny, devastating criticism, and a steady tearing down by your parents, it is no surprise that you, the adult, are paralyzed by fear.

Unfortunately, the world is not populated just by caring, loving parents. In dysfunctional families, children were taught to distrust, to attack rather than cooperate, or to lie constantly to cover up family problems.

Deep-seated beliefs can convey a sense of security when they conjure up sweet memories of the time when they were first introduced. Not only are the values important, but the legend of how they were introduced reinforces the security.

On the other hand, if chaos is what the child lived with while growing up, there can be little safety in adulthood.

With luck, we acquired a realistic set of expectations about how the world should treat us. We learned to strike a balance between giddy over-optimism and perpetual gloom and doom.

The last point we make about the parental role in establishing expectations is that most expectations have a moral tone to them. That is, if you should or ought to be doing something one way, then you had better feel guilty if that is not what you are doing.

The shoulds are also the product of:

1. The need to feel part of a group and to have the approval of others. The group has tremendous clout over the individual. When a group of co-workers uniformly turns on you, they put your version of who you are in direct conflict with the one they want you to believe. Most people yield to the group, as incredible as that sounds.

2. Our status in life or our role at work. People internalize hierarchies. Different views accompany different levels of organizations in our lives. Husband status activates one set of expectations, and wife status creates another.

We take the values and beliefs we learn from our parents to our jobs. If we learned to be overcritical in our family-of-origin, then those critical values are the values we take with us to work.

> Linda was recently fired from her job as an account representative. She tells her family and friends that she was stupid to ever consider, much less take, this job. She reports to her mother that the job was "demeaning, boring, and

181

*unchallenging. I've never met anyone in that line," she says, "who wasn't uneducated and stupid." She vows never to take another job like this. Her opinions are a rationalization created by her need to maintain her self-esteem. She must devalue her job and employer or see herself as a failure.*

*Shellie works hard at her job, often spending six to eight hours of overtime per week to ensure that her work is done. She is very vocal in her opinion that one must be completely committed to every job. She states she hates the smallest sign of laziness. However, another way to look at her actions are to consider that she works so hard to only show others that she doesn't need help from anyone. She needs to feel confident and safe and avoid the criticism of others. She stays in control by drowning herself in a pile of work.*

In these examples, both Linda and Shellie use their critical beliefs and values to judge themselves in their business lives. Their goals are unattainable, impossibly high with regards to their need for love, safety, and feeling good about themselves. When this happens, Targets need to be more realistic. Often the values that they have been taught have little to do with reality.

*Consider Sally. She has graduated from a college that strongly espouses that women are entitled to fulfill themselves personally and through their work. However, she has three strong needs that generate her beliefs about work. The first is the need to win the love of her father, who is very critical of what she does for a living. Her second need is to be able to work and give enough time to her family while she works. A third need is to set an example for her children that both women and men can find fulfillment in work and family. Unfortunately, her needs are in conflict.*

Sally has encountered the "tyranny of the shoulds." She operates under the belief that she should be able to be all things to all people (her father and her family), and the unforgiving sense of what is right (she should be able to please everyone) and wrong (if she doesn't, she is a bad person).

Why do we do this? We sometimes torture ourselves with guilt and self-blame over things we cannot change. This is why we become paralyzed when we are forced to choose between unbending rules (unattainable or unsustainable expectations) and genuine desire.

# Self-Defeating Shoulds

I should:

- be able to give to everyone all the time
- be the perfect partner, co-worker, team member
- never feel hurt
- always see the bright, positive side of situations
- always keep my negative emotions under control
- always be totally self-reliant, never depend on others
- be a complete, multi-faceted life partner
- anticipate my child's every need all the time
- never complain about being tired or sick
- never let the emotions—anger or jealousy—show
- be respectful and polite to everyone
- make no enemies
- never believe I'm good, but wait until others say so
- always put the needs of others before my own needs
- never be afraid
- never make a mistake

## The Tyranny of Totality Is Self-Defeating.

Think about it. We all torture ourselves with guilt and self-blame when we are unable to live up to standards that may be too high. We see ourselves as failures. The gap between the way we think the world "should be" for us and our perception of "what is" can generate a sense of worthlessness.

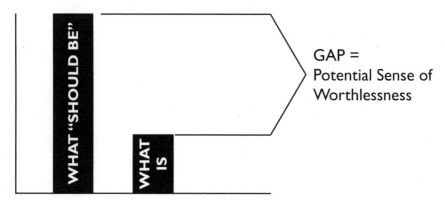

GAP =
Potential Sense of
Worthlessness

# Bullying and Standards

The bully's irrational, unrealistic hammering may be reminiscent of tyrannical parents who imposed and enforced martial law while growing up. The emotional cruelty was sufficiently evil. But the longer-lasting legacy is the deeply imbedded belief that you are never quite good enough, that you are always falling short.

Now that there is a bully at work, the parental voices resonate in your mind. It is as if it were yesterday—getting yelled at over trivial matters that "justified" a verbal assault. The bully is the bad parent come home again. As if you needed reminding that you are not a complete individual. The bully thinks her job is to police you so you don't miss an error or shortcoming. This is an outrageous intrusion into your life.

*Chapter Twelve:*

# Counter Your Inner Critic

*Keep away from people who try to belittle your ambitions. Small people always do that, but the really great make you feel that you, too, can become great.*
—Mark Twain

The inner critic is born during parental teaching of right and wrong. Later in life, it's that personal, negative, nagging little judge whose attacks only you hear in your head. Everyone has a critical inner voice. Some voices are more strident and demanding than others.

Your critic:

- blames you for things that go wrong
- compares you to others, especially achievements and abilities others have but you want
- sets impossible standards of perfection
- beats you up if you are not perfect
- sticks to a script that describes how you should live
- screams that you are wrong or bad if your needs drive you to violate its rules
- tells you to be the best, and if you're not the best, it tells you that you're nothing

- calls you names, leading you to believe they are true
- reads your friends' minds to prove to you that they are bored, turned off, disappointed, or disgusted by you
- exaggerates your weaknesses by insisting that you "always say stupid things," or "always screw up on the job," or, "never finish anything on time."

In other words, the inner critic is busy undermining everything you do. If you listen carefully, you might recognize the voice as that of your mother, father, or yourself.

The most important thing you need to know about your very special critic is that no matter how distorted or false the attacks may be, you always believe what is said. In almost every situation, the critic is there to find fault, blaming and judging you harshly in the process. The critic also reminds you of past failures, connecting them to the present, forever limiting your ability to start anew or to soar with newfound wings.

Our inner critic can be compared with Freud's super-ego. The super-ego is the internalized parent, the moral authority that develops supposedly to hold the pleasure-driven id in check. It's the self-righteous, pontificating, boorish part of our personalities.

The critic examines everything we do and puts its own spin on it. The critic is always there, whether tearing you down or helping you solve problems and meet basic needs.

Yes, there is a benefit to having an inner critic.

## Its Purpose

*The need to do right:* We all have our own values and morals that we learned in childhood. These serve to create an ethical frame-work for all activities in your life by defining how to act with family members, authority figures, co-workers, and friends. The critic helps you distinguish right from wrong. The critic also tells you how wrong or bad you are when you are tempted to act beyond your own ethical standard.

*The need to achieve:* The critic helps you achieve goals by whipping you like a race horse. It pushes you along—constantly telling you that what you thought was good is not good enough. It gives you the encouragement to reach goals others might feel are out of your reach.

*The need to feel right:* Even while the critic tells you you're no good, it helps you by evaluating how you stack up against others. Although it usually finds you lacking, once in a while it will confirm that you are stronger, more attractive, and smarter than others. Because this occurs rarely, it reinforces the critic by encouraging you to keep trying to reach unreachable goals.

Your inner critic can both hurt you and help you. The good news is that with practice you can learn to recognize, analyze, and refute the negative destructive criticism while keeping and using what is useful and helpful.

## Countering the Critic

You need to be realistic. Face the fact that the most painful criticism of your work might be coming from your own inner critic. Most people spend a good portion of every workday bombarding themselves with unrealistically high expectations, while bombarding you with harsh criticisms of the things you don't do well. It is a recipe for feeling like a failure. If you combine this with the critical statements and lies from a bully, you cannot help but feel like you are a failure.

You can improve the way you handle your own inner critic. Use the following questions to examine your attitudes toward yourself.

- When you make an error or an oversight at work, do you criticize yourself in a harsh manner?

- Before important meetings, job interviews, or work assignments, are your thoughts negative—do you focus on all that might go wrong?
- When you are running late, do you bombard yourself with harsh criticism, even before anyone else notices you are late?
- Do you worry you will be found out and others will discover you're not really able to do what is expected of you?
- Do you lie awake at night criticizing yourself for anything that went wrong during the day, even though you didn't have much control over what happened?
- Have you ever said or thought to yourself that you are your own worst critic?

If you answer yes to even one of these statements, your inner critic is working overtime.

## If You Invalidate Your Own Hard Work, Stop the Self-Destruction Immediately!

Instead of attacking yourself with criticism, take a moment to stop and catch yourself. Ask, "Is this self-criticism necessary and should I spend any time or effort on it?" or, "Would my time be better spent getting support and ideas for solutions?" or, "Does my supervisor's critical nature amplify my own doubts and leave me feeling doubly bad?"

Do not lose sight of all the good work you've done right on a project just because something has gone wrong. Ask yourself if you could address the problem without calling on your own critic. It is also important to keep in mind that you have done a lot of good work that got you this far.

> *Remind yourself each day or evening of*
> *three good things you did that day.*

Don't remember only the things that go wrong. Avoid focusing only on the things that you can't fix or control. Be good to yourself! At least once a day or at night when you are unwinding from work, take a few moments to acknowledge to yourself (or with a trusted friend) the hard work and worthwhile efforts you did that day. Even on projects that did not turn out as well as you planned, you need to take stock of the valuable planning, thinking, and actions that you've taken that day or that week.

> *Make sure you don't talk to*
> *yourself in a critical manner.*

If you notice you tend to talk badly to yourself, stop and say to yourself, "I don't need to be so mean to myself or anyone else. I don't need to listen to the negative remarks from the bully, I'm doing a good job."

Be aware of an increased susceptibility to be destructively self-critical in certain circumstances. You might try a "thought-stopping" technique to disrupt your train of self-defeating thinking. One way is to wear a rubber band on your wrist (hidden under your blouse or shirt sleeve, if you're self-conscious). When the "stinking thinking" starts, simply snap the band. Mindfully switch to another thought. Deliberately get yourself off the negative track. With sufficient practice, you can switch mental gears at will. Then, you can do it without the rubber band prop.

Know that the inner critic thrives in situations like these:
- ✓ Meeting new people
- ✓ When you have made a mistake—public or private
- ✓ At the start of a new job, project, or task
- ✓ When you feel criticized and defensive
- ✓ During interactions with management
- ✓ When you feel hurt
- ✓ When someone gets angry with you

## Chapter Thirteen:

# Control Destructive Mind Games

*Whatever you do, you need courage. Whatever course*
*you decide upon, there is always someone to tell you you*
*are wrong. There are always difficulties arising which tempt*
*you to believe that your critics are right.*
—Ralph Waldo Emerson

Initial reactions to a bully's misconduct are typically emotional. Scientists and philosophers have been speculating for years about what causes bad moods. Certainly there are stories about dysfunctional families and people who suffer from child abuse. However, the Greek philosopher, Epictetus, first observed that, "Men are not disturbed by things, but by the views they take of them."

The view that our thoughts, rather than the actual events themselves, create our moods has gained acceptance by psychologists, too. According to this view, emotions have two components: arousal (physical sensations—gut churning, butterflies, dizziness, profuse sweating, etc.) and a label so the mind knows what to call it.

Those who subscribe to this line of thinking believe that we become upset because of the way we think about these events. We have the ability to distort meanings related to dramatic events. This ability then helps define our emotional experiences—good and bad.

The distortions, or mind games, weave a protective net around ourselves that twists and colors our feelings according to what we think.

Self-defeating labeling forms the prison walls from which you yearn to break out. The bully brought the bricks and mortar. Through mind games, Targets are responsible for the prison's upkeep.

Distorted thinking styles can make you judgmental, can cause you to automatically apply labels to people and events before you get a chance to evaluate them. These distorted labels give you only one side of any situation and cause you to base your decisions on an emotional rather than a rational basis.

You or others can make you feel depressed, worried, or angry. But you are the only one who can elect to not have these feelings. You can choose to be happy.

If you lose your job, you may feel sad, angry at yourself, or self-critical. Your inner critic starts to whisper in your ear. Your thinking becomes distorted and you may tell yourself that you're no good, that there is something wrong with you. It would be less self-defeating to tell yourself that life is unfair, but for too many Targets, the choice of a label is mindless. It is an automatic process honed over years of practice.

These are mind games and they are very natural. When you choose to change the way you think, you turn negative, distorted thoughts into useful concepts.

Take a few moments to scan the following list of mind games we all play.

1. *Overgeneralization.* From one isolated event you make a general, universal rule. If you failed once, you'll always fail.

2. *Global labeling.* You automatically use pejorative labels to describe yourself, rather than accurately describing your qualities. "I'm a fool, a sucker, a patsy."

3. *Filtering*. You selectively pay attention to the negative and disregard the positive. "I won the award today, but tomorrow I have to start from scratch again to earn the respect of others."

4. *Polarized thinking*. You lump things into absolute, black-and-white categories, with no middle ground. You have to be perfect or you are left feeling worthless.

5. *Catastrophizing*. Worst-case scenario thinking. The danger is that expecting the worst helps it become a self-fulfilling prophecy. "Sure there was good news today, but it never lasts, just wait."

6. *Personalization*. You assume that everything has something to do with you, and you negatively compare yourself to everyone else.

7. *Mind reading*. You assume that others don't like you, are angry with you, don't care about you, and so on, without any real evidence that your assumptions are correct.

8. *Illusion of control*. You feel that you have total responsibility for everybody and everything, or feel that you have no control, that you're a helpless victim.

9. *Emotional reasoning*. You assume that things are the way you feel them to be. Others are assumed to have the same feelings as you.

*Chris was laid off of work with several other employees from the company because of a business slowdown. She felt rejected, worried, angry, and guilty. Her mind game distorted the layoff as a situation in which she had failed, that the layoff was directly due to her inability to do her work.*

Using the mind games list, let's analyze Chris's feelings that she is a loser.

- *Polarized thinking:* She's looking at herself in black-and-white categories because she sees herself as a loser.
- *Overgeneralization:* She lost her job, but she is generalizing to her entire life.
- *Filtering:* She is dwelling on her job loss and letting it color her entire view of life. Her choice of husbands is now clearly seen as a poor one.
- *Personalization:* She blames herself for the layoff, rather than the fact that business was slow.

We may say mind games are distorting as compared to the perceptions others might have of the same event. However, it is important to remember that there need not be an objective, "true" reality. Everyone has their own agenda, perspective, and eyes and ears.

Targets may fall into the trap of undermining themselves with destructive mental distortions that can slow down or block recovery from the bullying.

## Inside the Target's head

With workplace bullying in mind, note some of the internal monologues you typically hear.

Now, counter the echo of the bully's words with positive, balanced statements in rebuttal.

Try to identify the Distortions, Mind Games.

### Self-Statement

### Distortion

### Rebuttal

She's right. Nothing I do is ever accurate. I hate to agree with her, but the job I did on the project was not as good as before.

She's not right! She's just mean. It pleases her to tear into me. Wait a minute. The caliber of my work exceeded that of others then AND now. It may not be perfect, but it is better than this company has ever had.

*Overgeneralization*

*Filtering*

An internal rebuttal like the one above helps defeat the irrational thinking that plays into the hands of the bully.

*Chapter Fourteen:*

# Escape the Trap of Self-Blame

*The people who get on in this world are the people who get up and*
*look for the circumstances they want, and,*
*if they can't find them, make them.*
—George Bernard Shaw

When you are a Target, there is no doubt that the bully initiated the campaign to disgrace, defame, and demoralize you. This is certainty; it is an absolute fact. You did not invite ridicule or humiliation. When you tell friends and family, they believe you and stand by you up to a point.

However, witnesses, co-workers, the bully's allies, "institutional helpers" (Human Resources, Personnel, Employee Assistance, Legal, ombudsmen, mediators), senior managers, and lawyers are either less certain or call you a liar outright.

Yes, it is true that this wildly different version of reality stems from defensiveness, workplace politics, fear, timidity, lack of conscience, group dynamics, and sometimes evil, all of which we explain in this book. As strange as it sounds, in their eyes, it makes more sense to see you, the Target, as the cause of your misery rather than the menacing bully.

The lack of support resulting from myriad personal biases further undermines your sanity, increasing the self-doubt you did not deserve in the first place. Heinz Leymann credits this "secondary mobbing" for extending the bad times and postponing recovery from bullying and your ability to move on with your life.

# Power of Perspective

We also think it is important for you to understand another factor that explains the madness of blaming the recipient of direct, hateful assaults—perspective. The perspective we describe is a visual, physical vantage point, not a philosophical one. The determination of who caused what depends a great deal on where one sits.

It's this simple: there are two players in the destructive workplace bullying game—the bully and the Target. If I, as a witness, observe a nasty encounter between the two and am asked who caused it to turn out the way it did, I have three options: the bully caused it, the Target caused it, or they jointly caused it to happen.

We know from psychological research that the choice of explanations for events depends on a person's vantage point. The phenomenon is called causal attribution. The term *attribution* refers to the assignment of responsibility to the person, event, process, or thing that caused the behavior to happen.

Imagine two people seated across from each other in a TV studio. Position three cameras as follows: one camera peering over the shoulder of each of the two people aimed directly at the other person (call them bully-cam and Target-cam) and the third camera recording the situation from the side with both "actors" given equal amount of space in the picture.

We know from social psychological experiments using such a video setup that observers watching the encounter from the bully-cam tend to hold responsible the person they see, the Target. These observers have no preexisting biases or interest in the taped session and still take the side of the bully in blaming the Target.

To prove the power of visual perspective, other observers, also without bias, hold the bully responsible when watching the encounter from the Target-cam. They literally see the situation through the Target's eyes. Targets see the work environment that causes them to do the work as assigned, to work with supervisors over whom they have no control, and to deal with envious or destructive co-workers.

Guess who observers watching from the side camera think is responsible for what they see happening between the two people? Yes, each person was responsible. In all fairness, the researchers dealt with trivial conversations, not emotional altercations more likely in the bully-Target duo. In the real world, an equal split of responsibility would probably not happen. However, the research finding is so strong that we can safely predict some sort of shared responsibility.

This contradicts what you know about Targets. They did not invite their misery. However, the stark reality is that by merely not being the Target, other people get the false impression that Targets are somewhat to blame.

## Bias Begets Blame

Attributional biases are normal for humans. A person has to mindfully and deliberately fight the power of perspective to be fair. In the bully-Target situation, holding the Target even partly responsible when she did nothing to provoke the bully sounds fair to most observers. But it is unfair to the Target. Calling for "balance," as mediators do, underestimates the bully's role and discriminates against Targets who are the unwilling recipients of indefensible assaults.

As a society, we've had this discussion before. It was about rape victims. Is it fair to fault victims for dressing "provocatively" in the name of balance? That would be the equivalent of seeing the crime from the rapist-cam rather than from the victim-cam. Fortunately, reason prevailed and we have decided to fault the criminal rather than the victim (though the courts and defense attorneys have been dragged slowly to that conclusion). Blaming or denigrating the victim (she was "flirtatious") is showing a compassionless, attributional bias.

So, too, we should stop blaming Targets for their own plight that no one would voluntarily choose.

# Avoid the Trap of Self-Blame

As the Targets of most severe bullying tell us, the experience can be as destructive as the complete shattering of one's personality. The Target comes to believe the bully's false story about her. This can happen because the personal attacks are cumulative. Regardless of her initial strength, the Target gets worn down.

This is the beginning of the end of self-confidence in one's competence. It's her personal faith in her competence that enables her to confront the bully. When the inner strength is chipped away, the Target is most vulnerable.

Let's extend what we learned about attribution of responsibility to get a peek at how self-destruction happens and what can be done to avoid it.

As far as the delusional bully is concerned, the Target is the reason for the bullying, and those are the words the Target hears from the bully. "You, you, you." (Can't you just see the wagging finger now?)

Now, switch sides and see the world from the Target's perspective. The bully, operating in a workplace supporting the bully's misconduct, is rightfully seen as the cause of trouble. This is the way attributions normally work. Targets would be biased to blame bullies and the workplace culture that grows them. Bullies would be biased to blame Targets. It's a matter of perspective, depending on the angle from which the situation is viewed.

Targets exposed to verbal battering over time, however, mistakenly commit a sort of "reverse empathy." Normally, empathy is a valuable human trait to have—the ability to see the world from the other person's perspective and to share the emotions of the other person. In this twisted situation, it is the Target who sees herself as a defective unit in agreement with the bully.

Siding with the bully actually makes the bully's task easier. The Target inadvertently becomes an accomplice in the tearing apart of her own personality. Too many Targets come to accept the Bully's lies as fact. The campaign of destruction is made easier by the Target's paradoxical cooperation.

Family, friends, and co-workers witnessing this self-destruction find it hard to believe as they watch the individual spiral down. There's no objective reason for it, but the process is real. The pain the Target suffers while doing it can be severe. Extensive self-blame may require professional help from a counselor to correct.

A Target's explanatory style of assigning responsibility is related to mental health. For the sake of the remainder of this discussion, non-Targets will be referred to as "Self-Promoters." They tend to use an attributional bias that keeps them healthy. Call it hubris, vain self-glory, or justifiable confidence, they interpret causes of interpersonal behavior differently than do Targets.

## Explaining Success and Failure

When explaining their own success (taking a test, winning a job), Self-Promoters generally take credit. They point to either their talent or the effort put into preparation to make the success happen. That is, people usually see success as a result of something about them or some action they took. These causes are internal. To credit internal factors means to take personal responsibility.

Core internal factors are unchangeable personal characteristics that define who we are. Talent, ability, and personality are all internal, relatively constant explanations for events. Crediting personality as the reason for success provides quite an ego boost. Change in personality is very hard to accomplish, as you know if you've ever tried a major self-improvement campaign. (Changing someone else's personality is a recipe for misery—yours.) Your personality's stability, its constancy, is crucial to living an organized, chaos-free life.

Effort fluctuates with circumstances. Sometimes you prepare or rehearse hard; sometimes you do not. With each opportunity comes the chance to do it differently. Effort is internal, but changing.

| | CONSTANT | CHANGING |
|---|---|---|
| INTERNAL | Intelligence, Talent | Good Effort, Motivation |

Of the two internal sources of success, intelligence is preferred by most people because internal, stable causes are more predictable. Better to do well because you're smart than to have put forth a good effort. It is the higher self-compliment.

When it comes to explaining failure, Self-Promoters prefer external factors. External causes include the difficulty of a task. Why did the Self-Promoter fail the test or not get the job? She may reason, it "did not test for the important things;" "they hired only 1 percent and they all had friends on the inside." If no plausible explanations come readily to mind, the Self-Promoter points to bad luck: "It just wasn't my day."

Applying the same categories of constancy and changeability to external factors, the range of possible explanations (attributions) for events is complete.

| | CONSTANT | CHANGING | |
|---|---|---|---|
| INTERNAL | Intelligence, Talent | Good Effort, Motivation | ◁ Preferred for Success |
| EXTERNAL | Difficulty/ Ease of Task | Fate, Bad Luck | ◁ Preferred for Failure |

To blame external factors for failure, on the surface, may appear like ducking personal responsibility. Or it may be an accurate reflection of a reality only seen from the individual's point of view.

Attribution theory and the therapeutic approach that evolved from it are more about mental health and wellness than finding fault or fixing blame as a moralist would dictate. Moralists have a political agenda. Don't confuse the information they disseminate in a public arena with solid advice that has helped people recover from life-damaging events like bullying.

## The Positive Mental Health Bias

### *Success*: Take Personal Credit
### *Failure*: Blame Something "Out There"

# Unnecessarily Taking Blame

It is instructive to study depressed individuals and their explanations for why things happen. Bullied Targets often are depressed. Their pattern of explaining events is exactly the reverse of Self-Promoters. Failure is blamed on internal factors. One can beat oneself up for not trying hard enough (the internal effort explanation), but even the depressed person can be made to see that there will be other chances to try harder in the future.

However, when a person sees her or his personality as hopelessly flawed or defective, it is the strongest type of self-inflicted attack possible. That is what depressed people do. Their self-loathing somehow seems justified in their mind. All negative thoughts and lost confidence begin with the assumption that the person is irreversibly screwed up. It's not easy to escape from a pit like that.

In the same self-defeating manner, success is discounted by crediting external forces—"I passed only because it was an easy test." "I got the job because the interviewer was unskilled." "I was lucky." It is the glib writing-off of genuine wins for which that person should claim credit.

"Cognitive therapy" with depressed people attempts to reverse self-defeating attributions. Restoring self-confidence requires individuals to see that the core of their being has a solid, positive foundation. In addition, people have to be taught to look for environmental factors that can explain, if only partially, why they do what they do.

Here's how the table of explanations works for self-defeating Targets. The rows are swapped with the Self-Promoters' preferences. That is, success is discounted and minimized. Failure is taken on the chin, which is an unnecessarily harsh, disrespectful approach.

|  | CONSTANT | CHANGING |  |
|---|---|---|---|
| INTERNAL | Easy Task | Dumb Luck | ◄ Preferred for Success |
| EXTERNAL | Stupidity, No Talent | Poor Effort Low Motivation | ◄ Preferred for Failure |

Now relate this to being an unwitting Target of a series of bullying verbal assaults. The heart of the attacks is the lie that the Target is a worthless human being. This is not true and the Self-Promoting person knows this. Over time, doubt can creep into the minds of even the strongest. When bullies are shrewd (and this is often), they use subtle lies that are offensive only by virtue of their repetition. Only rarely does a single incident rise to the level of outrageousness. It's the pattern over time that proves effectively demoralizing. This wears through the Target's defenses.

Part of bullies' effectiveness in disrupting the lives of others is their ability to create chaos. Making statements that run counter to the reality everyone shares in a workplace certainly is the manufacture of madness. If the bully gets away with keeping everyone off balance so that no one can predict the next assault's timing or content, the bully achieves the control she desperately seeks.

Working in a chaotic, dangerous place can wear down the defenses of the "strongest" people. It is difficult for Targets to be close-minded, even when it comes to hearing the bully's pathological view of the world.

By somehow justifying the fit between lies and reality, the Target begins to let the bully define a darker reality of the bully's choosing. The Target who functioned well before the bullying gets lost in the process. [If you want to fundamentally change who you are, don't let the bully define your goals for you.]

## Bullies Win When Targets Accept Personal Criticism As If It Has a "Kernel of Truth" in It.

Finally, we witnesses see evidence that the self-blame process has taken hold. Successes are discounted or explained away. Setbacks are internalized, with a disproportionate amount of responsibility taken for events that were completely out of the Target's control.

In other words, the bully can goad the Target into adopting a depressed person's perspective. It's difficult to determine which comes first—the depression itself or the explanatory perspective of the depressive individuals.

## Suggested Interventions

Targets and their loving family and friends need to be aware of how attribution works. By recognizing the perspective shift Targets make, suddenly not taking credit for success while simultaneously blaming themselves for all failures, others can intervene to stop a Target's downward spiral into depression.

If it is you who is experiencing the mental and emotional shift, get help from a counselor now. (Read our advice about finding an understanding mental health professional in chapter 6.) Your awareness about how this happens will speed your recovery. Keep a written record of your thoughts, explanations, and feelings after events. The pattern of self-blame should become evident. You will have to deliberately retrain yourself to take credit for success and let failure roll off your back in order to get strong again. This may sound vain, but recovering from trauma requires dramatic corrective steps.

Ignore others who constantly urge you to take "personal responsibility" for the bullying that happened to you. You did nothing to bring on the assault from the bully. Take responsibility for shutting out the bully's lies; ignore others who side with the bully. Their advice is not good for your mental health, for your survival. The bully wants to steal your dignity at work. Appropriately explaining your actions is a first step toward reclaiming that dignity.

If it is someone you love who is going through the early stages of self-destruction, avoid at all costs agreeing with the dysfunctional explanations you hear uttered. You have to counter the person when she says she is defective, no good, a total loser, etc. It sounds easy, doesn't it? How could you not resist the lies yourself?

Over time, the bully can penetrate the psyche of the strongest, most optimistic person alive in an attempt to "convince" her that she is wrong. Eventually, dealing with wounded Targets challenges the staunchest supporters. Do not listen to lies; be a constant booster of the person's competence. Give specific examples. Don't simply say, "You are a good person." Say specifically that "volunteering to tutor immigrants in English is worthwhile and the students love you for it, they say so."

Finally, let a professional counselor help you help the Target if either of you gets in too deep with no apparent way out.

*Chapter Fifteen:*

# Satisfy Your Needs
# and Wants

*The vision must be followed by the venture. It is not enough to*
*stare up the steps—we must step up the stairs.*
—Vance Havner

After working through the preceding chapters, you now have the tools for minimizing emotional devastation by the bully. Now we will help you define your own needs and wants, so you can articulate what it is you deserve to have from others. Yes, you deserve to have certain basic needs met and a whole lot more. Your Targethood has convinced you that somehow you are less worthy than others. That kind of thinking has to stop. You are worthy.

## The Target's Declaration of Needs and Wants Signals the End of Targethood to All Past and Future Bullies!

## Fundamental, Basic Needs

We all have legitimate needs—environmental conditions, activities, and experiences important for physical and psychological health.

Targets often forget that they are entitled to have certain basic needs met. Needs are absolute rights to which every human being is entitled. During bullying episodes, when the bully's lies convince Targets that they are worthless, needs are ignored. Some Targets come to believe that they must relinquish their needs. Keep in mind that this exercise is not to prepare you to face the bully, but to give you skills to regain your confidence and faith in your competence.

The following list has examples to remind you about what you need in life. Feel free to add or omit the needs you decide are important to you.

*Physical needs*

- clean air to breathe
- clean water to drink
- nutritious food to eat
- clothing and shelter
- rest and enough sleep
- exercise
- physical safety, freedom from harm

*Emotional needs*

- to love and be loved
- to have companionship
- to feel respected
- sympathy and compassion from others
- to reciprocate that sympathy and compassion
- when you do well—recognition and appreciation
- when errors are made—forgiveness and understanding

*Intellectual needs*

- information
- stimulation

- challenge of solvable problems
- variety
- time for recreation and play
- space to grow and to change
- freedom to honestly express your thoughts
- authentic, consistent responses from others

*Social needs*

- to interact with others
- to be by yourself
- work, not necessarily a "job"
- a role in society that helps define an identity through which you make a positive contribution to others
- to feel that you belong to a group
- to not have confidences broken by group members

*Workplace needs*

- employer-provided resources to do the work
- accomplishment of tasks free from interference
- consistent application of internal rules and policies
- compliance with governmental regulations
- work environment free from health hazards
- freedom from retaliation if civil rights are exercised
- a psychologically stable workplace culture
- privacy with respect to matters unrelated to work

*Spiritual, moral, and ethical needs*

- to seek meaning in your life
- a way of putting a value into your life
- compliance with a higher moral code

# My Fundamental Basic Needs

Use the following worksheet to list your private needs.

Physical Needs:

Emotional Needs:

Intellectual Needs:

Social Needs:

Workplace Needs:

Spiritual, Moral, Ethical Needs:

Other Important Needs:

# Needs vs. Wants

The important distinction between needs and wants is that needs are the basics for living. Quality of life depends on going above and beyond fundamental needs. Wants reflect wishes.

For many Targets, it is hard enough to ensure that others honor and satisfy needs. One shouldn't have to beg for the basics. Bullies who violate a Target's rights also are interfering with the satisfaction of basic needs. When feeling passive, vulnerable, and assaulted, it is almost unthinkable for Targets to believe they also deserve to have their wants satisfied.

Ask yourself: Do you ignore your less vital needs and wants if they conflict with someone else's? Do you often identify essential needs as "extras" and neglect them? If you do, then you forego your own comfort. Would others do the same?

You have a right to have your needs met. At the same time, you need to recognize that you deserve to have wants met as much as anyone else. You do not need to be stoic or a martyr. You are just as important as anyone else. You have an inherent right to respectful, nonabusive treatment.

Sometimes you might absolutely need to talk to a co-worker (someone safe, but not the bully) about an aspect of your job. At other times, the job problem might seem less pressing and you want to discuss it, but you can postpone working on it until later.

You are the one, the only one, who can judge the importance of your needs and wants. If it is important to you, you have a right to ask for it. No matter what anyone else thinks!

The following inventory exercise can help you identify wants that you desire, but are afraid to ask for. They are divided into three parts: what you want, who can help satisfy your wants, and situations in which you would ask for what you want.

# Wants Inventory

Go through the list twice.

First pass: place a check beside all items that apply

Second pass: rate the checked items on a three-point scale

    1 = Mildly Uncomfortable

    2 = Moderately Uncomfortable

    3 = Extremely Uncomfortable

## WHAT

I have trouble asking FOR:

- approval for _____
- help with certain tasks
- someone to listen and understand
- respect
- time by myself
- answers to my questions
- permission to make my own choices
- acceptance of who I am by others
- acceptance of my mistakes
- other: _____

## WHO

I have trouble asking for what I want FROM:

- my husband/wife
- fellow workers
- clients
- strangers
- friends
- my boss at work
- salespeople and clerks

- authority figures
- a group of more than two or three people
- a person of the opposite sex
- other: _____

# WHEN

I have trouble asking for what I want WHEN:

- I want help
- I ask for service
- I need a favor
- I ask for information
- I want to propose an idea
- I feel guilty
- I feel selfish
- I ask for cooperation
- I negotiate from a one-down position
- a lot of people are listening
- others' tempers are high
- I'm afraid of looking stupid
- I'm afraid the answer will be "no"
- I might look weak
- other: _____

## *What Your Inventory Says*

Look over the inventory. Notice the things you want the most, the people from whom you want them, and when it is most difficult for you to ask for what you want. Look at the patterns that emerge. These are most likely the people and situations in which you need to acknowledge you feel less confident. List the problem areas in order of their rating and their importance to you.

## *Clarifying What You Want*

After you have identified the wants important to you, formulate an assertive request. If asking for things is hard for you, prepare your requests in advance. By preparing an assertive request ahead of time, you can get the facts clear in your mind and be better able to relate them to others clearly. The clearer you are, the more certain you will be that you are not misunderstood.

Use the following guide to prepare your requests.

*From* _____

Write the name of the person who can give you what you want. If there are several people from whom you want the same thing, write out separate requests for each of them.

*I Want* _____

Spell out what you want the other person to do. Avoid abstractions like "show respect" or "be honest." Don't ask others to change their attitude; instead, specify an exact behavior: "I want an equal vote in deciding the new overtime policy."

*When* _____

Specify a deadline for getting what you want. Give the exact time of day you want someone to do something, or the frequency with which you want something—use any aspect of time that will provide you a time table and won't allow for any misunderstanding. For example: "I would like to have my review the Friday following the day my three-month probation ends."

*Where* _____

Write down the places where you want something: "Please give me one half hour alone at my desk in the morning to organize my day."

*With* _____

Specify any people involved with your request: "I would like to meet with you (the supervisor) and Sue (the co-worker) when you decide what shifts we will have next month."

## Rules for Requests

1. Try to get the other person to agree on a convenient time and place for your discussion.

2. Don't attack the other person. Use firm "I" messages so you can stick to your thoughts and feelings. Remember to be objective and stick to the facts. Keep your tone of voice moderate.

3. Be specific. Don't hedge when you give exact times for what you want. Focus on asking for behaviors, not a change in feelings or attitude.

4. Use assertive words and high-esteem body language. Maintain eye contact, sit or stand straight, uncross your legs and arms, and make sure you speak clearly, audibly, and firmly.

5. Practice, practice, practice! Stand in front of the mirror to observe how you look when you request what you need. This will allow you to correct poor posture and to practice confident facial expressions. Remember, you are practicing the truth. The poor bully has to rehearse lying. Your job is ethical, thus easier.

When asking for change, start with a small request. Build one success upon another. Work slowly through your list of wants.

You need to work on your requests until they are as clear and direct as you can make them. Remember, the satisfaction of your needs and wants does not come at the expense of others. You are asking for no favors, you are simply taking back that which is rightfully yours.

# Clarify What You Want

FROM...

I WANT...

WHEN...

WHERE...

WITH...

## Chapter Sixteen:

# Anger and Shame: Emotions of Bullying

*Pain nourishes courage. You can't be brave if you've only*
*had wonderful things happen to you.*
—Mary Tyler Moore

Bullying brings strong feelings. If you are like the majority of Targets, your feelings are expressed as anger. But anger is not really the problem.

## Anger, the Mask

Anger is always the cover for another emotion. Lurking beneath the surface, waiting to be "outed" and confronted, is the real issue. It could be hurt, disappointment, jealousy, fear, shame, frustration, guilt, or some other emotion.

Anger is the wrong label. To stomp away in rage from an encounter with the bully serves only to hurt the Target about the resentment felt. If the Target stays angry and never confronts her real emotions, the golden opportunity to reclaim her dignity and self-respect vanishes in a cloud of unnecessary emotion.

As Targets know, bullies are sources of stress and anger. We lobby against anger because it postpones a Target's healing.

For Targets, anger is an index of the toxicity of a poisoned workplace. We have to quit blaming individuals entirely. Instead of searching for the perfect personality test to predict which individuals are most likely to be angry, those who care about workplace health should search everywhere at the company for people who enrage others and set off anger for their personal viewing delight. Bullies "burn people." Like arsonists, they love to watch conflagrations of their making.

Investigators and reporters see workplace anger as a malady inherent in disloyal, crazed employees from whom prissy senior management (aka "leaders") must be protected.

The obvious alternative is to eliminate anger by eliminating the source of the devastating emotions that the workplace creates, which drive people to hide the pain beneath a mask of anger.

## Anger Is the Target's Enemy.

The following indicate that you could be angry:
- flushed skin
- shallow breathing
- clammy skin
- rapid breathing
- tearfulness
- loud voice (if normally quiet)
- jitters
- light-headedness
- tensed muscles
- loss of concentration
- bulging veins

Anger can be turned inward and become self-destructive.

- Do you overeat?
- Overdrink?
- Overwork?
- Have you allowed yourself to become so stressed that you have trouble working and functioning adequately at home?
- Do you blame yourself for everything that goes on around you?
- Do you rage at your partner or children?

Sadness and feelings of loss often lie beneath anger. This happens when people are afraid of showing emotions of vulnerability. Anger, the more "socially acceptable" emotion, masks sadness. Some stereotypes are invoked. Men should not show emotion; women show too much "soft emotion." Anger is the great equalizer.

People are afraid of anger itself, too. Unresolved anger causes the bearer pain. Many people carry their anger for years but are not aware of it.

Some people are afraid of any intense emotions; anger scares them the most. They worry about consequences if they express their anger. Sometimes anger erupts with disastrous results—harming not only those who hold the anger, but their co-workers, partners, and children. The violent expression of anger is destructive, nonproductive, and essentially ineffective. Violence hurts—it does not heal.

The perception of anger as destructive comes from childhood. Many children, faced with their parents' anger, feel that the anger is directed at them. These children feel helpless and overwhelmed. They want to disappear.

To them, the parents are angry and raise their voices because of something the child did. Whether or not this is true or logical, it is how the child feels. This fosters the idea that somehow the child is at

219

fault. It is taken as a personal attack, even if not intended that way. Anger destroys the beginnings of self-esteem and feelings of self-worth. If the parents don't make a special effort to clarify why they were angry, the child could anticipate the worst. She assumes responsibility for the parents' emotions.

As an adult, this former child feels that if she disagrees with someone, if she needs to say "no" to someone, if she raises her voice in anger, that anger will hurt someone just as she was hurt by her parents.

This perception needs to be corrected. We all have times when we raise our voices. We all need to say "no" once in a while. We need to disagree. However, these incidents do not need to be destructive. Certainly no one should dread disagreement or being different.

Anger also can be a very constructive energy. To be constructive, it needs to be worked through and released. The goal is to let go of the anger, not to collect and hold it. The first step in letting go of your anger is to own it, to acknowledge that anger is the best name for what is felt inside. Unresolved anger accumulates over time and eventually eats away at your soul.

Although no two people are exactly alike in dealing with their anger, experts on anger have defined five general ways anger is managed. These are: with suppression, with open aggression, with passive aggression, with assertiveness, or by dropping the anger. The first three tend to perpetuate anger; the last two can lead to calm.

## Suppressing Anger

Because so many Targets have witnessed the destructive effects of anger, they hesitate to admit their own anger. They vow not to be lowered to emotions that seem overbearing or crude. They never want to appear rattled or weak, so they maintain a cool exterior of being above all problems associated with anger. When confronted with anger, they want to appear emotionless and pretend to feel no tension. They express surprise that anyone would assume they might be angry.

Most Targets who suppress their anger believe that anger is bad, that expressing it will cause them to be seen in a negative light. Holding in anger is the only way they feel they can interact with others. Unfortunately, there are serious heart health risks associated with the angry, hostile personality.

Check the lines that apply to see if you hold in your anger.

___ I am afraid I will look bad if I let others know my problems.

___ I tend to become resentful of others although I don't want others to know.

___ If I am flustered, I tend to keep it to myself.

___ If a co-worker upsets me, I tend to let days go by without mentioning it.

___ Sometimes I am frozen when faced with an unwanted situation.

___ I avoid mentioning conversations about sensitive topics.

___ I frequently suffer from headaches and stomach upsets.

If you checked three or more of these statements, you are very good at suppressing your anger.

Targets have been trained to think that anger is not normal. They have been invalidated when their perceptions are different than others. They fear retaliation if they express disagreement with others. However, suppression of anger only causes feelings of failure and personal defeat.

## Open Aggression

For many people, anger brings a mental picture of open aggression. They picture anger as taking a stand for personal worth and needs that comes at the expense of someone else. This anger brings images of explosive rage, intimidation, and blame. However, it is not limited to such violent pictures. It also includes bickering, criticism, and sarcasm. This type of anger springs from a focus on personal needs rather than sensitivity to the needs of others. Open, overt aggression is publicly displayed.

Check the lines that apply to see if you practice open aggression.

___ I can be blunt and forceful when someone does
      something to frustrate me.

___ As I speak my convictions, my voice becomes
      much louder.

___ When someone confronts me about a problem, I
      am likely to offer a ready rebuttal.

___ No one has to guess my opinion—it is known by
      everyone.

___ I overlook others' feelings because I focus so
      sharply on fixing the problem.

___ I am likely to argue with my family members.

___ When in an argument with someone, I tend to
      repeat myself.

___ If I think someone else is wrong, everyone knows.

___ I give advice, even when it is not solicited.

If you checked five or more of these statements, you probably have a pattern of open aggression.

## Passive Aggression

Targets who vow not to rage when they are angry recognize that open aggression creates a hostile environment. They refuse to explode loudly or get into a debate with a bully. They feel it is destructive to disagree. It is to be avoided at all costs. This leads to passive aggression, which involves expressing anger in a manner that preserves personal convictions at someone else's expense. The passive-aggressive person is being dishonest to others and to herself.

The following list has examples of passive-aggressive anger. Check the items that apply to you.

___ I use silence to let others know when I am frustrated.

___ I tend to sulk and pout.

___ I procrastinate when I do not want to complete a project.

___ I will never admit if I am frustrated, instead I will lie and pretend everything is fine.

___ Sometimes I avoid others so they won't bother me.

___ Sometimes I will deliberately ignore others when they try to talk to me.

___ I avoid face-to face conversations.

___ Sometimes I do things behind others' backs.

___ Sometimes I do things to others to irritate them.

If you check five or more items, you show the tendency to express your anger in such a way that you succeed in putting limits on your anger. But you are only communicating the anger in such a way that will cause everyone tension and stress at a later time.

## Assertive Anger

Anger defined as preserving personal worth and personal needs while also considering the needs and feelings of others represents a form of anger that truly helps relationships to grow. It shows maturity and personal stability.

It is important to distinguish between assertiveness and aggressiveness. In the past, assertiveness was often confused with pushy and abrasive behavior.

Assertiveness is not mean and is not meant to harm others. It allows a Target to address personal concerns about self-worth and personal needs. It leaves the door open to conversations about differences between the Target and the bully.

The following are examples of anger expressed in a non-hostile assertive way.

- When overworked, you can firmly and politely say "no" when asked to do more projects.
- As a supervisor, you can state project goals without resorting to harassment or being bossy.
- When overwhelmed by work, you can request help from co-workers without threatening retaliation if told "no."
- You can tell your boss or co-workers that you will take your lunch break and not answer the phone or solve any problems during that time.
- With co-workers, you can talk about differences and offer advice without raising your voice or altering your tone of voice.

To learn how to express assertive anger, remember two main points:

1. Make sure you expend your emotional energy on subjects that matter and concentrate your attention on matters that are not trivial. This is also true when reducing stress. Robert Sapolsky suggests that one needs to distinguish between genuine threats and imagined, possible threats.
2. Learn how to distinguish when you use tone of voice to convey your anger.

Remember, assertiveness is not always the easiest thing to learn. It takes time and practice to be able to manage your anger.

## Dropping Anger

The hardest decision to make is the choice of letting go of your anger. There are times when you hope to communicate without anger and you use your best assertive voice, but you still become locked in an angry debate with a bully. At this point, you have the option to choose to drop your anger.

Dropping your anger means you recognize your personal limits. You accept the inability to communicate with the bully. This choice allows you to walk away from the frustration and hurt that the bully has created.

Dropping your anger also indicates that you have accepted the fact that your anger control does not depend on someone else. However, you must remember that dropping your anger is not suppressing it. Suppressing your anger is only an exercise that will leave you with unresolved feelings of hurt and bitterness.

Most bullies bent on controlling the emotional climate at work will provoke Targets to rage. Consciously choosing to disengage from the angry, raging bully will probably infuriate the bully. Walking away is the Target's victory. Denying the bully what she wants is a positive step toward humanizing the workplace again.

## Final Thoughts about Anger

Reasonable responses to situations that cause anger are responses that help you maintain your cool and put the situation into your control, not to yield control to the bully.

Here are some ways to release anger:
- Reestablish your boundaries.
- Use active listening to communicate your willingness to understand any problem.
- Calmly tell the person that she is the source of your anger.
- Exercise by running, walking, working out, or swimming.
- Throw back your shoulders and arms as you say, "Get off my back."

- Talk to friends, family, a professional, or all of them to sort out your feelings.

When you take responsibility for your feelings and emotions, you are released from the bond that ties you to the bully and the ongoing feeling of inadequacy. You choose to take care of yourself, rather than use the bully's actions to dictate the destructive pattern of mistreatment.

## Shame

If you have been bullied, you will experience shame. The shame might be slight, but in many cases it is overwhelming.

It is important for a Target to understand that shame is not guilt.

### Guilt Is What You Feel When You Make a Mistake.

### Shame Is What You Feel When You Believe You Are the Mistake.

Shame is a very painful feeling, the result of the incorrect, internal assumption that there is something inherently wrong with who you are. Shame is the gut-wrenching feeling that you are bad, inadequate, or defective.

> After three years as a personal assistant to the vice president of her company, Pat lost her job. Her boss, Mary, always had been critical of Pat's work. Pat had tried her best to please Mary, working overtime and redoing projects when Mary complained that they weren't up to company standards.

> After months of her boss's torment, Pat lost her temper
> and screamed at Mary. The result was a corrective interview
> and Pat was fired three weeks later.
>
> Pat felt shame when she lost her job. She told herself,
> "I'm no good. I'm worthless. I'll never get another job."
>
> For Pat, the pain of her harassment dominated all her
> thinking. Shame came over her in waves. Her sense of
> unworthiness became so strong that no matter what others
> said, she was convinced she was flawed.

Many families use shame to control others. Parents continually make statements such as: "All you ever do is lay around." "You're going to be a bum, just like your father." "You'll never get a job; you have no skills." "Oh, Susie, you'll never get into college, your grades are not good enough."

Targets raised in families with shame carry that shame from childhood. When you are raised in a shame-based family, you don't know any other way to act. It's easy to understand how Pat might think, "I can't find another job, I'm just no good." Shelly, unemployed for ten months, truly believes she is a failure and reminds herself of this every morning as she looks into the mirror. These two women have retained the shameful messages of childhood and continue to reinforce them.

## To Heal from Shame

Feelings of shame are natural consequences of bullying. Healing from shame involves breaking the silence of pain. When you encounter a bully and you recognize that you feel shame:

- Contact past co-workers and ask them to remind you of your past good work with them.
- As you listen to the positive feedback you get, take time to let in the message that you are a good and competent worker.

- Identify the shaming messages you have internalized and the hurtful events you have experienced.
- Separate what is unreasonable and untrue from who you are.

Hurtful events and messages that have been internalized need to be challenged. You need to be able to say, "That's not about me! It's not about my worth or identity. It hurt me terribly, and it has caused pain in my life, but it's not about me. Shame is not my identity, I am a good and worthy person."

As you put your feelings about shame into words, as you identify how bad you feel, you will be able to let go of the shame and move on with your life. The more you talk with others you trust, the easier it will be to let go of the bad feelings. The more you acknowledge that the bullying isn't really about you, the closer you will be to leaving the bully behind.

# Section Three

......................................................

# What Can One Person Do?

## Chapter Seventeen:

# Make Yourself Safe

*It is better to die on your feet than to live on your knees.*
—Dolores Ibárruri

B y now you've decided to fight back. Do it for the sake of your long-term mental and physical health. The following suggestions are for information purposes only—the authors assume no responsibility for outcomes, good or bad. Be forewarned that the fight is uphill. Only a few successfully mount a challenge and enjoy a satisfactory result because powerful and vast forces are mobilized against you. Failing to fight back can render you bedridden, defeated, and suicidal.

Before we begin, consider things NOT to do after you discovered that you were bullied.

- Do not trust HR—they work for management and *are* management. Simple facts.
- Do not ask for relief from the bully's boss. That is the person who loves her or him most.
- Do not tell your story from a purely emotional-injury angle. It always scares away potential supporters, even family and friends.

- Do not share your voluminous documentation with anyone at work. No one cares as much as you do. In the wrong hands, it can be used against you.
- Do not ask others (HR, union reps, management) to make the bully stop for your sake. Their inaction will disappoint you. Rather, you will make the business case and ask them to stop bullying for *their own* self-interests.
- Do not pay a retainer to an attorney until you've exhausted cheaper alternatives to get your employer to take your complaint seriously.
- Do not confide in anyone at work unless they have demonstrated (and not just talked about) loyalty to you in the past and right now.

# Three Target Action Steps to Stop the Bullying

## Step One: Name It! Legitimize Yourself!

Choose a name for what is happening to you—bullying, psychological harassment, psychological violence, emotional abuse—to offset the effect of being told that because your problem is not illegal, and there are therefore no policies forbidding it, that no problem exists. This makes people like you feel illegitimate and the cycle of self-blame and anxiety begins.

The source of your problem is external; it's not you. The bully decides who to target and how, when, and where to harm people. You did not invite, nor want, the systematic campaign of psychological assaults and interference with your work.

The journey toward healing never begins until the discovery is made that something wrong is being done to you. As we said before, it could be your physician who first tips you off. Family members bemoan the loss of quality time with you and it suggests something is operating.

The discovery can take a long time. Our 2003 WBI Study found that Targets remain under a bully's control for an average of 22 months!

Discovery is confirmed when a friend or therapist gives you this book or you "stumble" onto the term "workplace bullying" when googling harassment at work. As soon as you learned that the phenomenon is real and that you were not alone, did you feel immediately better? That's the power of naming. Naming stops the descending spiral into unnecessary self-blame.

Educate yourself in-depth at the WBI website. Read the statistics, too. The second most relevant statistic after national prevalence is that 64 percent of bullied Targets lose their jobs simply because they were targeted. So, a realistic task is to plan on getting the next job even before you try to save this one using our three-step approach. Don't wait on the outcome of Step Three. If it fails, you have a backup. If you win a transfer or the termination or transfer of the bully, you can always turn down the job offer you procured elsewhere.

Your sense of injustice leads you to resist finding new work. ("I did nothing wrong. Why should I be the one to transfer or leave? Make the bully leave!") However, you give yourself power when you have the freedom to walk away with minimal economic and health damage. BullyBusting is about regaining control over your own life. The bully tried to steal it away. You are reclaiming it. By getting to safety, out of harm's way, you win.

## BullyBusting Is for Targets to Reclaim Dignity and Self-Respect.

## *Step Two: Seek Respite, Take Time Off*

Accomplish four critical tasks while on sick leave or short-term disability. Your physician holds the key to admission to the disability insurance system based on the observable job stress-caused physical symptoms. The tasks below are best done at home, a safe distance from work with its lack of privacy. And the intensive research demanded by some steps require more time than you could afford to take while still on the job.

*2a.* Assess your mental health with a professional and begin the restoration process to "put yourself back together" after being torn to shreds by the prolonged exposure to stress from bullying. Reread chapter 6 on how to select a person with whom you can be safe. Get emotionally stable enough to make a clearheaded decision to stay and fight or to leave for your health's sake. Your humanity makes you vulnerable; it is not a weakness but a sign of strength. Work Trauma, by definition, is overwhelming, an extraordinary experience.

You may want to engage your therapist in the effort to win long-term disability in the future. Connect the therapist early in your treatment with your physician. They need to be thinking alike to best support you.

Your ability to proceed with the action steps with any effectiveness depends on not being frozen by trauma. Remember when we told you about predictable stages of Targethood? You can only work on details and strategy when capable of high-level cognitive functioning. You must be able to think. Trauma renders coherent, sequential mental processing very difficult.

So, if you are stuck, now is the time to mark this page to come back to after you've undertaken some rebuilding exercises, either by yourself, with family and friends, or in concert with a cooperative therapist.

*2b.* Check your physical health. Stress-related diseases rarely carry warning signals (e.g., hypertension, cortisol levels). This a health preservation task. First, it is important to not ignore physical and emotional cues that the bully is affecting your health. Targets have a habit of thinking that it is a sign of toughness to shut out concerns about sleeplessness, anxiety, loss of appetite, lack of focus, or decreased sex drive. These are your body's warning signs that it is responding to stressors in your life. A harassing bully is probably the biggest stressor a person can experience.

Stress is a biological process. The ability to respond to threats is a remnant of our animal kingdom legacy. It happens at the lower, more primitive brain level. Your body responds to stress even when you try to trick it into thinking that nothing is wrong. This is a disservice to your health. Pay attention to the alarm reaction your body is having. Seek medical or psychological help or both. Don't wait. Bodily harm results from prolonged exposure to stress. Stress kills!

When your safety and health at work are compromised by a tyrant, you are in real danger. The only way to end the stress is to remove the stressor—the bully who dominates your work environment. Only by attacking the source will the pain stop.

If you are asked to sign a general release of your medical records by your employer, know that you have the right to limit employer access to your information to specific appointments with specific doctors and their notes concerning only job stress-related matters (diagnoses) that were discussed only at designated appointments. Never sign an unlimited general release unless advised by your attorney. Also, do not automatically file a workers' compensation claim until you have sought legal advice. Some states forbid lawsuits when a workers' comp claim is filed. That's why HR will steer you to workers' comp. WC is for employers, not you. Avoid WC!

2c. Check to see if your rights as an employee, however meager, were violated either according to an internal company policy or state or federal employment laws.

2c(1). First, look for internal policies that may apply to the mistreatment. Mid- to large-size employers have violence prevention policies. Verbal abuse is nearly always forbidden because it is thrown in with dreaded threats of homicide and physical battery. After ten years of the anti-bullying movement, your employer may actually have an anti-bullying policy that extends protections for workers beyond the civil rights list of protected group members. You have to read carefully. An anti-bullying policy's protection would not exclude any employees. These types of policies are rare. We know. We write them for progressive, early-adopter-type organizations in the United States and Canada. Of course, a written policy rings hollow if not enforced. You would have to dare them to enforce it against one of the jerks they likely consider indispensable.

Before you pursue the dramatic step of filing a formal complaint with your employer about one of its other employees, please know that you will not be believed. As incredible as this sounds, you will be called a liar, treated like a thief, and accused of harassing the wonderful person you dared to accuse of psychological violence. Robbing you of believability and credibility and discounting your record of stellar performance until the bully turned your life upside down is most traumatizing to ethical, conscientious Targets.

You, the complainant, will be unfairly branded a "troublemaker." Employers are complaint takers, investigators, jury, judge, and executioner. They own the process. All internal complaint systems, except the most extraordinary pro-employee ones, exist to protect the employer.

Close scrutiny of internal complaint systems reveals several anti-employee assumptions. They include beliefs that:

- complainants are liars, intent on defrauding the company for personal gain
- complainants are whiners, they deserve their fate
- harassment is not practiced here, therefore our managers are not harassers
- the process will give the employer power of discovery (of facts like your medical history)

while depriving the complainant of similar powers
(psychological testing of the bully is taboo)

- complainants rarely have legal representation
  without filing a lawsuit or paying expensive
  attorneys
- employers have access to staff legal counsel
  or defense firms as a routine matter
- deadlines are a double standard, inflexible
  and not to be missed by complainants, but
  nonexistent in the case of the federal
  government as employer
- bullies have the right to free speech, but Targets
  do not; whistleblowing is considered anarchy and
  therefore suppressible
- systems are based on the limited legal remedies
  available in the courts, namely Title VII of the
  Civil Rights Act violations and nothing else
- employers mount vicious defensive attacks against
  complainants (the "Target-is-nuts" defense),
  deflecting responsibility to respond to allegations
  and to sanction the bully/assailant.

Clearly, filing a complaint creates an adversarial relationship between you, the Target, and the employer, mirroring the sour relationship with your aggressive, destructive bully. The complaint system is not your friend. Approach it with skepticism and caution. They are the enemy. HR is not your friend—the department serves management, not you. HR and the internal anti-discrimination officer (EEO) are not impartial truth seekers.

Retaliation for complaining is predictably certain. Bullies can't stand being exposed. And if they enjoy a high enough rank, they can inflict career death on those who attempt to hold them accountable.

Our advice is to file a complaint immediately after the first deplorable incident. Waiting too long can be used against you, taken as evidence that either the bully's conduct was not as outrageous as you claim or that the impact on your health could not have been severe.

We suggest minimal filing. Give the complaint-taker only dates, times, and a dispassionate account of the bully's actions. Obsessing over the details only gives them ammunition to fight you. Be brief. Save your thunder for making the case yourself in a setting you orchestrate or for working with an attorney. Avoid giving witness names at this time to protect both you and them. Never give an emotional report about how your bully's assaults hurt your feelings or made you feel incompetent. Down the road, your supporting physician, psychologist, or psychiatrist can comment on psychological or physical health impact. Do not make yourself vulnerable in any way to the adversary in the early filing steps.

Filing takes away the employer's ability to deny that they were not aware of the bully's actions.

There may be talk of the employer launching an "investigation." Typically, this is comprised of one meeting or telephone call to the bully who says nothing happened, ending the investigation. Do not expect positive results. Expect the truth to not come out. Do not be surprised if disciplinary action begins against you as the result of filing the complaint. Do not cooperate with the employer's process except to repeat your account of the systematic mistreatment.

As one Target told us:

> I reported a co-worker after more than four personal, abusive attacks. I went to personnel and reported him. I was treated so nicely. I was sent home "on the clock" for two days so that "everything could be taken care of." I was called during the second day, Tuesday, and told, "Be patient, we are investigating and we will protect you. Enjoy your time

*off; you are on the clock." On Friday, I was fired with no reason given. Even when you think they are taking care of business, they may be taking care of YOU!*

Do not sign documents under duress. HR often gets Targets to sign away their rights to outside representation or private medical help, then mandate examinations by employer-paid (and therefore, biased) physicians, psychologists, or psychiatrists. Insist on taking all documents you are asked to sign to private legal counsel for an opinion. If HR refuses to give you time or a copy for review, know that your situation would have worsened had you signed. Block all threats the HR representative may make. Walk out of that meeting, noting date, time, and what threats were made.

We strongly encourage you to proceed with *Step 2d* of this action plan despite promises made to you about the pending results of any employer's investigation. Complaints filed with HR do not routinely receive the attention of senior management, executives, the board of directors, or the public. HR's actual role is to resolve apparent conflicts in "personality" at the lowest level so as not to take the precious time of higher-ups. They think this allows senior people to dodge accountability for in-the-trenches misconduct as long as they are unaware. The following steps prevent the ducking of responsibility and fix liability at the highest levels.

*2c(2)*. Second, check for violations of state and federal laws. If the employer potentially violated any law, you will have the leverage to negotiate a more dignified, respectable severance package than if you were "only" bullied with no hint of illegal discrimination. Use the selection process described in chapter 6 to find a plaintiff's attorney. Rent her or his time; pay for a 30-minute consultation. Prepare extensively beforehand. Know what you will require to be "made whole." In other words, what demands do you want to make of the employer. Tell your story very briefly. You are paying for legal advice, not to be listened to. Explore the possibility of limiting the attorney's role to writing a letter to the employer threatening a lawsuit and conveying your list of demands—several months compensation, prepaid health insurance, payment into your retirement account, a positive letter of recommendation for the next job at the next company, etc. Ask for anything, and be ready to negotiate. If discrimination is present, you have a bargaining chip—signing away your right to pursue litigation now or in the future.

Be aware that severance agreements routinely include a "gag clause." That is, the employer buys your silence about the often years-long history of mistreatment and degradation. It's up to you whether the offer is sufficiently attractive to give up your right to talk about your experience. You yourself or an attorney may be able to alter the clause slightly to enable you to tell your story. Revise the text so that you agree to never disclose the terms of the separation/severance agreement or the dollar amount paid you. Employers' attorneys are most interested in your waiver of the right to sue. They could easily miss the nuanced point about your agreement to stay silent. When we ask individuals with dramatic stories to appear on TV or to talk to a newspaper reporter, we get to see how many gag orders have been signed by formerly bullied Targets.

*2d.* Gather data about the economic impact the bully has had on the employer. Build the business case that the bully is too expensive to keep. First, a word about the reason for this task. You will do it to bring a dignified end to the bullying to be sure. However, the odds are against you. We've come to learn that the more important reason is to distract yourself from the oppressive emotional depression you are feeling. If you climb into bed now, it will be tough to get back up. But if you busy yourself with digging out facts and assembling them into a researched, non-emotional argument, you are doing yourself two favors. Your chances of a quicker recovery and landing the next job and getting on with your life are increased. Secondarily, you have a chance to find a sympathetic ear in the company to "make you whole."

Calculate the dollars and cents of each of the following consequences of bullying to estimate the total economic impact of bullies. *Turnover*—calculate the costs of recruitment, headhunters, advertising, lost productivity during the process, demoralization from understaffing, interviewing time of managers, lost time while the newbie learns the job, multiplied by the number of people chased out by all identifiable bullies. *Absenteeism*—number of people multiplied by the number of mental health days attributable to bullies times hourly compensation rate. *Lost productivity*—compare figures in a unit for a time period prior to the bully working there and after he or she came on the scene; estimate number of customers or contracts lost, members of the public not served, lost opportunities because of bullying-caused understaffing. *Litigation and settlement costs*—discover previous lawsuits, estimate legal defense costs, call former employees to discover the size of settlement agreement compensation (if they will tell you). Add it all up. That is the cost of doing business the way your employer has been doing business while protecting the bully's right to torment others and paying good workers like you to leave.

## Step Three: Expose the Bullying

The real risk was sustained when you were first targeted. You have a 7 in 10 chance of losing your job, involuntarily or by choice for your health's sake. It is no riskier to attempt to dislodge the bully. Retaliation can be expected, but what's new. Good employers purge bullies, but most employers promote them.

*3a.* Finalize the *business* case that the bully is "too expensive to keep." Present the data gathered (in *Step 2d*) to let the highest level person you can reach (not HR) know about the bully's impact on the organization. Obviously in family-owned or small businesses, this is impossible (so leave once targeted).

Start at the top. Find someone who is not related to your bully and has never declared loyalty to the bully. Obviously, the bully's boss is too close to the bully to see the perspective you will present. You have to find someone at least two levels above the bully's rank. We call this our "Rule of 2." So, aim high up the chart. Select someone with a reputation for fairness and known to be less autocratic.

*3b.* Rehearse your 15- to 30-minute presentation. Forget that you were ever an employee there. Act like a dispassionate consultant. You have news about significant financial losses in the trenches that any executive or owner who cares about the business (or the mission of public service in government) should want to hear. Prepare a single page leave-behind report that shows your cost accounting.

Stick to the bottom line. If you drift into tales about the emotional impact of the bully's harassment, you will be discounted and discredited.

Rehearse the transition near the end of your time to discuss solutions. This shows that you are a problem solver, in addition to the long-time valuable contributor you always were. The option to mention last is the termination of the bully, without calling her or him a bully. But before that, suggest transferring him or her. Suggest stripping the bully of supervisory responsibilities, not only to protect workers hurt by the bully but to free him or her to do the work again for which recognition was once honestly earned. The bully must have been good at something some time ago. Return the bully to that work, and don't let him or her touch other people's lives again. This last strategy is easily done in government but nearly unimaginable in other workplaces.

Prior to the scheduled presentation, lower your expectations of success. Consider the job offer taking you down the road in your career. Decide beforehand that no matter what is said to you, you will not be hurt or surprised by it. Prepare to be fired on the spot. Stay in control of your perceptions and you can't lose.

Prior to the presentation, clarify for yourself what demands you will make that will restore your health and safety. Your safety is paramount. Do not agree to return to the same position under the same supervisor no matter what promises about changes are made. As long as the bully has access to you, you will not be safe.

3c. Deliver your presentation. Give the executive a chance to adopt one or more of your solutions. If he or she sides with the bully because of personal friendship ("He's a great conversationalist and a lunch buddy") or rationalizes the mistreatment ("You have to understand that that is just how she is"), you will have to leave your job for your health's sake. However, some employers are looking for reasons to purge their very difficult bully. You are the internal consultant with the necessary information. Help good employers purge their assholes!

3d. OK, the presentation was brilliant. But the executive defended the bully, and you are banished. No surprise there. The key to your future is that you controlled how you left the place. You brought sunshine to the dark side. You let the employer know that the wrong-doing was entirely preventable and unjustified. You fixed responsibility where it should have been fixed—at the executive or senior management or owner level where the bullying is allowed to go unaddressed. If they chose not to stop it, that was their choice. But you are not stupid or a martyr. You will not subject yourself to such indignity and stupidity anymore. Leave with your head held high. Tell everyone about the petty tyrant for your health's sake. You have nothing to be ashamed about. You were only doing the job you once loved. Now go make yourself safe to heal.

## *Chapter Eighteen:*

# Facing the Future

*I decided it is better to scream… the last vestige of human dignity.
It's a man's way of leaving a trace…. He asserts his right to live,
sends a message to the outside world demanding help and calling
for resistance…. Silence is the real crime against humanity.*
—Nadezhda Mandelstam

We end the book where most Targets begin, with the question,
"Should I stay or leave?"

Only you know the answer. Only you know how the quality of your
work and personal life have fallen as the result of bullying.

You get no medals for "hanging in there." For you, toughness may
be one of those unattainable personal standards over which you beat
yourself up.

We suggest doing a cost-benefit analysis on a two-column sheet.
Review the Impact Assessment results from chapter 9. Let that information enter your decision-making discussions. Leaving a job is a
private decision to be made only by you and your life partner. Do the
required math yourself.

## Sacrifice Health and Sanity for a Paycheck?

## It Simply Doesn't Add Up!

For what it's worth, we coach people as long and as hard as we can to get them to save their jobs. However, the kiss of death for potential BullyBusters is when the bully has support all the way to the top of the organization. Targets facing unanimous opposition like that do not stand a chance. If no allies can be found above the bully, you'll never gain the leverage against him or her that you need to stop the bullying.

If your workplace is a convenience store and the bully is a co-worker but the owner hired her, polish your resume and hit the road.

However, if you decide to stay and you work in a large organization, you owe it to yourself to follow as many of the action steps as you can.

Targets seriously underestimate the consequences for their health. The cumulative nature of the bullying, combined with the tendency to procrastinate about seeing a doctor or telling others out of shame, lulls the individual into a barely perceptible decline. However, the strain may have already begun cardiovascular and gastrointestinal problems, several of which may be irreversible. Make your health the most heavily weighted, most significant factor in the decision-making process.

The major conflict for Targets is wanting to get out to save their sanity and wanting to stay so as to not seem to turn tail and run. Trust us, you can control the story of your departure if you don't accept a quiet exit. Leaving with dignity seems to quicken the healing process.

Let's assume you've decided to leave. You can leave the way your employer wants or you can try our suggested routine.

## A Quiet Exit

Thousands of traditional career counselors out there can advise you about leaving gracefully. They can tell you how to transition to the next job without ruffling anybody's feathers. To summarize their approach: burn no bridges, kiss the behind of the bully boss so she won't say bad things about you (she will anyway, don't they know?), never be negative (which we guess means to avoid the truth) about the job-ending turmoil you are leaving behind when interviewing for the next job, smile, and put your future in the hands of those who have ruined your life to date.

Accepting the humiliation inflicted by the bully, HR, and senior management, culminating in the "exit parade" or "plank walk," essentially leaving with your "tail between your legs," jeopardizes your ability to move on with your life, to start anew somewhere else. The circumstances under which you leave seem to predict the length of time needed to completely heal and be able to function at 100 percent in another job. When you control the terms, damage is minimized. When the bully and employer set the agenda, Targets are left doubting for months about what they could or should have done differently.

## An Alternative Departure

It involves guile, cynicism, and paranoia. But the bully pushed you into this mess in the first place. Never forget that. Clearly we think you will do best following our three-step action plan described in detail in the previous chapter. But here are some additional thoughts regarding the transition from this job to the next.

### 1. Arrange for Positive References and a Great Letter

Ask for a positive reference from colleagues, allies up the chain, and customers who will verify that your performance record was impeccable. You need people to confirm that you are a skilled, competent person. Some employers insist on talking with your ex-supervisor (often the bully) regardless of the glowing reference list you produce. If that next employer is more obsessed with your subordination and willingness to sell your soul to a tyrant, would you want to work there? Choose carefully where you work next. Go with open eyes.

Write your own letter of recommendation and make the employer sign it before you leave. Even if they hate you, just maybe their fear of confrontation will convince them to sign. Plus, this might balance the practice of making you sign forms against your will (such as stating that your departure was voluntary to cut you out of unemployment benefits). Then you can threaten them with legal action if they renege on the letter or choose to state anything more than employment dates if and when contacted. If they go along with this letter, you can skip the next suggestion. Hire a reference checking service to verify compliance. Check the WBI website links for firms we recommend.

Warn the bully and all bully supporters, including HR, that they are to provide the next employer with dates of employment only or face legal action. Use the legal language about defamation.

## 2. Know the Law Regarding Defamation of Character

Goad the bully into defaming you to others. Get it on the record. (Most bullies will actually boast of the smear campaign they launch against you.)

David Hurd, attorney and author of the *California Employee Survival Handbook*, states that it is illegal for an employer to make a "misrepresentation which prevents or attempts to prevent a former employee from getting a new job…. A misrepresentation can include any act, suggestion, or inference that leads the listener to believe something untruthful or misleading… (even) gestures, or tone of voice, or a raising of an eyebrow could qualify as an illegal misrepresentation." Proof can be provided by a reputable reference checking firm.

According to Hurd, if an employer "volunteers to another person or another employer the reason or reasons for an employee's discharge or reason for quitting, that employer is guilty of a crime…. The past employer is only permitted to disclose the truthful reasons for the discharge or voluntary termination of the employee if the past employer is specifically asked without prompting."

Because warnings don't stop liars and cowards, consider using a pro-employee reference checking service (our recommendations appear in the links list at the WBI website). The company calls your ex-employer as someone checking your references. Since they are working for you, for a modest fee, they transcribe exactly what is said. The defaming statements give an attorney ammunition to exact your pound of flesh from them for continuing the bullying after your departure. Using this service doesn't stop them, but it might help you get a settlement from them large enough to cushion the economic blow of being "constructively discharged" from the job you once loved.

## 3. If the Employer Insists on an "Exit Interview," Deliver or Send an Attorney's Letter Instead

You are leaving. So you control the meeting agenda for once. Be prepared for Gestapo-like tactics. Produce a letter from an attorney representing you (pay for one hour's time) to the employer in a way that proves receipt. The letter warns all those listed that they, as individuals and as representatives of the employer liable for the mistreatment you endured, will be held liable for the release to future employers of any information prohibited by law regarding your employment there.

## 4. Worst-Case Scenario—Launch a Preemptive Strike about Your Version of the Bullying Fiasco at the Interview for the Next Job

Prospective employers are always desperate to talk to your exemployer. Convince them not to do this. Tell them there was conflict and positive news from the bully is not likely. If you then let them know how you expect to be smeared, you will have "self-published" the defamation you anticipate. According to Hurd, your statement would be admissible in court to show you have been defamed by disclosing the false statement made against you by the ex-employer. Direct their attention to the positive comments from others. Emphasize the skills you bring. Compliment them on their reputation as a humane, progressive employer who cares about employees, if they enjoy this reputation.

## 5. Review Your Record of Bullying Incidents and the Response by the Employer; Consider Legal Action Against the Company

Scan the record and your memory for potential invasions of your privacy while there. There is no explicit right to privacy. Courts always question whether or not the person watched or recorded had the "reasonable expectation" of privacy.

In the workplace you should expect that the employer's property would be considered public (except for toilet stalls, and even then, there seems to be some doubt). Call the Privacy Rights Clearinghouse in San Diego [(619) 298-3396] for advice on privacy questions.

Pursue legal or EEOC complaints, if applicable. Your departure is imminent when complaints are filed. As a rule, retaliation is swift, severe, and persistent for those who dare to complain. If your rights have been violated as a member of a "protected class" under Title VII Civil Rights Act, call the Federal Government's EEOC for a free consultation and preliminary determination of your status.

If you are not Title VII eligible, consult a plaintiffs-only attorney or an attorney concerned about employee rights. There may be "tort" law that applies—e.g., intentional infliction of emotional distress (see IIED in chapter 20), constructive discharge, defamation, wrongful termination, breach of contract, reckless indifference, employer negligence. We're not lawyers, so seek legal advice about the various alternatives. Now that you are out, the power of a lawsuit would be to create a nuisance for the ex-employer to let them know they messed with the wrong person. Justice happened the day you stepped away from your tormentor's grasp. Lawsuits can make public the dirty tactics they tried to accomplish behind closed doors. Do not expect to get rich from bringing a suit. Also consider how your current employer feels about someone on staff who has sued a boss. You have to expect retaliation.

Admittedly, these steps sound like hardball, but doesn't that describe accurately what the employer and bully conspired to do to you? It's an alternative to the quiet exit. It's time to live the richly rewarding life you were enjoying before the uninvited bully distracted you temporarily.

# Work Shouldn't Hurt!

# Section Four

..................................................................................

# Making Employers Responsible

*Chapter Nineteen:*

# The World Declares War on Bullying

*In the societies of the highly industrialized western world, the workplace is the only remaining battlefield where people can "kill" each other without running the risk of being taken to court.*
—Heinz Leymann, MD

Bullying may be running rampant through the United States, but it certainly doesn't stop at the borders. In fact, when it comes to acknowledging bullying's destructive effects on the workplace, America could stand to take a few notes from the rest of the world. We are dead last among the western democracies to democratize the workplace. We may think we are exceptional. The record suggests otherwise.

## International Roots of the Anti-Bullying Movement

### The European Pioneer

Heinz Leymann treated Swedish victims of workplace "mobbing" in Sweden's RehabCenter clinic at Violen for individuals traumatized at work. He held the equivalent of two doctorates (MD and PhD), which enabled him to not only work to heal victims but to conduct research at the same time. His scientific publications on the topic began in the 1990s. Research was funded as part of a national commitment to understand psychosocial stressors and their impact on workers.

He defined "mobbing," his term for workplace bullying, as:

> *Psychological terror or mobbing in working life involves hostile and unethical communication which is directed in a systematic manner by one or more individuals, mainly toward one individual, who, due to mobbing, is pushed into a helpless and defenseless position and held there by means of continuing mobbing activities. These actions occur on a very frequent basis (statistical definition: at least once a week) and over a long period of time (statistical definition: at least six months' duration). Because of the high frequency and long duration of hostile behavior, this maltreatment results in considerable mental, psychosomatic, and social misery.*

Note that Dr. Leymann focused on the health impact on the Target. He writes that the level of PTSD (post-traumatic stress disorder) suffered by mobbing victims is more intense and persistent than that felt by train operators who witnessed suicides by people leaping onto railroad tracks in front of them.

Leymann's concern was the set of medical stress consequences of bullying for the Target rather than with classifying personality types or reengineering organizations.

Leymann also claimed that the chances of healing from acute trauma from bullying are reduced if the individual faces continuing threats. As long as the perpetrator goes unpunished, or the victim does not receive effective support, he or she can be torn to pieces again at any time.

The trauma is sustained by loss of income, spouses leaving due to discomfort in the marriage, pro-management Employee Assistance (EAP) counselors, uncooperative Personnel departments, insensitive managers, uncooperative co-workers, doubting union stewards, doctors in general practice, the company's insurance carrier, state disability agencies, and lawyers and the courts, if legal steps are pursued.

Leymann died of cancer in Spring 1999.

## In the United Kingdom

British journalist Andrea Adams coined the phrase "workplace bullying" based on her 1988 investigation of the mistreatment of employees in a bank. She reported on bullying for BBC radio and wrote the first book in the United Kingdom (*Bullying at Work: How to Confront and Overcome It*) on how to confront and overcome bullying in 1992. She also died too young.

In the United Kingdom, unions have assumed the mantle of leadership after Adams's passing, along with the nonprofit Andrea Adams Trust. It is they who provide national awareness campaigns, telephone hotlines to report mistreating employers, and support. There are several individual pioneers and crusaders who also contribute much to the public movement—Andrew Ellis (who hosts the legal information website www.workplacebullying.co.uk) and the late Tim Field.

Academic researchers in the United Kingdom include Charlotte Rayner, PhD; Helge Hoel, PhD; Duncan Lewis, PhD; and transplanted Australian Michael Sheehan, PhD; all of whom were instrumental in founding The International Association on Bullying and Harassment in the Workplace in 2008. (Details about this new group, combining researchers and practitioners, can be found at the WBI website.)

## In Australia

In 1994, four Australians—two business school professors, a psychiatrist, and a school psychologist—convened their country's first conference on bullying. The four founders of the Beyond Bullying Association had concluded that bullying was a major problem in schools, homes, and workplaces. The BBA works to create codes of conduct for schools, prisons, and workplaces and to develop guidelines for laws protecting individuals from harassment. Michael Sheehan, PhD, is one of the founders.

## In South Africa

Dr. Susan Steinman, co-author of the 1997 book *Hyenas at Work*, launched the Work Trauma Foundation. She has become an expert in workplace violence in the health care sector in her country.

## In France

The psychiatrist Marie-France Hirigoyen launched the national movement with the 1998 publication of her book, *Stalking the Soul*, which sold 500,000 copies immediately after its publication in its native French language before translation into English. She writes about the "perversity," the cruelty, of bullying. By 2002, there was a national anti-bullying law in France.

## In New Zealand

The movement there was led by Andrea Neeham, a transplanted Californian. Her book, *Workplace Bullying: The Costly Business Secret*, was published in 2003. She is not only a brave pioneer and anti-bullying advocate but the survivor of a double lung transplant.

## In Ireland

In 1999 a Task Force on the Prevention of Workplace Bullying was chartered by the Minister for Labour Affairs for the Government. In 2001, the first national survey was conducted. The Expert Advisory Group on Workplace Bullying produced its report and recommendations in 2004, followed in 2005 by the amending of the national Safety, Health, and Welfare Act of 2005 to suggest that employers create explicit anti-bullying policies because workplace bullying is a societal problem. According to the second national survey conducted in 2007, reflecting a 7.9 percent prevalence, nine out of ten Public Administration organizations and three-quarters of those working in Education have such a policy.

## In Finland

Katri Kytöpuu tells of a Finnish association that supports Targets of bullying, both at school and in workplaces. In Finland, they use the term "bullying" to describe at-school mistreatment and the term "psychological violence" to describe workplace terror. Though Sweden is a neighbor, the word "mobbing" is not so familiar, even though most Finnish research is based on Leymann's work.

## In Italy

Harald Ege, PhD, with a background in work and organizational psychology, is the president of PRIMA, the first Italian Association against Mobbing and Psychosocial Stress. A nonprofit organization founded in January 1996 in Bologna, Italy, it was the first one in the Mediterranean area to speak about mobbing. Ege wrote several books in Italian on the topic.

## In Germany

The KLIMA Association was founded in 1998 in Hamburg, Germany, to help victims of mobbing, to provide counseling, and to prevent mobbing in businesses, the state, and society. KLIMA operates independently of any employer, employee organization, or ethnic, political, or religious group. Its members are chosen by a governing Board and Advisory Council. Its primary contact is Dr. Alfred Fleissner.

# International Laws against Bullying

Bullying at work is increasingly seen as an important issue throughout Europe. Scandinavian countries in particular have recognized bullying as a work environment or health and safety issue and have introduced measures to prevent it.

In Sweden, an ordinance on measures against victimization at work came into force in March 1994, making it the world's first law against what we call workplace bullying. This defines victimization as "recurrent reprehensible or distinctly negative actions which are directed against individual employees in an offensive manner and can result in those employees being placed outside the workplace community."

The ordinance makes clear that this includes adult bullying, mental violence, social rejection, harassment, and offensive administrative sanctions. The ordinance requires employers to:

- Plan and organize work so as to prevent victimization.
- Make clear that victimization cannot be accepted.
- Provide routines for the early detection and elimination of such unsatisfactory working conditions, problems of work organization, or deficiencies of cooperation as can provide a basis for victimization.
- Implement countermeasures without delay if signs of victimization become apparent, including investigation of whether the way in which work is organized may be a cause.
- Have special routines to provide rapid help and support to employees who are subjected to victimization.

The Swedish legislation makes it clear that bullying is an organizational issue and that employers have a duty to organize work and the work environment so that it does not provide the sort of climate in which bullying is likely to occur.

## *In Britain*

Laws in the United Kingdom indirectly prohibiting bullying invoke either Health and Safety or Employment Law codes.

Employers have general duties to protect employees' health and to consult safety representatives about health and safety matters. Furthermore, every employer has a legal duty to make a suitable and sufficient assessment of the risks to the health and safety of their employees while they are at work.

Although not explicitly stated, the employer's duty to protect employees' health should be taken as referring to both physical and mental health and the employer should assess the risks to both.

The British Health and Safety Executive (HSE) has published guidelines for employers on preventing stress at work that makes it clear that bullying can be a cause of stress and that preventive measures must include action to eliminate bullying where it exists.

According to UK tort law, employers also have a general duty of care for their employees. The victim can claim damages where the victim suffers some injury.

In certain circumstances, those in which bullying leads to a fundamental breach of the employment contract and is serious enough for the employee to terminate without notice, an employee may be able to pursue a claim of constructive dismissal. Contractual terms can be expressed in written form—as in a labor agreement—or implied. Typical examples of implied contract terms would be "mutual trust and confidence" or the statutory term to "provide a safe system of work." Employees can take their claims to employment tribunals.

Final provisions of the *Protection from Harassment Act* enacted in 2001 define harassing conduct as alarming a person or causing the person distress on at least two occasions. Conduct includes speech. Putting people in fear of violence is also actionable under this law.

Sometimes, the English judiciary can be far-reaching and imaginative when it comes to interpreting a statute. For instance, if an individual manager or a company is found responsible for causing psychological harm (a recognized psychiatric illness like PTSD, for instance), the mistreatment may constitute either Actual Bodily Harm (a violation of the *Offences against the Persons Act*, punishable by up to five years imprisonment) or Grievous Bodily Harm if committed with intent. The latter offense qualifies the perpetrator for a life sentence, a sentence rarely imposed.

In August 2006, Helen Green, a former employee of Deutsche Bank Group Services (UK) Ltd. in London, was awarded a $1.5 million judgment for her pain and suffering and loss of past and future earnings. It was a bullying case in which her legal team invoked the *Protection from Harassment Act*. She claimed to have been subjected to "offensive, abusive, intimidating, denigrating, bullying, humiliating, patronizing, infantile, and insulting words and behavior," including crude and lewd comments from her former colleagues and having her workload increase to unreasonable and arbitrary levels. Justice Robert Owen ruled that the behavior at the international banking firm was a "relentless campaign of mean and spiteful behavior designed to cause her distress."

## In Australia

The government of Queensland issued "An Employer's Guide to Workplace Bullying" that summarizes the status of state laws related to bullying.

Workplace bullying is defined as "the repeated less favorable treatment of a person by another or others in the workplace, which may be considered unreasonable and inappropriate workplace practice." It includes behavior that intimidates, offends, degrades, or humiliates a worker, possibly in front of co-workers, clients, or customers.

Employer obligations—under common law, an employer is under a duty to protect workers from workplace bullying. This duty exists:

- in tort; for example, negligence—failure to provide a safe workplace
- as an implied term in the employment contract that the employer would not, without reasonable cause, destroy or seriously damage the relationship of trust and confidence between employer and worker.

Employers who do not take suitable precautions to protect workers from workplace bullying may be liable for any physical and psychological injury suffered by the victim. Recent cases at common law are setting precedents for workplace bullying to be dealt with under personal injury claims.

The *Public Sector Ethics Act 1994* states five "ethics obligations," including "respect for persons." These obligations are intended to provide the basis for codes of conduct for public officials, to be developed by government departments and other public sector entities.

The *WorkCover Queensland Act 1996* allows a worker to submit a claim for workers' compensation if an injury or disease is suffered as a result of workplace bullying.

The *Workplace Relations Act 1997* entitles a worker to make a claim under the unfair dismissal provisions of the WRA when a worker is dismissed or is forced to resign as a result of workplace bullying.

The state of South Australia passed in 2005 one of the toughest anti-bullying laws—*SafeWork SA Amendment* to the *Occupational Health, Safety, and Welfare Act*. For the purposes of this section, bullying is behavior—(a) that is directed toward an employee or a group of employees, that is repeated and systematic, and that a reasonable person, having regard to all the circumstances, would expect to victimize, humiliate, undermine, or threaten the employee or employees to whom the behavior is directed; and (b) that creates a risk to health or safety. State Government departments and private organizations can now be prosecuted and fined up to $100,000 for failing to "adequately manage" bullying behavior by breaching their duty of care, including failing to have appropriate systems in place to stop bullying at work.

## In France

In 2002, the French introduced the Social Modernization law to directly address bullying. Mobbing (bullying) is defined as "the perverse implementation of power… a means of subjugation and persecution of the other, questioning his fundamental rights to the respect which is due him or her… Consequences… can be detrimental to the good functioning of the company: disorganization of production, both quantitative and qualitative, and financial effects."

French law treats public sector employees differently. There are two jurisdictions: one for civil servants, one for private sector employees. The latter group, when bullied, may request timely mediation, be represented in courts by unions, are forbidden to be retaliated against in financial or other ways, and the law shifts to the accused the onus for proving that misconduct was not bullying. Public sector employees are subject to having their annual income cut by as much as half by arbitrary retaliation by the supervisor for complaining under the new law.

## In Canada

Canada shares with Britain and Australia an implied duty of care for employers. Part of the implied employment contract requires the employer to treat the employee with civility, respect, and dignity. Constructive dismissal actions based on bullying behavior represent a breach of the implied contract.

However, the big news is that the first North American anti-bullying law was passed in Quebec. Workers there have the right to be free of "psychological harassment."

The province of Quebec passed a new *Labour Standards Act*

effective June 2004, giving workers several new protections. Balancing the good news about legal progress is the unfortunate lack of precision in the law's language that offending bullies may be able to exploit to defend themselves.

The law protects employees against "any vexing behavior in the form of repeated and hostile or unwanted conduct, actions, or gestures that affects an employee's dignity or psychological or physical integrity." There is a cumbersome resolution process that first mandates mediation between the parties. After the initial 4,000 complaints were received, only 3 cases made it to the final stage of adjudication. As University of Quebec at Montreal professor Angelo Soares, an expert on the provincial law, concluded at conferences where he reported on the law's progress, the most influential aspect of the law is that the province declared the unacceptability of bullying *in principle*.

In Saskatchewan, effective October 2007, the provincial *Occupational Health and Safety Act* was amended to include harassment as a prohibited health hazard for workers. Harassment is defined as:

> *Any inappropriate conduct, comment, display, action, or gesture by a person that is based on status/grounds of illegal harassment (race, creed, religion, color, sex, sexual orientation, marital status, family status, disability, physical size or weight, age, nationality, ancestry or place of origin) or harassment which adversely affects the worker's psychological or physical well being and that the person knows or ought reasonably to know would cause a worker to be humiliated or intimidated; and that constitutes a threat to the health or safety of the worker.*

In other words, health-harming harassment from actions that we define at WBI as bullying.

*Chapter Twenty:*

# America Wakes Up

*Some way must be worked out by which employer and employee,
each recognizing the proper sphere of the other, will each be free
to work for his own and for the common good, and that powers of
the individual employee may be developed to the utmost.*
—Justice Louis Brandeis

The United States is far behind the rest of the world in recognizing workplace bullying. The pattern worldwide has been to have the movement first led either by social pioneers, a significant book, academic researchers, or some combination of them all. Lawmakers typically follow.

Lawmakers are persuaded to act on the social dilemma based on convincing statistics coupled with the very vivid, anecdotal tales from bullied Targets who testify at legislative hearings.

The American anti-bullying movement began in mid-1997 informally, and officially in January 1998. Much progress has been made. But it is has been an uphill battle when it is characterized as "anti-employer" instead of its rightful designation—freedom at work from abusive mistreatment.

## U.S. Academic Pioneers

Traditions within schools of business naturally promote management as a profession. It takes a bold individual to declare bullying-related phenomena as one's research specialty. The study of illegal violence and sexual/racial harassment are safer topics for academics. Most approach the area timidly, with euphemistic labels. Our heroes are the ones with the courage to call it bullying.

David Yamada, JD, professor at Suffolk University Law School in Boston, is the lead reformer inside the legal education community. His work is at the center of the U.S. movement and is summarized in detail later in this chapter.

The emergent and most prolific U.S. academic behavioral researcher is Pamela Lutgen-Sandvik, PhD, at the University of New Mexico. As a middle-aged post-doctoral professional, she brings real-world work experience to her studies. Her studies span methodologies like few other researchers. She relies on paper-and-pencil questionnaires, online surveys, intensive interviews, case studies, and innovative projective techniques. She explores every aspect of Targets' experiences, from bullying frequency to the stages of emotional repair that must be undertaken before and after bullying invades their lives. At the 2008 biennial meeting of the world's workplace bullying researchers, Dr. Lutgen-Sandvik was chosen to serve as the sole U.S. representative on the inaugural governing Board of the International Association on Bullying and Harassment in the Workplace. Visit the WBI website to read several of Dr. Lutgen-Sandvik's studies.

Judith Richman, PhD, and Kathleen Rospenda, PhD, at the University of Illinois at Chicago study the role substance abuse plays as an ineffective coping strategy for those harassed at work. They conducted a study comparing the mental health effects of sexual harassment and bullying (called "generalized workplace abuse"). Early in her career, Rospenda is not afraid to tackle workplace bullying directly.

Suzy Fox, PhD, and Lamont Stallworth, PhD, of Loyola University in Chicago actively study workplace bullying as it relates to both illegal discrimination and whether or not mediation and techniques of alternative dispute resolution are useful in bullying incidents.

Loraleigh Keashly, PhD, at Wayne State University in Detroit reviewed the collection of bullying-related research. In a 1998 report, she chose the label "emotional abuse at work." She defines it as the hostile verbal and nonverbal behaviors, independent of racial or sexual content, directed at a person to gain control over, even subservience from, that person. Keashly and Karen Jagatic presented at the WBI Workplace Bullying 2000 U.S. conference, offering the best estimate at the time of the prevalence of mistreatment in the U.S. workplace. It was 16.5 percent.

Joel Neuman, PhD, at the State University of New York at New Paltz explores organizational conditions related to the frequency of workplace aggression and factors, both personal and workplace-related, that predict a bully's hostility. Many of his studies of aggression point to the increasing rate and extent of change facing employees and managers. His work bridges the gap between macroeconomics and impact on individual lives.

## There Oughta Be a Law

Employers, especially American employers, take care of their workers only when pushed by laws that compel compliance with standards of decency. Laws lead to the creation of internal policies. If, and only if, those policies are faithfully enforced, an employee has the chance of being protected against negative conduct by others. Employers beg to be allowed to deal with bullying voluntarily. Because bullies are too expensive to keep, you would think rational employers would purge them. Good employers do purge bullies; bad ones promote them! Waiting on employers to voluntarily stop bullying is an endless wait. A law will move employers more quickly.

On the shoulders of the researchers named previously and with a mixture of our WBI studies conducted in 1998, 2000, 2003, 2007, and 2008, the U.S. movement was launched. The catalyst for actually declaring our "Campaign Against Workplace Bullying" in 1998 with its own website was Ruth's personal and Gary's vicarious experience with a bully supervisor of Ruth's. We funded a toll-free crisis line until we went broke. It didn't help that the call for bullied Targets to dial up appeared in feature articles in *The Washington Post* and *USA Today*. But in the process, we gathered nearly 5,000 stories told by Targets averaging an hour each. We've heard every version of imaginable cruelty racing through corporate cubicles, executive suites, hospital floors, government agencies, do-gooder nonprofits, and small family-owned businesses. We wondered what was the next step. Then we got a call from Boston and WBI doubled its workload.

Thanks to a Herculean research effort by David Yamada, professor at Suffolk University Law School in Boston, we know that the favored legal basis for addressing emotionally abusive workplace mistreatment is to sue for Intentional Infliction of Emotional Distress (IIED). IIED cases seem the most applicable legal remedy to bullying as described by WBI and this book. If IIED cases brought by workers hurt by bullies are successful, then we already have a legal solution.

Professor Yamada reviewed the records of several hundred state court IIED decisions for the period from Summer 1995 through Summer 1998. The record of success for plaintiffs (the employees who file the lawsuits asking for relief) is dismal.

The legal criterion used by several courts to define IIED is: "One who by extreme and outrageous conduct intentionally or recklessly causes severe emotional distress to another is subject to liability for such emotional distress, and if bodily harm to the other results from it, for such bodily harm." Which is translated into the requirements that the perpetrator's conduct must be intentional or reckless, outrageous, and intolerable (according to the unrealistically high standard of the conduct beyond the bounds of societal decency and morality), that conduct be shown to be the cause of the emotional distress. In turn, the impact must be severe.

Unfortunately, the court decisions researched by Yamada proved that the threshold for holding the employer liable is high, often impossibly high, as understood by a rational layperson.

Here's one example from a 1996 Arkansas Supreme Court case that involved a female employee, Holloman, who worked for a male physician, Keadle, for two years. Holloman claimed that her boss "repeatedly cursed at her and referred to her with offensive terms, such as 'white nigger,' 'slut,' 'whore,' and 'the ignorance of Glenwood, Arkansas.'" The physician repeatedly used profanity in front of his employees and patients, and he remarked that women working outside of the home were "whores and prostitutes." He told Holloman "he had connections with the mob" and mentioned "that he carried a gun," allegedly to "intimidate her and to suggest that he would have her killed if she quit or caused trouble."

The bullied employee claimed that she suffered from "stomach problems, loss of sleep, loss of self-esteem, anxiety attacks, and embarrassment."

The Arkansas Supreme Court agreed with a summary judgment (dismissal without proceeding through the entire case) in favor of the doctor. The Court said the Target had failed to make the doctor "aware that she was 'not a person of ordinary temperament' or that she was 'peculiarly susceptible to emotional distress by reason of some physical or mental condition or peculiarity.'" In other words, she was obligated to state during the hiring process that if she were to be abused in the work environment by the physician, she might suffer stress-related harm. How ridiculous is that? All of the burden falls on the Target, none on the employer!

You can see the problem with courts being the only forum to which bullied individuals are expected to turn for relief from unbearable emotional, physical, and economic damage using IIED.

## The First "Bullying Trial" in the United States

On October 25, 2001, Joe Doescher, who was acting as a perfusionist in an open-heart surgery being performed by Dr. Beth Ashworth at St. Francis Hospital in Beech Grove, Indiana, left during the surgery to attend to personal business. As a perfusionist, Mr. Doescher operated the "heart/lung" machine that kept the patient alive during the surgery. Prior to the beginning of the procedure, Doescher had arranged for Jennifer Lee, another perfusionist, to fill in for him after his departure. The combination of Doescher's absence, Jennifer Lee's commitment as Doescher's replacement, and the involvement of the third perfusionist, Joe Borondy, in a scheduled surgery left the hospital with no available perfusionists for a short amount of time. Accordingly, Dr. Dan Raess, who was a cardiac surgeon at St. Francis, was not immediately able to conduct an emergency heart surgery. Raess became angry and yelled at both Lee and Borondy.

The following day Joe Borondy told Joe Doescher about Raess's outburst. Doescher testified that he then resigned his Chief Perfusionist position as a form of "protest." However, Doescher continued working as a staff perfusionist at the hospital.

On November 2, 2001, Joe Doescher acted as a perfusionist in a surgery performed by Raess. Afterward, Raess approached Doescher to talk about "coverage issues" such as the one caused by Doescher's previous absence. Doescher informed Raess that he was no longer Chief Perfusionist and that coverage issues were not his concern. The two men separated without further discussion.

Later in the day, Doescher and Raess were together in the "pump room" located between the operating rooms in the hospital's open-heart surgery area. An argument ensued and Raess became angry, causing his body to stiffen, his face to turn red, and his jugular vein to extend. Raess walked toward Doescher and exited out the door close to Doescher. At trial, Doescher testified that Raess walked toward him in a manner that caused Doescher to think that Raess was going to "smack the s*** out of me." Doescher also testified that although Raess's balled fists were at his side, Raess's demeanor and purposeful walk caused Doescher to back up against the wall and raise his hands in defense. Doescher then declared an end to the conversation, and Raess walked out after yelling, "You're over. You're history. You're finished." Doescher further testified that he felt assaulted because of "the advancement, the look in [Raess's] eye, [and] his body positioning."

After the November 2, 2001, incident, Doescher testified that he became depressed and anxious, exhibited heightened anxiety, developed sleep problems, and experienced loss of appetite. Doescher further testified that he lost his confidence and did not return to his position as a staff perfusionist. Doescher presented medical experts who testified as to Doescher's mental and physical health.

On June 26, 2002, Doescher filed a complaint against Raess for assault, intentional infliction of emotional distress (IIED), and intentional interference with his employment relationship. The trial court entered summary judgment in Raess's favor, dismissed the intentional interference with an employment relationship claim, and the suit went to trial on the remaining issues.

Prior to the jury trial, Raess filed a motion in limine seeking to preclude any witness, including any expert witness, from giving testimony depicting Raess as a "workplace bully." Raess also filed a motion to exclude the testimony of Doescher's "workplace bully" expert, Dr. Gary Namie. The trial court ruled that Namie could testify that Raess was a workplace bully as to Doescher, but not "against the world." Over Raess's objection, Namie testified that the November 2, 2001, altercation was an "episode of workplace bullying" and that Raess is "a workplace abuser... a person who subjected [Doescher] to an abusive work environment."

The six-person jury found for Raess on the intentional infliction of emotional distress claim and for Doescher on the assault claim. It awarded damages of $325,000, based on Raess's guilt for assaulting Doescher. [*Doescher v. Raess*, Marion Superior Court, Indianapolis, IN, No. 49D01-0206-PL-1116, Cale Bradford, Judge, March 2005]

Raess's attorneys appealed the trial court decision principally because of the testimony that Raess was a "workplace bully" and the fact that Doescher's attorney had referenced "workplace bullying" in both his opening and closing statements to the jury.

Quoting the Appellate Court: "Assuming, without deciding, that the trial court correctly determined that Doescher presented evidence sufficient to establish Namie's opinion was based on reliable scientific principles, we still must address the issue of whether the probative value of the testimony is substantially outweighed by the danger of unfair prejudice, confusion of issues, and/or misleading the jury. Here, the question of whether Raess is a 'workplace bully,' as it pertains to the ultimate issue of whether Raess committed assault or intentional infliction of emotional distress, is relevant only to the extent that it bears on Doescher's perceptions at the time of his argument with Raess. Given Doescher's admission that he had no prior fear of Raess, the probative value of Namie's testimony is nil. On the other hand, Namie's testimony labels Raess as a bad person, a 'workplace bully' who commits assault. Even as limited by the trial court, Namie's testimony allowed the jury to infer that Raess committed assault because that is what 'bullies' do." [*Raess v. Doescher*, Indiana Court of Appeals, No. 49A02-0506-CV-490, December 8, 2006]

However, the Indiana Supreme Court heard oral arguments on October 10, 2007, and rendered its 3–1 decision on March 8, 2008. The Court reversed the appeal and reinstated the original trial verdict and award in Joe Doescher's favor.

Before trial, the defendant filed motions in limine to exclude Dr. Namie's testimony and to prevent him and any other witness from offering testimony or evidence depicting or referring to the defendant as a "workplace bully."

Quoting the Supreme Court transcript: "... the trial court likely understood the defendant's 'not qualified' objection to be claiming that Dr. Namie wasn't qualified, due to his failure to personally interview the defendant and due to the witness's unusual professional function as a consultant rather than a diagnostician. We find nothing in the trial court colloquy to have informed the trial judge of the claim that Dr. Namie's testimony was based upon unreliable scientific principles, that it violated Evidence Rule 702, or that it would not assist the jury to determine a fact in issue.... In determining whether the defendant (Raess) assaulted the plaintiff (Doescher) or committed intentional infliction of emotional distress, the behavior of the defendant was very much an issue. The phrase 'workplace bullying,' like other general terms used to characterize a person's behavior, is an entirely appropriate consideration in determining the issues before the jury. As evidenced by the trial court's questions to counsel during pre-trial proceedings, workplace bullying could 'be considered a form of intentional infliction of emotional distress.'" [*Raess v. Doescher*, Indiana Supreme Court No. 49S02-0710-CV-424, April 8, 2008]

## The Needed Anti-Bullying Healthy Workplace Bill

It is David Yamada's contention that new laws are necessary that extend the protection against hostile workplaces to all individuals, regardless of membership in a "protected class." Existing anti-harassment and anti-discrimination state and federal laws require the mistreatment to be based on gender, race, religious creed, color, national origin, ancestry, physical disability, mental disability, medical condition, marital status, sex, age, or sexual orientation. The recipient must be protected, but legal complications abound when the harasser is also protected—as in woman-on-woman bullying. We know from the WBI-Zogby Survey that 61 percent of bullying is same-gender harassment. Therefore, most bullying is legal. Discrimination laws apply in only one out of five situations.

The history of IIED decisions and the proposal for new public policies comprise Yamada's article published by the *Georgetown Law Journal* in Spring 2000—"The Phenomenon of 'Workplace Bullying' and the Need for Status-Blind Hostile Work Environment Protection."

Based on Professor Yamada's work, we heeded the call for new and specific anti-bullying legislation. He wrote the text for state legislatures, which we dubbed the *Healthy Workplace Bill*. It precisely defines abusive conduct, malice, health harm, and negative employment decisions (economic harm such as termination, demotion, unfavorable assignments). It states that it shall be unlawful to subject an employee to an abusive work environment that results in health or economic harm. It's an anti-bullying bill that when passed into law will not even contain the term "workplace bullying" in the text.

The *Healthy Workplace Bill* is employer-friendly, not a draconian anti-employer piece of legislation as the opposing business lobbyists portray it to be. It does not mandate any government regulation of businesses. Instead it dangles the threat of financial penalties for employers who do not bother to prevent or correct bullying. Simultaneously, employers who voluntarily do the right thing by not ignoring bullying will be rewarded with an escape from liability clause. Thus, the goal of the bill is to get employers to create and enforce anti-bullying policies without being sued to do so.

Good employers will use the law to purge themselves of bullies whose conduct will now be indefensible, regardless of how well liked he or she may be by the CEO. Reluctant employers who choose to support bullies over Targets should fear litigation.

The Drs. Namie, with Professor Yamada's brilliantly crafted language in hand, accompanied by articulate veteran Targets (initially Carrie Clark and Moe Tyler) as citizen lobbyists educated California lawmakers about workplace bullying. The first bill in the nation was introduced in 2003 in California. As fate would have it, the curious political ascendancy of Arnold Schwarzenegger cowed California Democrats into subservience, and the bill was ignored.

WBI started a new organization, the WBI-Legislative Campaign, to standardize our approach to lawmakers and to call for volunteer citizen lobbyists from throughout the country to help in their states. Super lobbyists are designated as Coordinators and spearhead local efforts by organizing repeated trips to the state capitols. They repeat the message loud and often to new and veteran lawmakers until the *Healthy*

*Workplace Bill* is introduced by cooperative sponsors. Affiliated groups have formed in several states—the California Healthy Workplace Advocates were first and they have their own website. New York State followed, and in the province of Ontario another group is underway.

As of this writing, thirteen U.S. states have introduced some version of the Workplace Bullying Institute-Legislative Campaign's anti-bullying *Healthy Workplace Bill*. Both Republican and Democratic sponsors have carried the bill. It has passed several committees (video of hearings can be viewed at the WBI-LC website), but has not yet become law.

Why no U.S. anti-bullying law for workers yet?

Strong business lobbyists led by state Chambers of Commerce are organized, effective opponents of workers' rights.

- they contribute to candidates election campaigns (which we do not), buying credibility
- they blackmail states by threatening to move companies and jobs to another state if lawmakers dare to regulate or hold accountable employers with unsafe business practices
- they falsely brand the anti-bullying *Healthy Workplace Bill* (HWB) a "job killer"
- they define all workers' complaints as potentially "frivolous" lawsuits
- they claim that current laws are adequate, that "hostile work environment" is actionable by everyone (it is not)
- they misrepresent the bill by claiming that the HWB will mandate compliance (it specifically does not)
- they used to claim that bullying did not exist; now they admit it happens but implore lawmakers to allow employers to deal with it voluntarily, to just be patient, more time is needed...

Weakened unions deprive lawmakers from hearing the workers' perspective.

- unions are too busy struggling to survive (only 7.5 percent of non-government workers are unionized); a quality of work issue like bullying is easy to ignore
- unions are ambivalent; member-on-member bullying paralyzes unions

Widespread misunderstanding about the phenomenon.

- confusion of serious, health-harming abusive conduct (in the HWB) with incivility, rudeness, awkward glances, an inadvertent slighting of one person by another, which is not bullying
- the erroneous belief that bullying cannot be defined precisely ("bullying" does not appear in the HWB)

Occupational health/epidemiological research findings are undervalued.

- the well-established scientific literature buried in obscure academic journals remains inaccessible to politicians who respond to crises and societal issues that dominate headlines, little else
- most of the studies originate in Europe; state lawmakers tend to be Euro-phobes, or at least to discount findings from other countries
- the necessary conservatism of scientists (refusal to draw causal conclusions in non-experimental studies such as surveys based on self-report data) is misportrayed and exploited as equivocation by political opponents

Political partisanship.

- though bullying ignores membership in political parties when it finds its targets, pro-worker protections are rarely supported by Republican lawmakers (though we have had Republican prime sponsors for the HWB)
- workers' rights, women's rights, and human rights have been defined as "liberal" issues, a label tainted from thirty years of right-wing reactionary mudslinging
- to date, committee votes on the HWB follow strictly partisan lines

## A Post-Bullying Opportunity

For Targets who have sufficiently recovered from the distress or trauma of their personal bullying experience, working to pass a law in your state or province can be healing and invigorating volunteer work. It is a way to work for the justice you were denied. Inquire at the WBI-LC website (www.workplacebullyinglaw.org).

If any employment law is to provide genuine protection for employees, it must force employers to take seriously the problem addressed in the law. Without laws like the one proposed by the WBI-LC, employers can discount, denigrate, and deny complainants whose harassment is horrific but not quite illegal. The truth is that until there is a law, employers do nothing. The way our law can affect millions of bullied Targets is to compel employers to notice bullying and to do something about it.

Thanks to the American media obsession with success mantras—"globalization," "competitiveness," and "productivity"—our attention gets diverted from the mistreatment of colleagues at work. We are bamboozled into mistaking the Dow Jones average for an index of the national mood, while completely ignoring personal accomplishments that feed our souls rather than our pocketbooks.

Let's recruit competition to do some good. The United States had better catch up with the rest of the world to stop bullying as a demonstration of America's parallel leadership in the arenas of economic dominance and compassion for those who do the work!

Another distraction is the widely popular comic strip *Dilbert*, where many of the problems with the cubicled world are sketched. Scott Adams, the creator, populates his strip with idiot bosses, idiot co-workers, and names of the latest management fads foisted on unsuspecting workers. It's great to laugh. Newspaper columnist Norman Solomon's book, *The Trouble with Dilbert*, takes the comic's popularity as proof that employees recognize that the way corporations currently operate has to change (we assume this would include stopping bullies). The tragedy, according to Solomon, is while fans vent their anger, they only symbolically thumb their nose at the boss or employee without taking any real steps to improve their workplace.

We interpret *Dilbert*'s popularity as proof of the number of people facing frustrating problems at work. It's a problem of immense size.

## U.S. Courts Frown on Employees

The least helpful people on your side are judges and juries. Do not believe employer groups who warn their members that frivolous lawsuits brought by disgruntled employees will put owners out of business.

According to this type of disinformation propaganda, cases that bottleneck the courts are filed by fun-loving employees who suffered nothing more than irreparable "personality conflicts" with benevolent, but misunderstood, bosses. This is pure fiction, a mythology that unites business owners and large employers against employees.

Here are some facts that should buoy employer confidence in the court system. At the same time, it should scare the hell out of an employee like you who deserves legal redress for suffering at the hands of a workplace bully.

- There's been a steady decline in the number of class action suits against employers filed by the Equal Employment Opportunity Commission (EEOC), the federal agency responsible for ensuring that the federally protected classes of employees are not discriminated against. In 1976, 1,174 suits were filed. The anemic, understaffed EEOC had only 68 class-action cases active in 1996.

- How about those costly accommodations for the disabled? The *Americans with Disabilities Act* (ADA) was supposed to drive many large companies out of business. On the contrary, it was found that Sears spent an average of only $45 per person to adjust the workplace to meet the needs of seventy-one workers. Not a budget buster, if done wisely!

- Sexual harassment is not the plague employers portray it to be. A recent study by the University of Illinois found that despite efforts by women's groups to educate the public, few women who are harassed, according to the legal definition, recognize it. Fewer report it and fewer still file a claim.

- In 1994, the median jury award in a sexual harassment case was $100,500. The median award granted to those who claimed job discrimination in federal court was $100,000.

- The number of people who actually file a claim with the EEOC for discrimination of any kind is less than six in ten thousand employees.

- The 1991 *Civil Rights Act* made possible both jury trials and punitive damages for discrimination cases. For the dozen years prior to the act, just 24 percent of the cases went before a jury. Employees (plaintiffs) won 24 percent of the time. Between 1991 and 1995, the employee win rate crept up to 30 percent despite a doubling of the percentage of cases heard by juries. Still, less than half the cases ever go before a jury!

Do the math. Employees 30, Employers 70. Who wins? A most unsettling comparison is made by Theodore Eisenberg, a Cornell University law professor stating that "job discrimination cases remain one of the single most unsuccessful classes of litigation for plaintiffs. They settle less and lose more than almost anything else." The only class of complaints with a lower success rate is the one filed by prisoners.

- Pre-trial settlements are not typically expensive for employers. True, the amounts paid by Texaco ($176 million), Publix Markets ($80 million), and Home Depot ($80+ million) grab headlines and fuel employer apprehension. The statistical reality is much different. A methodical analysis of wrongful termination cases in California courts during a recent seven-year period resulted in the following: 17 percent were dropped, costing employers on the average of less than $500; 40 percent were settled before a trial, costing an average of $60,000 including attorneys' fees.
- As always, headlines are deceiving. Dramatic awards like $50 million to a single Wal-Mart employee are often drastically reduced on appeal. In that 1995 case, $50 million became $385,000. Judges often set aside jury generosity.

A rare, true success story:

*Carla was fresh out of graduate school and eager to launch a research career. She won a low-paying position at the massive, prestigious state university working for a scholar with an international reputation in her field. Carla loved research more than teaching; it was her calling. She planned on a decades-long career collecting data, authoring journal articles, writing books, giving symposia, the flurry of activities that announced that this academic had made a mark in her field.*

*Then, the highly esteemed scholar-boss asked Carla for her shoebox of raw data for a certain project. Not thinking twice, she handed it over. There was some talk of publishing articles based on the data, but Carla began to feel left out of activities. The boss refused to return Carla's data when asked. When the scholar-boss's boss was told about the theft, he threatened to fire Carla if she continued to complain. She did and he fired her. For four years, Carla was without a full-time academic job to replace the one stolen from her. She taught courses on campus on a part-time basis, while simultaneously pleading with university administration to retrieve her data and give her job back.*

*At the end of the fifth year, she finally took the two supervising professors—the thief and the hatchet man—to court. A jury found them guilty of theft and illegal retaliation (see what can be done when a lawyer can see possibilities beyond the narrow scope of the law against discrimination). The initial jury award for damages was over $1.5 million. The university legal eagles dug in and appealed. It took a total of ten years from the date of the original bullying acts before the case ran its course through the appeals process. The university never gave up, nor did it ever acknowledge* *blame. The thief and hatchet man still work there. Carla has completely given up on the academe. But, she finally got her award... with interest!*

# Toward an American Legal Solution for Bullying

The law is attentive to harassment or discrimination when it relates to sex and race. Title VII of the 1964 (revised in 1991) *Civil Rights Act* created "protected classes" of individuals. Members of protected classes have a lower burden of proof than members of other groups when harassment or discrimination is claimed.

Many ostensibly "disadvantaged" individuals who harass others consider themselves immune to punishment for their deeds. Protected class members are often the worst bullies. Too often, they threaten lawsuits, based on race or gender, to scare away co-workers and employers who want them to stop harassing. The classic formula is for a woman or minority bully to shout discrimination as Targets or responsible employers begin countermeasures. Organizations then settle for cash with the bully, allowing her to stay on the job and force the Target to leave. The message sent is that the bully has the full backing of the organization, and gets paid for tyranny, backed by U.S. federal law.

## *Relevant U.S. Supreme Court Rulings*

There is little reason for optimism that a federal prohibition of general harassment is forthcoming. In fact, in the 1998 season of rulings by the U.S. Supreme Court, there were three rulings relevant to bullying. All focused exclusively on pervasive, hostile workplaces created by sexual harassment.

On June 26, the Court ruled on two cases putting employers on notice that they can be held responsible for misconduct by supervisors even if they knew nothing about it. Legally speaking, these were rulings on the issue of "vicarious liability."

Buried deep in the legalese of the rulings was evidence about how the Court defines the employer-employee relationship. In both rulings, references were made to the employer as "master" and the employed harassing supervisor as the "servant who purported to act or speak on behalf of the principal and… reliance on apparent authority, or he was aided in accomplishing the tort (wrongdoing) by the existence of the agency relation." Master-servant terminology at the new millennium in the United States? This is a huge hurdle to overcome if the dreams for employee dignity of Justice Brandeis are ever to be realized.

The good news appears in the following excerpt from the Beth Ann Faragher decision. She was sexually harassed while working for the city of Boca Raton, Florida, as a lifeguard. The Court held the city "liable for the harassment of its supervisory employees because the harassment was pervasive enough to support an inference that the city had 'knowledge, or constructive knowledge' of it; under traditional agency (that master-servant hierarchy reference again) principles… and a third supervisor had knowledge of the harassment and failed to report it to city officials."

Both rulings by the Court said employees have to first "take advantage of any preventive or corrective opportunities provided." This is exactly what we tell those who seek our advice to counter bullying. Comply, in a minimal way, with the frustrating internal procedures to protect all future claims—unfortunately, at this stage, complying with the system is a necessary evil. The worst thing a Target can do is to keep secret all that she is going through.

If a complaint is filed, thus providing "constructive knowledge," then the employer is liable for the mistreatment. Because of this, more credence is now being given to "hostile environment" cases (as long as it is outlawed by the *Civil Rights Act*). Much of the repeated mistreatment that characterizes bullying relies on a poisoned, sick workplace to permit and sustain the madness.

However, the Supreme Court's March 1998 decision dimmed hope that harassment's definition will ever be broadened by the Court. Justice Antonin Scalia, writing for the unanimous Court in the

*Oncale* decision, explicitly stated the law "does not prohibit all verbal or physical harassment in the workplace.... And there is another requirement that prevents Title VII from expanding into a general civility code... the statute does not reach genuine but innocuous differences in the ways men and women routinely interact.

"Common sense and an appropriate sensitivity to social context will enable courts and juries to distinguish between simple teasing or roughhousing... and conduct which a reasonable person in the plaintiff's position would find severely hostile or abusive."

This means the Court turned away from using discrimination law to enforce a general code of civility banning all workplace harassment. Looking from the top down, rather than through the eyes of a bullied Target, much harassment looks "innocuous," like mere personality conflicts.

A *Washington Post* editorial reaction to the Court's ruling saw the coupling of harassment to discrimination as missing the point. The *Post* called for Congress to write specific anti-harassment laws that do not require sex, race, or national origin protections, but instead require only that a work environment be sufficiently abusive. The editorial stated, "what bothers people about abusive workplace conduct, after all, is not the fact that it may be discriminatory but that it is abusive in the first place."

Employers see themselves as "reasonable people" who can then define a harasser's conduct as hostile rather than the simple teasing of a Target who needs to have thicker skin. Stephen Bokat, spokesman for the National Chamber Litigation Center, the business defense arm for the U.S. Chamber of Commerce, believed the ruling would actually make it easier for employers to defend themselves. He felt that more complaints will be dismissed as boisterous horseplay or casual flirting.

Bokat trivialized workplace harassment and discrimination problems with a glib comment to the Associated Press, "I don't think it happens that often."

*Appendix A:*

# U.S. Workplace Bullying Survey—September 2007

**B**ULLYING**G** WORKPLACE INSTITUTE™    Zogby International

## Research Report Contents

Polling of adult Americans by Zogby International, sponsored by a generous gift from the Waitt Institute for Violence Prevention, Cindy Waitt, Executive Director

## 1. Methodology and Sample Characteristics

### Methodology

Zogby International conducted online interviews of 7,740 adults. A sampling of Zogby International's online panel, which is representative of the adult population of the U.S., was invited to participate. The online poll ran from August 10, 2007, through August 13, 2007. The margin of error is +/−1.1 percentage points. Margins of error are higher in sub-groups. Slight weights were added to region, party, age, race, religion, and gender to more accurately reflect the population.

| Sample Characteristics | Frequency | Valid Percent* |
|---|---|---|
| Sample size | 7,740 | 100% |
| East | 1,721 | 23 |
| South | 1,946 | 26 |
| Central/Great Lakes | 2,320 | 31 |
| West | 1,497 | 20 |
| Did not answer region | 256 | — |
| 18-29 | 1,543 | 20 |
| 30-49 | 3,087 | 40 |
| 50-64 | 1,775 | 23 |
| 65+ | 1,312 | 17 |
| Did not answer age | 23 | — |
| White | 5,728 | 75 |
| Hispanic | 764 | 10 |
| African American | 840 | 11 |
| Asian/Pacific | 153 | 2 |
| Other/mixed | 153 | 2 |
| Did not answer race | 103 | — |
| Roman Catholic | 2,033 | 27 |
| Protestant | 3,765 | 50 |
| Jewish | 226 | 3 |
| Other/None (religion) | 1,506 | 20 |
| Did not answer religion | 210 | — |
| Member of union | 1,440 | 19 |
| Not member of union | 6,179 | 81 |
| Parent of child under 17 | 2,026 | 27 |

| Sample Characteristics | Frequency | Valid Percent* |
|---|---|---|
| Not parent of child under 17 | 5,599 | 73% |
| Married | 4,615 | 61 |
| Single, never married | 1,642 | 22 |
| Divorced/widowed/separated | 1,052 | 14 |
| Civil union/ domestic partnership | 284 | 4 |
| Did not answer marital status | 147 | — |
| Less than $25,000 | 468 | 7 |
| $25,000–$34,999 | 604 | 9 |
| $35,000–$49,999 | 967 | 14 |
| $50,000–$74,999 | 1,612 | 24 |
| $75,000–$99,999 | 1,208 | 18 |
| $100,000 or more | 1,848 | 28 |
| Did not answer income | 1,034 | — |
| Male | 3,664 | 48 |
| Female | 3,938 | 52 |
| Did not answer gender | 138 | — |
| Women—work outside home | 2,297 | 59 |
| Women—no work outside home | 1,578 | 41 |
| Works full-time | 3,925 | 51 |
| Part-time | 483 | 6 |
| Self-employed | 855 | 11 |
| Unemployed | 360 | 5 |
| Retired | 1,496 | 19 |
| Student, not working | 293 | 4 |
| Other employment/Not sure | 329 | 4 |

\* **Numbers have been rounded to the nearest percent and might not total 100.**

*Which of the following best describes your employment status?*

| | |
|---|---|
| Full-time | 51% |
| Retired | 19 |
| Self-employed **(Survey ends)** | 11 |
| Part-time | 6 |
| Unemployed | 5 |
| Student, not working **(Survey ends)** | 4 |
| Other/not sure **(Survey ends)** | 4 |

# 2. <u>U.S. Prevalence Statistics</u>

**2a.) 37% of American Workers have been bullied at work; nearly half (49%) of adult Americans are affected by it, either through direct experience or by witnessing it.**

*Question:* At work, have you experienced or witnessed any or all of the following types of repeated mistreatment: sabotage by others that prevented work from getting done, verbal abuse, threatening conduct, intimidation, humiliation?

| Responses | Percentage | Rounding |
|---|---|---|
| Yes, I am experiencing it now or have in the last year | 12.6% | 13% |
| Yes, it has happened to me in my work life, but not now or in the last year | 24.2 | 24 |
| I've only witnessed it | 12.3 | 12 |
| I've been the perpetrator myself | 0.4 | (n = 22) |
| Never had it happen to me and never witnessed it | 44.9 | 45 |

Bullying affects individuals who are directly, currently under assault. However, it also continues to affect them unless the mistreatment is corrected in a way that is perceived as just and fair. Thus, the bullying experience lingers. It is fair to say that **37% of American workers have been bullied, combining the current + ever bullied categories.**

According to the Bureau of Labor Statistics (U.S. Department of Labor), 146 million Americans were employed in July 2007. An estimated **54 million Americans have been bullied at work** using the 37% rate. Even the more conservative 13% rate (those currently or within the last year experiencing it) places 19 million American workers at risk. It's an epidemic.

Witnessing the humiliation and degradation of others can be vicariously traumatizing. Therefore, it is a conservative statement to say that **bullied individuals and witnesses** are all affected by bullying. In our survey, **nearly half of adult Americans (49.1%)** reported these experiences.

Extrapolating the BLS employment estimate to the total of bullied people + witnesses—**71.5 million workers** can be estimated to be affected by bullying.

Significant differences in reported experiences of different racial groups emerged. The comparison of combined bullying (current + ever bullied) prevalence percentages reveals the pattern from most to least:

| Combined Bullying | Percentage | Rounding |
|---|---|---|
| Hispanics | 52.1% | 52% |
| African Americans | 46 | 46 |
| Whites | 33.5 | 34 |
| Asian Americans | 30.6 | 31 |

The reported rates of <u>only witnessing</u> bullying were:

| Witnessing Only | Percentage | Rounding |
|---|---|---|
| African Americans | 21.1% | 21% |
| Hispanics | 14 | 14 |
| Whites | 10.8 | 11 |
| Asian Americans | 8.5 | 9 |

The percentages of those claiming to have <u>neither experienced nor witnessed</u> mistreatment were among:

| Never Experienced It, Never Witnessed It | Percentage | Rounding |
|---|---|---|
| Asian Americans | 57.3% | 57% |
| Whites | 49.7 | 50 |
| Hispanics | 32.2 | 32 |
| African Americans | 23.4 | 23 |

Slight differences in bullying experience rates occurred across <u>age groups</u>. The likelihood that a person ever experienced bullying naturally increased with age:

| Bullied in Worklife | Percentage | Rounding |
|---|---|---|
| 50–64 | 29.7% | 30% |
| 30–49 | 25.5 | 26 |
| 18–29 | 18.7 | 19 |

Conversely, the rates of <u>currently experiencing bullying or within the last year</u> were:

| Currently Bullied (<12 mths) | Percentage | Rounding |
|---|---|---|
| 18–29 | 18.5% | 19% |
| 30–49 | 16.8 | 17 |
| 50–64 | 9.9 | 10 |

The rates of never witnessing or experiencing bullying were relatively constant across the groups.

A pattern of differences across <u>U.S. geographical regions</u> also emerged. The combined prevalence rates were as follows:

| Combined Bullying | Percentage | Rounding |
|---|---|---|
| West | 41.1% | 41% |
| South | 37.5 | 38 |
| East | 34.9 | 35 |
| Central/Great Lakes | 26.3 | 26 |

<u>Self-identification by political party</u> seemed to affect prevalence reporting rates. The comparison of combined bullying (current + ever bullied) prevalence percentages reveals this pattern:

| Combined Bullying | Percentage | Rounding |
|---|---|---|
| Democrats | 42.8% | 43% |
| Independents | 39.1 | 39 |
| Republicans | 28.9 | 29 |

There was wide variation among the <u>never saw it or experienced it</u> rates across political party self-identification:

| Never Experienced It, Never Witnessed It | Percentage | Rounding |
|---|---|---|
| Republicans | 56.6% | 57% |
| Independents | 43.2 | 43 |
| Democrats | 35.8 | 36 |

The overall finding that 45% of Americans claim to not have experienced or seen workplace bullying emboldens the Institute's resolve that more public education must occur. As was true in the domestic violence movement, observers stayed in denial because of the personal discomfort or fear that acknowledging battering a spouse can arouse. After DV's criminalization, people felt freer to talk, appropriately blaming the perpetrator. Anecdotally, we believe workplace bullying is a "silent epidemic," a view confirmed by the ILO (International Labor Organization, a UN agency). It is an "undiscussable" topic at work because of its career-jeopardizing potential. Eventually, the shame and fear associated with it will diminish and bullying will lose its taboo status. Over time, it will be easier to speak about its occurrence and to shame its perpetrators to stop.

**2b.) Most (54%) bullying involves public humiliation of targets; 32% of bullying happens behind closed doors.**

*Question:* Where did the majority of the mistreatment occur?

| Responses | Percentage | Rounding |
|---|---|---|
| Out in the open, in front of others | 53.9% | 54% |
| Behind closed doors, in silence | 31.6 | 32 |
| Behind doors kept open so others could hear | 10.2 | 10 |
| Not sure | 4.3 | 4 |

Perhaps the choice by bullies to hide much of the bullying accounts for the 45% of the public who report to have never seen it.

Gender differences among bullies emerged. Men bullies more than women bullies prefer public bullying (57.8% vs. 48.6%). And women bullies prefer to bully behind closed doors (47.2% vs. 38.3%).

# 3. Gender and Bullying

**3a.) Both men and women are bullies; women are targeted more frequently.**

*Question:* What is the gender of the person primarily responsible for the mistreatment?

*Question:* What is the gender of the person targeted for mistreatment?

|  | **Men** | **Women** |
|---|---|---|
| Gender of the Perpetrators, Bullies | 60% | 40% |
| Gender of Targeted Individuals | 43.3 | 56.7 |
| When the bully is a woman, she targets... | 28.7 | 71.3 |
| When the bully is a man, he targets... | 53.5 | 46.5 |

Note that women prefer to bully other women, 2.5 times more frequently than they target men. Men divide their cruelty, showing a slight preference toward same-gender harassment.

In rank order, from most to least frequent, these are the gender pairings with respect to bullying at work.

| **Categories** | **Percentage** | **Rounding** |
|---|---|---|
| Male who bullies a male target, **Man-on-Man**, same gender | 32.1% | 32% |
| Female who bullies a female target, **Woman-on-Woman**, same gender | 28.5 | 29 |
| Male who bullies a female target, **Man-on-Woman** | 27.9 | 28 |
| Female who bullies a male target, **Woman-on-Man** | 11.4 | 11 |

**3b.)** Most, **68% of bullies, operate alone**, at least in the beginning.

*Question:* Did the harasser work alone or were there several people involved in the mistreatment?

| Responses | Percentage | Rounding |
|---|---|---|
| Solo harasser | 68.4% | 68% |
| Several harassers | 26.7 | 27 |
| Not sure | 4.9 | 5 |

Slight gender differences apply. Women bullies are slightly more likely than men bullies to enlist the help of others to "gang up" on their targets.

# 4. Bullying: A Different Kind of Harassment

When we say "harassment," most of us automatically think of sexual harassment, which we all know is illegal by state and federal laws. In order for harassment to be illegal and actionable in court, the recipient/victim/target's civil rights must be violated. Further, that person must be a member of a recognized "protected status" group. In the U.S., there are seven Civil Rights protected status groups (with gender and race most prominent) to which a person may belong in order to file a discrimination complaint or lawsuit. In addition, discrimination is prohibited if age or disability can be shown to be the reasons for the harassment. Illegal harassment is status based.

Bullying cuts across boundaries of status group membership. Bullying is status-blind harassment. It must be distinguished from illegal varieties of harassment. Bullying happens when harassment is same-gender or same-race or when the bully enjoys potential legal protection because he or she is a member of a status-protected group.

**4a.) Bullying is four times more prevalent than illegal, discriminatory harassment.** (Based on the 80:20 ratio in which only 20% of cases would the targeted person have been eligible for a potential discrimination complaint or lawsuit.) **Bullies enjoy civil rights protection in 31% of all cases.** And from WBI's anecdotal experience, they are the ones to threaten employers with lawsuits to stop investigations or attempts to curb the mistreatment.

*Question:* Sometimes mistreatment is based on discrimination due to race, gender, ethnicity, religion, disability, or age. Based on those categories, some people enjoy protected status by law. Now considering the mistreatment you endured, witnessed, or participated in, compare the target's status regarding membership in a protected group with that of the harasser's status.

| Responses | Percentage | Rounding |
|---|---|---|
| The **target only** is in a protected group | 20.2% | 20% |
| **Neither** harasser nor target are in protected group | 40.2 | 40 |
| Harasser and target were/are **both** in protected group | 16.7 | 17 |
| The harasser only is in a protected group | 14 | 14 |
| Not Sure | 9 | 9 |

4b.) Employers must respond appropriately when employment laws exist. Since bullying is not currently illegal, how do employers react to bullying? **In 62% of cases when employers are made aware of bullying, they escalate the problem for the target or simply do**

**nothing.** Doing nothing is not a neutral act when an individual explicitly asks for help. When nothing is done, the employer becomes the bully's accomplice, whether deliberately or inadvertently, by allowing it to continue unabated. In less than a third of situations, employers rendered help.

*Question:* When the mistreatment was reported, what did the employer do? (Asked only of those who said the targeted person filed a complaint or lawsuit, or complained informally.)

| Employer Action | Percentage | Rounding |
|---|---|---|
| Did nothing | 43.7% | 44% |
| Worsened the problem for the target | 18.4 | 18 |
| Completely or partially resolved the problem in a way that helped the target | 31.9 | 32 |
| Not sure | 6 | 6 |

Gender differences occurred. Men bullies were more likely than women bullies to enjoy employer protection by having the organization do nothing in response to reported mistreatment (47.5% vs. 38.8%).

# 5. Bullying Is Top-Down

**5a.)** Not all bosses are bullies, but most bullies are bosses. **72% of bullies are bosses.** The bully boss stereotype is real.

*Question:* What was the principal harasser's rank relative to the targeted person?

| Responses | Percentage | Rounding |
|---|---|---|
| Harasser ranked higher (Boss) | 72.3% | 72% |
| Target and harasser same rank (Peer) | 17.7 | 18 |
| Harasser ranked lower (Subordinate) | 8.5 | 9 |

Slight gender differences surfaced. Women targets were bullied more by bosses (74.7% vs. 69%) and less by subordinates (6.1% vs. 11.6%) than men targets. Of the subordinate bullies, a higher percentage were women than men (9.5% vs. 7.8%) and men bullies were more likely to be bosses than women bullies (72.9% vs. 71.3%).

5b.) Bullies operate with confidence that they will not likely be punished because they enjoy support from higher-ups who can protect them if and when they are exposed. For those bullies to whom support is given (excluding the "No one" and "Not sure" categories), **43% of bullies have an executive sponsor**; 33% thrive because of support from their peers, mostly fellow managers; and 14% get help from human resources.

*Question:* Who supported the harasser? (Check all that apply)

| Responses | Raw Percentage | Rounding | Adj. Percentage |
|---|---|---|---|
| One or more senior managers or executives or owners | 35.2% | 35% | 43% |
| The harassers' peers | 26.7 | 27 | 33 |
| Human Resources | 11.2 | 11 | 14 |

| Responses | Raw Percentage | Rounding | Adj. Percentage |
|---|---|---|---|
| The target's peers | 7.8% | 8% | 10% |
| No one | 30.2 | 30 | |
| Not sure | 13 | 13 | |

There were no gender differences in support for bullies.

**5c.)** Bullying is primarily top-down. **Nonsupervisory employees are the most frequently bullied, accounting for 55% of the total,** with managers (from supervisors to mid-level to senior-level) second most frequently bullied (35%). Temps and contractors (whose livelihood is less vulnerable to an employer's control) represent only 5% of the bullied. Executives, Board members, and owners represented 4.8% of the bullied.

*Question:* What was the targeted person's position?

| Respondent Rank | Currently | Ever Bullied | Combined | Witness |
|---|---|---|---|---|
| Non-Supervisory Employees | 57.1% | 54.3% | 55.3% | 62.6% |
| Supv/Mid/ Senior Managers | 31.2 | 36.8 | 35 | 29.1 |
| Executives and Owners | 4.4 | 4.8 | 4.8 | 3.7 |
| Temps/ Contractors | 7.3 | 3.8 | 5 | 4.6 |

# 6. Tactics of Bullies

**6a.)** Bullies can be cruelly innovative. They often vary their tactics hour to hour, day to day. Survey respondents were asked to choose any or all families of tactics from the list provided.

*Question:* Please describe the forms of mistreatment (choose all that apply).

| Responses | Percentage | Rounding |
|---|---|---|
| **Verbal abuse** (shouting, swearing, name calling, malicious sarcasm, threats to safety, etc.) | 53.3% | 53% |
| **Behaviors/actions** (public or private) that were threatening, intimidating, humiliating, hostile, offensive, inappropriately cruel, etc. | 52.5 | 53 |
| **Abuse of authority** (undeserved evaluations, denial of advancement, stealing credit, tarnished reputation, arbitrary instructions, unsafe assignments, etc.) | 46.9 | 47 |
| **Interference with work performance** (sabotage, undermining, ensuring failure, etc.) | 45.4 | 45 |
| **Destruction of workplace relationships** (among co-workers, bosses, or customers) | 30.2 | 30 |

| Responses | Percentage | Rounding |
|---|---|---|
| Other (See list on next page) | 5.4% | 5% |
| Not sure | 0.5 | 1 |

*Other responses:* (Number in parentheses denotes frequency of similar response.) Sexual harassment, inappropriate contact/conduct/favors (39); Slander, lying misrepresentation, false accusation (20); Physical assault, battery, fighting (12); Reduced income, denying benefits (11); Fired, terminated employment without cause (10); Invasion of privacy, email abuse, identity theft (6); All of the above (6); Threaten job loss (5); Passive-aggressive, perform no work, incompetent (5); Religious prejudice/discrimination (4); Racial prejudice/discrimination (4); Age (2); Theft, took lunch money (2); Property damage, arson (2)

*One each:* Alcohol created unsafe work environment; Headhunting; Illegal drugs planted in target's vehicle; Subverted OSHA regulations

Slight gender differences surfaced. Men targets were more likely than women to experience verbal abuse (60.1% vs. 48.1%); women targets were sabotaged more frequently (47.1% vs. 43.1%). Women bullies more frequently than men engaged in sabotage (53.7% vs. 39.9%) and abuse of authority (50.2% vs. 44.7%); men bullies were more frequently verbally abusive than women bullies (57.5% vs. 47.1%).

**6b.) Why does bullying happen?** The preferred explanations focus on personality, the bully's and the target's. It's the American culture firmly rooted in individualism and myopia about invisible factors that have little to do with the players in the bullying drama. The overall result is **56% because of the bully's personality, 20% because of the target, only 14% because of the system, the work environment run by the employer.**

*Question:* Why was the target mistreated? Primarily because of...

| Responses | Percentage | Rounding |
|---|---|---|
| Some aspect of the **target's** personality | 12.8% | 13% |
| The **target's** unacceptable level of performance | 7 | 7 |
| Some aspect of the **harasser's** personality | 56.3 | 56 |
| The tolerance for, or admiration of, aggression in that particular workplace | 8.6 | 9 |
| Orders or suggestions from senior managers or executives or owners | 5.7 | 6 |
| Not sure | 9.7 | 10 |

Systemic causes of bullying include whether or not hyper-aggression is rewarded by promotions or forbidden. Survey respondents, however, only credited these types of factors with 14% responsibility.

The 20% responsibility attributed to the target is lower than the bully's responsibility (56%). There is still a tendency, however, to blame the victim somewhat for her or his fate, much like what was historically done for victims of domestic violence. The 20% could also reflect a societal desire to define bullying as a form of conflict with shared responsibility by the two parties. But in violent incidents, we do not make that assumption. Society realizes that perpetrators determine who is targeted, when, by what method, and for how long. Control is unilaterally driven by the aggressor. And so it is with bullying.

There were <u>gender differences</u> in the attribution of responsibility for bullying. Survey respondents held men more than women bullied targets more responsible for their fate (24.4% vs. 16.1%). When the bully was a woman, her negative personality was given more weight as a causal factor than when the bully was a man (62.4% vs. 52.1%). Also, the blame was shifted to systemic factors (see previous) that were assigned more responsibility when the bully was a man than when the bully was a woman (16.9% vs. 10.3%).

# 7. <u>Targets' Reactions</u>

**7a.) Bullied individuals rarely confront or act in an adversarial manner. They sued in only 3% of cases and filed a formal complaint in only 4% of cases, 38% *informally* notified their employers, and 40% did not even tell their employer.**

*Question:* What action did the targeted person undertake to solve the problem?

| Target Action | Percentage | Rounding |
|---|---|---|
| Took **no action,** formal or informal | 40.1% | 40% |
| Complained **informally** to employer/superior | 38.4 | 38 |
| Filed a **formal** complaint with Human Resources, senior management, or owner | 14.6 | 15 |
| Filed a **formal** discrimination complaint with a state or federal agency | 3.5 | 4 |
| Filed a **lawsuit** in court | 2.7 | 3 |

Other actions not counted in the percentages above: Retired, resigned, quit (64); Complained to union, filed grievance (45); Confronted harasser, attempted resolution (39); Stood up, fought back (28); Transferred, requested reassignment (22); Sought legal counsel, advice (15); Initiated job search, got a new job (14); Coped, minimized interaction, ignored harasser (13); Complained informally to peers (13); Worked hard/improved performance/good attitude (11); Joined class action group effort (11); Complained informally to state or federal agency (10); Harasser was fired, terminated (9); Sought support, EAP, outside help (8); Took responsibility, changed ways (7); Documented thoroughly, compiled copious notes (7); Medical leave, under Dr.'s care (6); Covert actions to expose harasser, make him look bad (4); Target fired, terminated (4); Called police, filed report (4); Truce, cease-fire, uneasy peace (3); Severely reprimanded/punished for complaining (2)

One each: Partied "when the bitch transferred"; He died

Some <u>gender differences</u> surfaced. Men targets were more likely than women to take no action (37% vs. 45.5%). Targets were more likely to informally complain to their employer when the bully was a woman than when a man (42.6% vs. 35.6%) and to do nothing when the bully was a man than when a woman (43.8% vs. 36%).

**7b.)** Bullying can occur with or without harming the health of the bullied individuals. However, when proposing legislation, WBI–Legislative Campaign State Coordinators insist on the proof that health has been harmed to provide a high standard to meet before legal action should be initiated. **For 45% of bullied targets, stress affected their health.**

*Question:* Did the mistreatment result in stress-related health complications, psychological or physical, for the targeted person?

| Stress-Related Health Impact? | Percentage | Rounding |
|---|---|---|
| Yes | 45.2% | 45% |
| No | 35.9 | 36 |
| Not Sure | 18.9 | 19 |

Large gender differences resulted. A higher percentage of bullied women suffered stress-related health harm than did men targets (52.6% vs. 35.6%). And women bullies inflicted more health harm than did men bullies (55.1% vs. 38.6%).

**7c.) How long does the bullying last?** In 75% of bullying cases, mistreatment was experienced repeatedly by targets. When the 25% of respondents who reported only nonrepeated mistreatment (only "once or twice") are negated, the adjusted percentages reflect that **73% of bullied targets endure bullying for more than six months, 44% for more than one year**

*Question:* How long did the mistreatment continue?

| Responses | Percentage | Rounding | Adj. Percentage |
|---|---|---|---|
| More than 12 months | 33.4% | 33% | 44% |
| 6–12 months | 21.6 | 22 | 29 |
| Less than six months | 20.3 | 20 | 27 |
| Just once or twice | 24.8 | 25 | — |
| | n = 3101 | | n = 2187 |

Critics of the phenomenon of workplace bullying and of bullied targets, in particular, posit that targets are "thin-skinned," "whining complainers." In reality, targets endure mistreatment for long periods of time. They do not readily flee. Staying in harm's way can contribute to the onset of emotional injuries from unremitting exposure to a stressful work environment.

# 8. Stopping It

**8a.) Targets lose their jobs to make the bullying stop in 77% of cases. Bullies bully with near impunity, experiencing negative consequences in only 23% of cases.**

*Question:* What stopped the mistreatment?

| Response | Percentage |
|---|---|
| It has not stopped | 17.2% |

The following response percentages exclude the 17% of respondents for whom the bullying is ongoing and the 26% of respondents who checked either "Not Sure" or "Other" (remaining n = 1763). Therefore, for the individuals for whom the bullying stopped, here is their report about what stopped it.

| Responses | Percentage |
|---|---|
| Target was terminated, driven out | 24.2% |
| Target voluntarily left the organization | 40 |
| Target transferred and stayed with the same employer | 13 |
| Target lost job, combined percentages = | 77 |

| Responses | Percentage |
|---|---|
| Target fired or quit, combined percentages = | 64% |
| Harasser stayed but was punished | 9 |
| Harasser was terminated | 14 |
| Negative consequences for bully, combined percentages = | 23 |

Bullying generates turnover. When 40% of bullied individuals quit, that represents the **preventable loss of 21.6 million workers** [based on the estimated 54 million who are bullied, Section 2, page 291] at a time when employers face critical shortages of skilled workers. Further, if one makes the conservative estimate that half of the bullied employees' terminations are the result of a bullying boss and not just cause separations, an additional 6.5 million employees lose their jobs to preventable bullying. The **total turnover estimate** attributable to bullying can be reasonably stated to be **28 million American workers**.

One gender difference in what stops bullying is that bullied women targets were more likely to quit than men (45% vs. 32.3%). WBI has found that the sooner targeted individuals restore safety by any means, the healthier they remain or the more quickly they recover from their injuries.

| Other Responses Reported | Percentage |
|---|---|
| Harasser voluntarily left company | 79% |
| Harasser transferred, stayed with employer | 44 |
| Target fought back | 36 |
| Confrontation, worked for resolution | 30 |
| I retired/quit | 30 |
| Issue resolved, it stopped | 24 |

| Other Responses Reported | Percentage |
|---|---|
| Harasser reprimanded, given serious warning | 18% |
| Medical leave, disability retirement | 17 |
| Legal action, lawsuit initiated | 16 |
| Truce, cease-fire, uneasy peace | 14 |
| Harasser was promoted | 14 |
| Target worked hard, improved performance, changed | 12 |
| Company closed | 11 |
| Minimized interaction, ignored harasser | 11 |
| Coworker intervention/counseling | 10 |
| Complained to union, filed grievance, arbitration | 10 |
| Equal treatment—Both fired/reassigned/disciplined | 9 |
| Reorganized/new management | 8 |
| Contract ended, project canceled | 7 |
| Time passage | 6 |
| I was promoted, transferred | 5 |
| Target was promoted | 5 |
| Sought help, EAP, rehab, time-off | 4 |
| Harasser died | 4 |

One each: Target died; Target committed suicide; Harasser arrested by police

© 2007, Workplace Bullying Institute

Citations of survey results must credit WBI

Research Director: Gary Namie, PhD—360-656-6630

# Employer and Co-worker Response Survey— Labor Day 2008

The **definition of bullying** used in the study:

*Question asked:* **At work, have you experienced any or all of the following types of repeated mistreatment: sabotage by others that prevented work from getting done, verbal abuse, threatening conduct, intimidation or humiliation?**

This same question was asked of a nationally representative sample of adult Americans in the 2007 WBI-Zogby survey. 37% of Americans reported its direct experience; 12% witnessed it.

For this 2008 WBI study, there were two separate 400-person respondent groups who visited the WBI website and completed one or both of the surveys, asking about either their employers' responses to bullying (data collected in June–July), or asking what co-workers did (data collected in August).

## Principal Findings from the Employers' Response Study

*Question asked:* **When the employer was told about the bullying, what did the employer do?**

1.7%—Conducted fair investigation and protected target from further bullying with negative consequences for the bully

6.2%—Conducted fair investigation with negative consequences for the bully but no safety for the target

8.7%—Inadequate/unfair investigation; no consequences for bully or target

31%—Inadequate/unfair investigation; no consequences for bully but target was retaliated against

12.8%—Employer did nothing, ignored the complaint; no consequences for bully or target

15.7%—Employer did nothing; target was retaliated against for reporting the bullying but kept job

24%—Employer did nothing; target was retaliated against and eventually lost job

- Bullied workers report that employers predominantly <u>did nothing</u> to stop the mistreatment when reported (53%) and actually <u>retaliated against the person</u> (71% of cases) who dared to report it.

- In 40% of cases, targets considered the employer's "investigation" to be inadequate or unfair, with less than 2% of investigations described as fair and safe for the bullied person. Filing complaints led to retaliation by employers of bullied targets leading to lost jobs (24%). Alleged bullies were punished in only 6.2% of cases; bullying is done with impunity.

- Bullied individuals are not whiners, nor do they complain at the slightest provocation.

*Question asked:* **Was a formal, written complaint filed with management or Human Resources?**

50.7%—No

44.8%—Yes

4.5%—Not sure

Recall that in the 2007 WBI-Zogby Survey with a national representative sample, only 15% of bullied individuals ever formally complained to their employers, only 4% filed EEO state or federal claims, and a miniscule 3% filed lawsuits against bullying employers!

## Principal Findings from the Co-workers' Response Study

**Question asked: Did the target's co-workers (of any rank—peers or managers) SEE the mistreatment, at least once?**
95% said "Yes"

**Question asked: Were the target's co-workers AWARE of the mistreatment?**
97% said "Yes"

**Question asked: What did (at least one of the) co-workers DO in response to the mistreatment?**

    0.8%—They banded together and confronted the bully as a unit; stopped the bullying

    7.1%—They offered specific advice to the target about what he or she should do to stop it

    28.4%—They gave only moral, social support

    15.7%—They did and said nothing, not helping either the target or bully

    13.2%—They voluntarily distanced themselves from the target, isolating him or her

    4.8%—They followed the bully's orders to stay away from the target

    12.9%—They betrayed the target to the bully while appearing to still be friends

    14.7%—They publicly sided with the bully and acted aggressively toward the target

    2.5%—Not sure

- Co-workers were nearly as unhelpful as employers, though nearly all were aware of what what was happening. In 46% of bullying cases, co-workers abandoned their bullied colleagues, to the extent that 15% aggressed against the target along with the bully. Co-workers did nothing in 16% of cases.

- Co-workers did do positive things in 36% of cases—mainly limited to offering moral support. The rarest outcome (less than 1%) was for co-workers to band together to stop the bullying through confrontation. Co-workers' personal fears were the preferred explanation by bullied targets (55%) for the actions taken or not taken by witnesses.

### Additional Facts from the Employers' Response Study

95% of respondents were self-described targets of bullying (past or current)

59% of the bullies were women; 80% of targets were women

74% of cases, the bully enlisted others; 26% bully worked alone

### Question asked: Bully's rank relative to the targeted person:

7.6%—Bully ranked lower than the targeted individual

18.7%—Bully was a co-worker, colleague, a peer of the targeted individual

73.6%—Bully ranked above the target by one or more levels in the organization

### Question asked: Was the bullying illegal? Did the conduct violate anti-discrimination rights laws because the target was a member of a legally protected group and the bully was not?

32.6%—Yes, it was at least partially illegal

42.7%—No, it was not illegal

24.7%—Not sure

*Question asked:* **Did the targeted person tell the employer that the bullying occurred?**

75.8%—Yes

20.5%—No

3.7%—Not sure

Types of employers described by survey respondents:

27.7%—Government: Federal, State, County, City, Quasi-Govt

31.1%—For-Profit Corporations, Large and Medium and Small

10.6%—Nonprofit Organizations and Churches

18.8%—Education: K-12 thru Universities

8%—Healthcare provider

## Additional Facts from the Co-worker Study

95% of respondents were self-described targets of bullying (past or current)

85% of targets were women

*Question asked:* **If co-workers were AWARE, HOW were they made aware?**

73%—Co-workers witnessed it directly

16.5%—Target explicitly told coworkers what happened

5.1%—Co-workers saw the target react in ways that they themselves had reacted

5.4%—Not sure how they learned about it, but they were certainly aware

*Question asked:* **WHY did co-workers do what you said they did above?**

23.7%—Co-workers made conscious, deliberate choices on their own, right or wrong

12%—Co-workers did what they thought MANAGERS wanted them to do

7.1%—Co-workers did what MANAGERS explicitly told them to do

2.3%—Co-workers did what they thought the TARGET wanted them to do

0.3%—Co-workers did what the TARGET explicitly told them to do

54.7%—Co-workers acted out of personal fear, whether or not they recognized the fear

# Bibliography

Adams, Andrea, and Neil Crawford. *Bullying at Work: How to Confront and Overcome It.* London: Virago Press, 1992.

Brink, Betty. "Transforming the truth: How TU Electric twisted the medical facts after an employee working with PCB got sick." *Fort Worth Weekly,* 26 March 1998.

Brown, Stephanie. *Safe Passage: Recovery for Adult Children of Alcoholics.* New York: John Wiley & Sons, 1992.

Frank, Robert H. and Philip J. Cook. *The Winner-Take-All Society: Why the Few at the Top Get So Much More Than the Rest of Us.* New York: Penguin, 1995.

Harvey, Jerry. *The Abilene Paradox and Other Meditations on Management.* New York: Lexington Books, 1989.

Hirigoyen, Marie-France. *Stalking the Soul.* Paris: Editions La Decourverte & Syros, 1998.

Hornstein, Harvey. *Brutal Bosses and Their Prey: How to Identify and Overcome Abuse in the Workplace.* New York: Riverhead Books, 1996.

Hurd, David J. *The California Employee Survival Handbook.* 3rd ed. Placerville, Calif.: Pro Per Publications, 1998.

Keashly, Loraleigh. "Emotional abuse at work: conceptual and empirical issues." *Journal of Emotional Abuse* 1 (1998).

Keashly, Loraleigh, and Karen Jagatic. "Workplace abuse and aggression." Paper presented at Workplace Bullying 2000: Redefining Harassment. Oakland, Calif., 27 January 2000.

Kramer, Roderick. "The Great Intimidators." *Harvard Business Review*, February 2006.

Labor Occupational Health Program. "Violence on the Job: A Guidebook for Labor and Management." University of California, Berkeley, 1997.

Lutgen-Sandvik, Pamela. "Intensive remedial identity work: Responses to workplace bullying trauma and stigmatization." *Organization* 15 (1) (2008): 97–119.

Marais, Susan, and Magriet Herman. *Corporate Hyenas at Work: How to Spot and Outwit Them by Being Hyenawise.* Pretoria, South Africa: Kagiso, 1997.

McCarthy, Paul, Michael Sheehan, and William Wilkie. *Bullying: From Backyard to Boardroom.* Alexandria, NSW, Australia: Millennium Books, 1996.

Meichenbaum, Donald, PhD. *A Clinical Handbook/Practical Therapist Manual for Assessing and Treating Adults with PTSD.* Waterloo, Ontario: Institute Press, 1994.

Nader, Ralph, and Wesley Smith. *No Contest: Corporate Lawyers and the Perversion of Justice in America.* New York: Random House, 1996.

Namie, Gary. "Create a blueprint for a bullying-free workplace." *The Complete Lawyer* 4 (2008), online at *www.thecompletelawyer.com.*

———. *Report on abusive workplaces.* Bellingham, WA: Workplace Bullying Institute, 2003. Posted at www.bullyinginstitute.org.

———. U.S. Workplace Bullying Survey. Conducted by Zogby International. Bellingham, WA: Workplace Bullying Institute, 2007.

———. "Workplace bullying: challenges for employment relations professionals." *Employment Relations Today* 34 (2007): 43–51.

————. "Workplace bullying: escalated incivility." *Ivey Business Journal*, a publication of the Ivey Business School, University of Western Ontario, Canada.

Namie, Gary, and Ruth Namie. "Anti-bullying advocacy: an unrealized employee assistance opportunity." *Journal of Employee Assistance* 33 (2003): 9–11.

————. "Workplace bullying: How to address America's silent epidemic." *Employee Rights and Employment Policy Journal* 8 (2004): 315–333.

————. "Workplace bullying in healthcare." *Clinician News* 9 (2005): 14–15.

Needham, Andrea. *Workplace Bullying: The Costly Business Secret.* Auckland: Penguin, 2003.

Neuman, Joel H., and Robert A. Baron. "Workplace violence and workplace aggression: Evidence concerning specific forms, potential causes, and preferred targets." *Journal of Management* 24 (1998): 391–419.

Nisbett, R. E., C. Caputo, P. Legant, and J. Maracek. "Behavior as seen by the actor and as seen by the observer." *Journal of Personality and Social Psychology* 27 (1973): 154–164.

Office of Civil Rights, Oregon Department of Transportation. "Anti-Harassment Policy." Salem, Oregon, 1999.

Privacy Rights Clearinghouse, Dale Fetherling (Ed.). *The Privacy Rights Handbook: How to Take Control of Your Personal Information.* New York: Avon Books, 1997.

Queensland Government, Division of Workplace Health and Safety, Department of Employment, Training & Industrial Relations. "An Employer's Guide to Workplace Bullying." Queensland, Australia.

Richman, Judith, et al. "Sexual harassment and generalized workplace abuse among university employees: Prevalence and mental health correlates." *American Journal of Public Health* 89, no. 3 (1999): 358–363.

Schaef, Anne Wilson, and Diane Fassel. *The Addictive Organization: Why We Overwork, Cover Up, Pick Up the Pieces, Please the Boss & Perpetuate Sick Organizations*. New York: Harper & Row, 1988.

Scott, Michael J, and Stephen G. Stradling. "Post-traumatic stress disorder without the trauma." *British Journal of Clinical Psychology* 33 (1994): 71–74.

Solomon, Norman. *The Trouble with Dilbert: How Corporate Culture Gets the Last Laugh*. Monroe, Maine: Common Courage Press, 1997.

Storms, N. D. "Videotape and the attribution process: Reversing actors' and observers' points of view." *Journal of Personality and Social Psychology* 27 (1973): 165–175.

Sutton, Bob. *The No-Asshole Rule*. New York: Warner Business Books, 2007.

Tobias, Paul, and Susan Sauter. *Job Rights & Survival Strategies: A Handbook for Terminated Employees*. NERI, 1997.

Waggoner, Martha. "Study: Workplace incivility rising." Associated Press, May 29, 1998.

Yamada, David. "The phenomenon of 'workplace bullying' and the need for status-blind hostile work environment protection." *Georgetown Law Journal* 88, no. 3 (2000).

# Index

Ethics gap, 59
Exhaustion, 139
Exit interview, 249

F
Failure, 201–203
Family interaction, 169–172,
    180–181
Faragher, Beth Ann, 285
Fear, 87, 91, 94
Festinger, Leon, 89
Field, Tim, 257
Fighting back, 122–128, 232–244
Finland, 259
Fleissner, Alfred, 259
Flight or fight response, 138, 148
Fox, Suzy, 268
France, 258, 264
Frank, Robert, 91

G
Gatekeeper, 40–44
Gender, 5, 297–299, 301, 302,
    305, 307, 308, 309, 311
Germany, 259
Great Britain, 257, 261–262
Groupthink, 88–89

H
Harassment. See Discrimination
Harvey, Jerry, 68, 86, 87
Health consequences. See
    Physical reactions;
    Psychological reactions
Healthy Workplace Bill, 275–279
Hirigoyen, Marie-France, 258
Hornstein, Harvey, 142
Human resources, 231, 235, 237,
    239
Humor, 31, 35
Hurd, David, 248

Hypocrisy, 59

I
Identity boundaries, 165–168
Incivilities, 15–16
Inner critic, 185–190
Integrity, 59
Intentional Infliction of Emotional
    Distress, 110, 134, 270,
    273
Intervention, 205
Invasion of privacy, 177–178, 250
Ireland, 258
Italy, 259

J
Jagatic, Karen, 269
Journaling, 31, 206

K
Keashly, Loraleigh, vix, 268–269
KLIMA Association, 259
Kytöpuu, Katri, 259

L
Lawsuits, 107–108
Lawyers, 109–114, 239–240
Leaving, 245–251, 310, 311
Legal advice. See Lawyers
Legal system, 134, 270–275,
    280–282. See also
    Supreme Court, U.S.;
    individual countries
Letters of recommendation,
    247–248
Leymann, Heinz, 198, 255–256
Lutgen-Sandvik, Pamela, 268

M
Meddling, 164
Meditation, 30

331

# The Drs. Namie:
## North American Workplace Bullying Pioneers

Gary Namie (PhD, social psychology) was a professor at several universities in departments of management and psychology. He also designed the first college course on workplace bullying in the United States. Ruth Namie (PhD, clinical psychology) specialized in chemical dependency treatment services before encountering her bully supervisor. She now helps develop training and consulting programs to stop bullying. Together, the Drs. Namie are founders of the nonprofit research and education Workplace Bullying Institute (WBI), which introduced workplace bullying to the United States in 1998. WBI provides voluminous self-help information on the web for millions of bullied individuals. In 2003, the WBI-Legislative Campaign began the national initiative to pass the anti-bullying *Healthy Workplace Bill*. To date, it has been introduced in several states thanks to the many volunteer citizen-lobbyist WBI-LC coordinators. The Namies' bullying-related research and work have been featured numerous times on network TV—CNBC, *The Today Show*, *Good Morning America*, *The Early Show*, *Nightline*, CNN—on local TV, in the national press—*New York Times*, *Washington Post*, *Wall Street Journal*, *National Post*, *Financial Post*, *Toronto Star*, *Los Angeles Times*, *San Francisco Chronicle*, *Chicago Tribune*, *Maclean's*—and on radio across the United States and Canada. Their guest appearances and interviews now total over 700 across all media. They educate the scientists via conference presentations and peer-review publications. Gary Namie serves as an expert witness in litigation. He testified in the nation's first "bullying trial" where the plaintiff's verdict and award were upheld by the Indiana Supreme Court in 2008. Work Doctor, Inc., is the family's consulting firm for employers.

The Namie Blueprint to Correct and Prevent Workplace Bullying is the program adopted by the national demonstration project to curb adult bullying in schools and in corporations and government agencies in the United States and Canada.

The Namie network of eight websites reflects the breadth of their services and available information on the topic. The portal site is *www.workplacebullying.org.*